PENGUIN BOOKS

MAIN BATTLE TA

D1136566

'An emotional rollercoaster . . . the retelling of the Challengers' devastating displays of firepower in tense, close-quarter battles in and around Basra which will awe every reader . . . Fast-paced and charged with action' *Soldier Magazine*

'A breathtaking insight into the heaviest fighting experienced by British troops in Iraq. Powerful, terrifying, relentless – the action comes at you like the Challenger itself' Ross Kemp

'An intimate, vivid and action-packed account of armoured fighting in the heavily defended "complex terrain" of urban Basra' *Military Times* (Book of the Month)

'This graphic, compelling account . . . an engrossing insight into the experiences of those who lived and fought on the frontline with Britain's oldest surviving Cavalry Regiment of the Line' General Sir David Richards, Chief of the Defence Staff

'Edworthy steers with a sure and steady hand through the plunging drama and roiling violence in his detailed, gripping account of the tank's final battle. Essential reading for anyone with an interest in the smoke-wreathed belly of mechanized war' Anthony Loyd, War Correspondent, *The Times*

'Told in the style of a thriller' *Northern Echo*

'An enthralling account . . . Loaded with tales of incredible heroism, Edworthy's book reveals how the Royal Scots Dragoon Guards helped bring Saddam's regime to its knees. Reads like the finest fiction but ranks as an outstanding work of narrative journalism' Stephen Stewart, *Sunday Mail*

'Awesome. An explosive story' *Sun*

Niall Edworthy conducted hundreds of hours of exclusive interviews with the officers and men of the Royal Scots Dragoon Guards. He lives in West Sussex with his wife and two children.

Main Battle Tank

NIALL EDWORTHY

PENGUIN BOOKS

PENGUIN BOOKS

Published by the Penguin Group
Penguin Books Ltd, 80 Strand, London WC2R 0RL, England
Penguin Group (USA), Inc., 375 Hudson Street, New York, New York 10014, USA
Penguin Group (Canada), 90 Eglinton Avenue East, Suite 700, Toronto, Ontario, Canada M4P 2Y3
(a division of Pearson Penguin Canada Inc.)
Penguin Ireland, 25 St Stephen's Green, Dublin 2, Ireland (a division of Penguin Books Ltd)
Penguin Group (Australia), 250 Camberwell Road, Camberwell, Victoria 3124, Australia
(a division of Pearson Australia Group Pty Ltd)
Penguin Books India Pvt Ltd, 11 Community Centre, Panchsheel Park, New Delhi – 110 017, India
Penguin Group (NZ), 67 Apollo Drive, Rosedale, Auckland 0632, New Zealand
(a division of Pearson New Zealand Ltd)
Penguin Books (South Africa) (Pty) Ltd, 24 Sturdee Avenue, Rosebank,
Johannesburg 2196, South Africa

Penguin Books Ltd, Registered Offices: 80 Strand, London WC2R 0RL, England

www.penguin.com

First published by Michael Joseph 2010
Published in Penguin Books 2011

1

Typeset by Palimpsest Book Production Limited, Falkirk, Stirlingshire
Printed in Great Britain by Clays Ltd, St Ives plc

A CIP catalogue record for this book is available from the British Library

ISBN: 978-0-141-04191-9

www.greenpenguin.co.uk

Contents

List of Illustrations

Foreword

This graphic, compelling account of a British tank regiment at war in Iraq in early 2003 shows our armed forces at their very best. Faced with rapidly changing conditions on the ground and operating in extremely complex terrain, the Challenger II crews rode roughshod over all the obstacles in their path.

Up against a desperate enemy who often hid amongst the local population, the Royal Scots Dragoon Guards, and the other armoured units of the Desert Rats, carried out their tasks with tremendous professionalism, resourcefulness and courage. Ruthless against the enemy but ever mindful of the civilians they were endeavouring to liberate, our tank squadrons more than proved their worth in the intense and febrile circumstances of the modern battlefield.

It has been many years since British armour has been involved in such a sustained, intense period of combat, and no regiment saw heavier fighting, or were tasked to carry out such a wide range of operations, than the Royal Scots Dragoon Guards. *Main Battle Tank* provides an engrossing insight into the experiences of those who lived and fought on the frontline with Britain's oldest surviving Cavalry Regiment of the Line.

General Sir David Richards
Chief of the General Staff

Acknowledgements

This is a military history, albeit very recent history and albeit one that is told, I hope, more in the style of a thriller than a dry chronicle of events. There is only so much that an operational record or log book can reveal about the truth of a soldier's experience of combat – these provide only a faint, flat, factual outline of events. For the colour, the noise and the emotion of the drama, you must turn to the recollections and reflections of the men themselves. In that, I have been very fortunate to have been given permission to spend many hundreds of hours talking to over fifty of those men whose experiences make up an enthralling story of a British tank regiment at war in the Gulf. I hope I have managed to repay their generosity with an account that is faithful to their experiences, captures the magnitude of the challenges they faced, and impresses on readers the courage and professionalism that helped them rise to those challenges.

Every detail of the narrative has come from the first-hand accounts, diaries and operational records of the three squadrons of the Royal Scots Dragoon Guards, also known as the SCOTS DG, who deployed as part of the 7th Armoured Brigade 'Desert Rats' in early 2003. In Operation TELIC 1, British tank crews had their first experience of sustained combat since the Second World War – and no regiment experienced more drama, more fighting and more variety of operational experiences than the SCOTS DG.

To a man, they recounted their experiences with honesty,

graphic vividness and unfailing modesty. Quick to pass on the credit for a success or accept responsibility for a failing, in telling the story of their deployment to the Al Faw, the men of SCOTS DG unwittingly showed all the qualities that make up their reputation as an especially tight and loyal regimental family. It has been a genuine pleasure to have spent time in their company and a true honour to have been given the opportunity to produce a record of their experiences that, I hope, their families will be able to read with pride, now and in generations to come.

Special thanks for overseeing the book project to Major Roger Macmillan – the Ops Officer of the SCOTS DG Battle Group in TELIC 1 – and to the three Squadron leaders in the story: 'A' Squadron's Major Tim Brown (now retired from the Army), 'B' Squadron's Major Chris Brannigan (now Lieutenant Colonel) and 'C' Squadron's Major Johnny Biggart (now Lieutenant Colonel and CO of the regiment at the time of this book going to print). The SCOTS DG worked and fought alongside the Irish Guards, who comprised the infantry element of their battle group, the 1st Battalion Black Watch, to whose battle group 'A' Squadron was attached, the Royal Marines of 3 Commando Brigade and the REME, whose fitter sections made an invaluable contribution to the operational efficiency of all the Challenger squadrons. With so many other units involved, it was clear that a line had to be drawn in the editorial sand and the decision was taken early on to keep the story within the SCOTS DG. Based on my interviews with the Challenger crews, I have endeavoured to record the events involving other units accurately and truthfully, but I am very happy to put right in any subsequent editions of the book any errors that may have slipped through in this one.

I owe a very special debt of gratitude to Rowland White,

who commissioned me to write the book after many years negotiating with the MOD to get the project off the ground. As ever, his wisdom was gratefully received. I am also indebted to Daniel Bunyard, Rowland's successor at Michael Joseph, who picked up the project at the production stage and carried it through to publication with such enthusiasm. Thanks too, as always, to my agent Araminta and her highly efficient new sidekick Harry at Lucas Alexander Whitley (LAW).

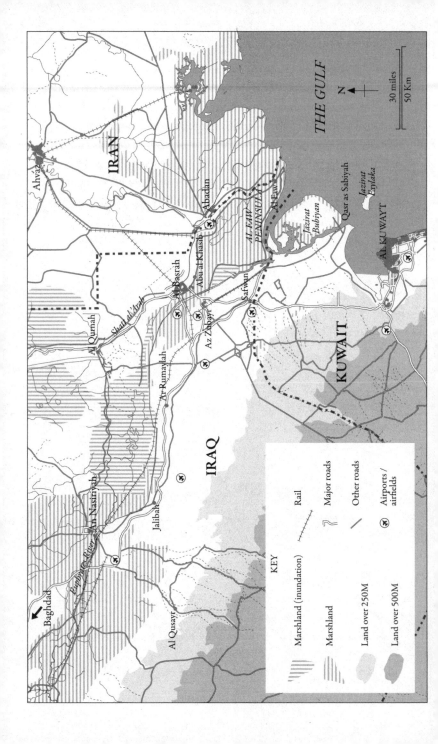

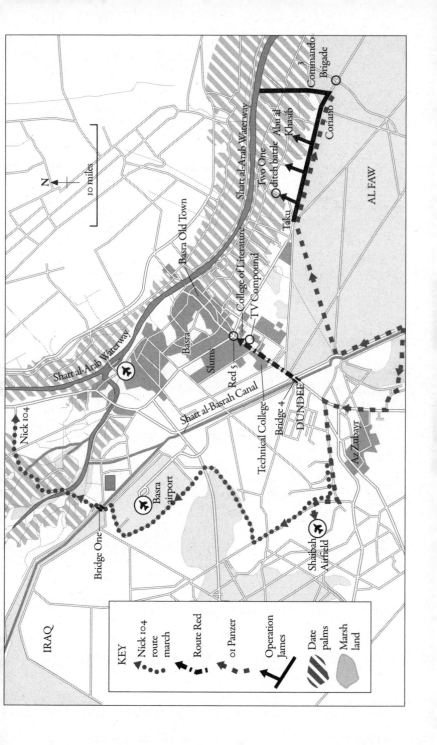

1. Alert to All Possibilities

The thump of the tandem rotor blades filled the air above Adler's Nest as the Chinook emerged above the tent tops in a cloud of pale dust, banked sharply to the right and disappeared towards the massive copper sun melting over the horizon of the Kuwaiti desert. To the pilots, the scene below was an extraordinary one: a patchwork of khaki and green merging into a single dark vastness, hemmed by white sands, like a giant oil slick on an otherwise unspoilt beach. The higher the helicopter climbed into the late-afternoon sky, the more military camps came into view; dozens of canvas cities, each arranged over a grid of thoroughfares and squares, spilling and seeping into the far distance. The windscreens of tens of thousands of vehicles flashed and sparkled in the last rays of the dying sun. Some of the vehicles were moving through the maze of makeshift streets, leaving trails of dust in their wake, no more than tiny puffs to the airmen above; others were lined up in perfect order, as if for inspection, column after column of them, row after row, block after block: Challenger 2 and Abrams tanks, armoured personnel carriers, self-propelled artillery guns, fuel tankers, ambulances, supply trucks, reconnaissance vehicles, Land Rovers, Pinzgauers, Humvees ... The British alone had brought enough vehicles to form an eighty-mile convoy that would stretch from London to Southampton.

In amongst the tents and the vehicles, hundreds of thousands of men and women, their numbers equivalent to the entire population of Edinburgh or Pittsburgh, hurried to and fro, making their final, frantic preparations. Two months earlier there had been nothing to see there but sand, no life but vipers, scorpions and lizards. Natural selection has persuaded only a few creatures to carve out an existence in this empty, unforgiving wilderness. For a few brief weeks after the rain has come in the spring, the desert bursts with flowers but the townsfolk no longer come to enjoy this extraordinary spectacle of nature. Iraqi mines, scattered twelve years earlier by fleeing troops, still litter the landscape, responsible for the bizarre sight, every now and then, of a stray goat spiralling into the air in a plume of sand.

In Camp Adler's Nest, a stream of soldiers in an assortment of T-shirts, green combats and heavy black boots, gas masks swinging from their necks and belts, jogged towards a small crowd forming inside the supplies distribution area, where the SQMS (Squadron Quartermaster Sergeant) packets were unloading large boxes from the back of a Bedford truck. The rumour had spread like a brushfire among the men of the Royal Scots Dragoon Guards – 'SCOTS DG' as they were known for short – that the desert combats and boots had finally arrived. Staff Sergeant Tam McVey whipped out his Stanley knife and sliced through the cardboard. The men pressed a little closer as McVey bent back the flaps of the box and lifted out a pair of blue-and-white chequered chef's trousers from the top of the pile, triggering an uproar of laughter and cursing.

'You're kidding! . . . Great, well that's going to frighten the life out of the Iraqis isn't it? Six hundred men in white tunics and checked trooz . . . They'll be giving us spatulas to fight with next . . . How the hell do you lose a whole battle group's worth of clothes, rations and ammo? . . .' The men muttered and joked as they melted back into the surrounding tents. It was not the first time they had left the SQMS area hiding their disappointment behind the banter.

It had been a frenetic, sometimes frustrating, time for the whole battle group. From the moment they had stepped off the planes from Hannover straight into a violent hailstorm, nothing was quite working out as they had imagined. A whole squadron of tanks and dozens of other vehicles had yet to arrive in dock, meaning they were unable to practise live firing at the Udairi ranges up by the Iraqi border or run through dry field-training exercises. What's more, the tanks still had to be up-armoured with extra protection panels, spray-painted in desert colours and, as a precaution against blue-on-blue (friendly-fire) incidents, fitted with the Identification Friend or Foe (IFF) and Blue Force Tracker systems. After the experiences of the last Gulf War, nobody wanted to be crossing that border in an unmarked tank below a sky screeching with jets and attack helicopters. Since their arrival, the only rations the troops had been issued were the dreaded American MRE rations ('Meal Ready to Eat') while the 'loggies' of the Royal Logistics Corps tried to track down the consignment of British rations which were still in their sea containers on a ship floating around somewhere in the Gulf, or somewhere in the docks, or the desert . . . along with the desert combats, the ammunition for the tanks and the small arms, the spare parts, the new NBC filters to protect the crews in the event of an anthrax or nerve agent attack . . . the list ran and ran.

For the men of the SQMS packets tasked with supplying all the equipment for the men and the machines of the battle group, it had been an especially trying period, driving back and forth to the other side of the concentration area all day long to join in the scrum of other sergeants and their men from the rest of Brigade, all doing their utmost to bring back the kit their boys so desperately needed. No one knew when the war was to begin, but the flurry of orders from above and the sudden acceleration in preparations suggested it was to be days rather than weeks. Every day, the SQMS packets begged, borrowed and stole for their battle groups, but often they returned empty-handed with no news when the consignments of essential equipment were going to arrive. It was just pot luck what turned up at the docks that day, or as the SQMS boys put it to the increasingly frustrated troops they turned away: 'Sorry, lads, it's a bit like making chicken soup out of chicken shit right now.'

But it was a similar story for the whole of 7th Armoured Brigade, the 'Desert Rats', and the air of anticipation and the flow of banter among the SCOTS DG told the officers and NCOs that morale was still solid as H-hour approached. Lieutenant Colonel Hugh Blackman, Commanding Officer of the battle group, had been writing up his plans based on the nod from Brigade that the SCOTS DG were to form one of the three attack battle groups, behind the 1st Battalion Black Watch and the 1st Royal Regiment of Fusiliers. The 2nd Royal Tank Regiment, who made up the fourth battle group of the Desert Rats Brigade, was to be held back in reserve, the last to cross the border. This had been the hope and expectation of everyone in the SCOTS DG since their deployment had been announced, two months earlier. No soldier wants to work round the clock for two months to get combat-ready, only to sit on his helmet in the rear and watch his brothers-in-arms disappear to the frontline.

The four battle groups of the Desert Rats were all structured and organized in the same way. 'B' and 'C' Squadrons formed the armoured element of the SCOTS DG Battle

Group, with each of them comprised of fourteen tanks and a hundred men, including non-combat personnel. Two companies of Irish Guards made up the infantry element of the 1,200-strong unit, which also included the men and vehicles of Command troop, the nexus of the regiment centred round the Commanding Officer. Completing the itinerant military community were the Reconnaissance troop, the medics of the Regimental Aid Post, the Quartermaster's Department responsible for supplying the armoured units, and the technicians from the Light Aid Detachment of the Royal Electrical and Mechanical Engineers (REME).

Briefings and drills of all kinds were underway across the concentration area as 'B' Squadron leader, Major Chris Brannigan, and 'C' Squadron leader, Major Johnny Biggart, strode at a brisk pace through the streets of tents, taking the salutes of the men they would soon be leading into battle, as they headed towards the Battle Group HQ. It was not difficult for approaching troopers to distinguish the two men, with Biggart tall and rangy, and Brannigan stocky and bustling.

The Battle Group Operations Officer, Captain Roger Macmillan, had been on the radio to summon them to a meeting with Lieutenant Colonel Blackman, and there had been a hint of urgency or uneasiness in his voice.

'What's your guess?'

'Could be anything. Perhaps there's been a political breakthrough . . . new Intelligence about the WMD threat . . . who knows? The flow of information from on high has hardly been overwhelming . . . The BBC reporters seem to know more than we do!'

'There's talk of reported sightings by air of 170 Iraqi T-72 tanks massing near the border.'

'Now, that would be interesting.'

To pass through Adler's Nest in early March 2003 was to witness a world stuck in fast-forward mode. Soldiers rushed between tents, Land Rovers and trucks jammed the roads and the air was filled with the shouts and orders of men and the occasional roar of an aircraft overhead. Even without the tanks to work on, there were still dozens of tasks and exercises to be completed – not all of them rewarding experiences for those ordered to carry them out. In one of the tents, a dozen SCOTS DG were kneeling on the floor embroiled in the tedious task of cutting up thousands of small maps, arranging them into larger ones and taping them together so that all members of the battle group had identical maps that covered the entire area of operation in which they were to be fighting over the coming months. They had been there for days, working late into the night, and any soldier putting his ear to the canvas side of that tent was treated to a stream of expletives and cries of frustration from his colleagues inside. The floor was littered with piles of similar-looking pieces of map and the men were walking and crawling amongst them to find the relevant parts to put together their Ordnance Survey jigsaws – 500 of them in total. 'Has anyone seen the pile of Az Zubayr sections? . . . Who's got the border areas? . . . Damn, I've put Basra in upside down . . . I'm not sure what's going to pop first: my head or my kneecaps . . . They'll be signing the peace treaty by the time we finish this lot . . .'

In a neighbouring tent, a junior medic stood before a seated audience running through the procedure in the event of casevac being needed to take casualties from the frontline: 'Give the location of the Landing Zone . . . the number of casualties by precedence. "Urgent" means less than two hours, "priority" more than two hours . . . you need to assess the security of the LZ and give details of the marking . . . give name, rank, number, age and unit of the casualty . . .'

Next door, a staff officer from Brigade HQ addressed a small group on the threats the Coalition forces were expected to face. 'The enemy is likely to exploit the country's oil infrastructure to discredit and disrupt the Coalition. He will try and do this by pumping oil into the Gulf, by igniting oil wells to create confusion and by damaging installations to prevent exploitation of the oilfields and resources for the rebuilding of the country . . . The enemy's critical capabilities facing the Brigade are WMD, as you know only too well by now, Corps level artillery, deception operations, the tanks of 6th Armoured Division, mainly T-55s but possibly augmented by the far more competitive T-72s. The Challenger 2 may be a superior tank but the enemy has the upper hand in terms of numbers . . . The enemy has many weaknesses however: lack of air defence, lack of logistic lift, low morale amongst its regular army, poor Intelligence and a fractious population unhappy with the current regime . . .'

Towards the centre of the concentration area, soldiers were starting to queue up for the last meal of the day at the largest field kitchen constructed in modern military history. The chefs' troops of all the regiments within the battle group had combined forces and equipment to create a giant cooking and dining area catering for the 6,000 men of the Brigade. In adjoining tents to the side, the temperature had started to drop a little, to the relief of the scores of chefs, who had the hottest jobs in the Brigade, going about their work under canvas in the heat of the desert alongside banks of ovens and refrigeration equipment. The upside of the system was a more efficient use of resources and a less complicated logistic chain but the risk with centralized cooking was a food poisoning outbreak that laid low half the army on the eve of war. Napoleon once said that an army marches to war on its belly, but as the planners for Operation 'TELIC' knew only too well it can also crawl on its hands and knees to the Portaloo. To the relief of the Brigade command and the troops themselves, as yet there had been no hint of the debilitating 'soldier's bug', D&V – or diarrhoea and vomiting to the man in the street.

If there was a hygiene problem brewing it was in the small amount of Portaloos that had arrived so far. There were far too few of them for the men, and although the engineers were working hard to solve the problem, 'where to crap?' was becoming a pressing and irritating issue. A trooper walked in and burst straight back out of one of the plastic kiosks, gagging and exclaiming in a great guffaw of disgust: 'I'm nae sitting doon in there. It's heaped tae the brim with bangers 'n' mash. I'm away to the desert for mine.' Collecting his spade, he strode out into the sands bordering the camp and joined the group of other soldiers spread over an area the size of a football pitch, crouching on their haunches with their combat trousers round their boots. This was what the troops called the 'scattered mine' approach because it was just plain bad luck if they stood in another man's waste.

'Later symptoms of nerve agent poisoning include headache and dizziness . . .' – the loud voice of the medic, trying to make herself heard at the back of the tent, reached outside as Brannigan and Biggart walked by – '. . . increased saliva, drooling at the mouth, excessive sweating, involuntary urination and defecation . . .'

Two NCOs saluted as they approached the officers from the other direction. 'I think she must be talking about the 2nd Royal Tank Regiment, don't you, sir?' one of them said as the two officers took the salute and acknowledged the wit with a smile.

'Steady, boys. Just because they're reserve battle group, doesn't mean they're not a valuable element of the Brigade!'

Close to the sleeping quarter tents, a dozen bare-topped men were bent over buckets of water on wooden tables, shaving and washing themselves and their clothes. Behind them, two men with their top halves visible above the poncho screen, stood beneath solar shower bags with their heads tilted backwards to let the water run over their faces and wash away the sand and grimy sweat of another day. Sergeant 'Larry' Lamb was holding a small mirror in one hand and running an electric razor over the stubble on his head with his other – to the great amusement of the others around him. 'Are you going to cover yourself in tattoos as well, Larry? . . . I don't know what the Iraqis will make of you, but you sure frighten me . . .' Many of the men had decided to shave their heads so that they would be that little bit cooler out in the field when the real heat arrived. It was warm enough already during the day, but in a couple of weeks the temperature was expected to rocket to 35 degrees Celsius and beyond. Cropped hair and shaven heads were also more hygienic and they made it easier to maintain the high grooming standards demanded in the SCOTS DG. Smart appearance, even holed up in a battle zone, was essential for strong discipline and good morale and it was strictly enforced. Long hair and beards were strictly for Special Forces only.

Men were coming and going from the two giant tents serving as sleeping quarters for 'B' and 'C' Squadrons. Through the open flaps, they could see a few curled up on top of their sleeping bags, grabbing what rest they could, with their Bergens and rifles stowed at their heads along the edge of the canvas. Some were lying on camp bed-style cots but most slept on the floor using a pullover or their combat jackets as pillows.

Others were sitting on the carpet tiles with their backs against the big wooden poles that ran down the length of the tent in two columns. Some were reading letters, others writing them, scribbling away on pale blue aerograms, 'blueys', to their loved ones back home. A final few were getting round to writing their wills. This was a disheartening experience for the soldiers and many put it off till the very last moment. Captain Richard Le Sueur (pronounced *Swer*) was kneeling on one leg, helping two of his men to write theirs. It was up to the troop leaders to make sure that their men had written one, reminding them that they put their families at financial risk if they didn't, and Le Sueur was keen, just like the other officers, that his men had squared away their personal lives before crossing the border. There was going to be plenty to concentrate the mind in the field as it was and the last thing a commander needed was for his troops to be distracted by private worries.

The two Squadron leaders walked another 200 yards in silence, each running through a mental checklist of the tasks he had to complete before the day was out. As they approached the entrance of the Battle Group HQ tent, a Land Rover slammed to an abrupt halt churning up the dust around the wheels. Captain Macmillan cranked up the handbrake as Lieutenant Colonel Blackman jumped from the passenger door and marched into the tent clutching a dossier under his arm.

The Ops Officer gave the two Squadron leaders a look as if to say: 'Don't ask.' As he disappeared into the tent, Major Peter MacMullen and Major Ben Farrell, the two company commanders of the Irish Guards, were stepping from their own command vehicle and heading towards them. The four men, who had known each other for years, shook hands and walked in. Biggart and Farrell were particularly close friends as were Brannigan and MacMullen. Their close affinities were likely to be an asset on the battlefield. They trusted and understood each other and were able to speak frankly.

There was no natural light in the Operations tent, which had been sealed as tightly as possible to prevent the dust from infiltrating the machinery. This was the temporary nerve centre of the battle group and there were half a dozen soldiers crouched over computer keyboards and radio sets. A hot-water boiler for brews and two cases of bottled water sat amongst mugs and boxes of tea on a general-purpose table in the middle of the tent. Lieutenant Colonel Blackman stood with his back to his senior officers, rubbing clean the whiteboard next to his desk with a sequence of vigorous swipes.

'I've just come back from Brigade HQ,' he said turning round to face them. If he was angry, he didn't let his voice betray it. He sounded, to his audience, every bit as composed and gracious as ever. 'The rest of the tanks are still not here. Their ship was bumped to the back of the queue of traffic heading through the Suez Canal. The other battle groups now have a full fleet of vehicles. Brigade's line is that the whole war effort can't wait for us.'

He paused as if summoning the effort to get the words out.

'I think you know what's coming . . . we are now the reserve battle group, the last in the order of march into Iraq. I'm sorry to have give you this news after all the hard work you and your men have put in over the last two months. Break it to your men as gently as possible – and as soon as possible. You know how news like this . . .'

Silence filled the tent for several moments and the four senior officers of the battle group were absorbing the Commanding Officer's bombshell announcement when the air was suddenly rent by the sound every man had come to dread since arriving in Kuwait: the blare of Land Rover horns and the cries of 'Gas! Gas! Gas!' Mostly the alerts came in the night, a deliberate move to deny the soldiers their sleep and undermine morale, but this was the fourth that day alone. Instinctively, everyone in the tent jumped to their feet and seized their helmets and rubber gas masks with their big bug-eye lenses. Outside, men and women were jogging in all directions, attaching their 'face wellies' as they scrambled into the nearest Scud pit. Even the men who had been showering had no choice but to head in the nude for the safety of sandbags. Within a minute, a quarter of a million men, with faces like giant insects, lay in the dust of the Kuwaiti desert and waited.

In spite of the UN inspectors' failure to find tangible evidence of weapons of mass destruction capable of striking targets in the West, the prospect of conflict with Saddam Hussein's rogue regime had become increasingly inevitable by the day. With a third of a million troops in theatre, there was a momentum to the military build-up that only the most dramatic political or diplomatic development could stop in its tracks. But such was the determination of the US administration under President George Bush to flex its muscles against undesirable regimes and terrorist organizations in the wake of the 11 September attacks on New York and Washington, there seemed little chance of that – short of Saddam appearing live on television draped in the Stars and Stripes and singing 'America the Beautiful'. There was no surprise, only a global intake of breath, when the invasion was launched on 20 March 2003.

The protests and public scepticism over the war, back home and across the world, were an unenviable backdrop for an army preparing for combat in a conflict without a clear-cut *casus belli* and lacking widespread backing. It's easier for a soldier to spill blood if he knows he's fighting for a noble cause endorsed by the overwhelming majority of his country-men. But in the frenetic rush there was little thought let alone talk of politics among the SCOTS DG as they put together the final touches to their preparations. Zeroing the weapons and maintenance of the tanks was the priority.

Their notice to move had been upgraded from twelve hours to one hour following aviation reports of large columns of Iraqi armour on the move, and the pace of preparation, already furious, was now frantic. The 200 vehicles of the SCOTS DG Battle Group had congregated at a location three miles south of the Demilitarized Zone, and crate after crate of ammunition was being unboxed from the back of Bedford trucks and laid out across the sands as fast as the men could shift it. The pristine pale sands of the Kuwaiti desert were covered with row upon row of stubby, yellow-based high-explosive shells (HESH) and anti-armour APFSDS rounds – known as 'FIN' to the troops – with their distinctive tung-sten darts at the head and orange protective caps at the base. The colours, shapes and symmetry of the ammunition against the spotless white backdrop of the desert gave the arrange-ment a strange beauty that wouldn't have looked completely out of place as a modern art installation. There was, however, nothing creative or lovely about the purpose of these sleek-looking tank rounds. Combined, they had the power to reduce an average-sized market town to rubble.

Anticipating traditional armour-versus-armour desert warfare, the planners had allocated considerably more FIN than HESH rounds for each of the 120 tanks of the Desert Rats' four battle groups. Every Challenger 2 was loaded with 29 FIN, 18 HESH and 3 smoke rounds as well as 20 smoke grenades, 6 regular grenades, 22 boxes of 7.62mm 'coax' (a total of 4,400 rounds) for the fixed coaxial chain gun and the anti-aircraft GPMG – general-purpose machine gun – or 'gimpy' (pronounced *jimpy*), mounted on the turret. Each tank also had a hundred rounds of 5.62mm for the SA80 assault rifles issued to the driver and the loader, the only two of the four crew with the room to store the assault rifles near their seating area. The aggregate of this inventory gave the Challenger more firepower than an entire company of infantry. Twelve rounds were also provided for the Browning pistols worn by the commander and gunner. It was a measly amount, but the thinking was that if a tank crew was reduced to using its two pistols, its number was already up. Hand-held guns generally have proved of little use in armoured engagements across the world's deserts and plains.

The men of the SQMS packets and the crews of each tank had formed small chains and were quickly shifting the rounds into the bowels of the Challengers as sergeants strode between the vehicles barking orders.

'What's the bloody rush now that we're the tail-end Charlies?' muttered one of the troopers as he handed a HESH round up to his loader in the turret. 'It'll all be over by the time we cross the border.'

The Coalition invasion had begun two days earlier and the other three battle groups of 7th Armoured (the Desert Rats) – the Black Watch, the Royal Regiment of Fusiliers and the 2nd Royal Tank Regiment – were already thirty miles into Iraq, pushing up to the southern outskirts of Basra. As part of the 1st (UK) Armoured Division, the Desert Rats, together with the Royal Marines of 3 Commando Brigade and the Paras of 16 Air Assault Brigade, had been tasked with securing Basra and the south of Iraq, while the Americans streamed through their positions to seize Baghdad 300 miles to the north. Immediately the invasion was launched, 3 Commando Brigade, attempting the first full-scale opposed landing since the Second World War, had seized the huge oil complex at the south of the Al Faw peninsula in a brilliantly executed air and amphibious assault from HMS *Ocean* and HMS *Ark Royal* floating out in the Gulf. The Paras, meanwhile, were lining up to take the oil fields of Al-Rumaylah twenty miles to the north-west of Basra.

The immediate objective for the British troops as a whole was to secure every key military, civilian and economic asset and location in the south, including the oil wells of the Al Faw and the pumping stations at Az Zubayr, defeat any resistance they might meet in achieving that and then start pouring in the humanitarian aid as quickly as possible. They had also been tasked to seal off Basra by putting in screens to the north-west of the city and to block routes in and out of it by securing the five bridges over the Shatt Al Basra. This former shipping canal, as wide as the Thames in London at Tower Bridge, runs on a south-east to north-west diagonal a couple of miles below Iraq's sprawling second city, marking a natural boundary for an invading force to seize and secure.

Once these immediate assignments had been completed, the planners were to assess the strategic situation and hand out the tasks and missions accordingly. From the outset – as they could only be as they headed into a realm of infinite possibilities – the plans were fluid and flexible and relied heavily on the resourcefulness and adaptability of the British troops to react quickly to events unfolding on the ground. In effect, this meant no British soldier crossing the border had more than the vaguest idea of what he was going to be doing in the coming days and weeks. Or months.

The hope, at the heart of general strategy, was that by sitting on the outskirts of Basra for a few days and showing the locals that they were there to help and not harm, drawing out and defeating any resistance as they did so, the troops would be able to walk into Basra without bloodshed. That was the theory at least. With just 28,000 combat troops to secure the whole of the south, what the British wanted to avoid at all costs was to get drawn into a Stalingrad or Grozny-style siege, fighting through a dense maze of streets and alleys in a city the size of Birmingham with a population of 2 million.

From the little that the SCOTS DG had been able to glean from their embedded journalists and their own channels of information, none of the Coalition forces had experienced anything other than light sparring since the invasion had begun thirty-six hours earlier. There had been a few potshots with small arms and the odd RPG – rocket-propelled grenade – but no significant weaponry or co-ordinated resistance had been encountered. There was, it seemed, no sign of the 200 T-72s and the hundred or so BM-21 truck-mounted multiple rocket launchers said to be roaming the south in search of British forces. If there had been, that was the kind of major news that didn't need a grapevine to travel along. Shocking news has its own way of finding its target audience and the SCOTS DG would have known about that back in Kuwait almost immediately. The fact that the Americans were already well north of Basra, massing on the south side of the Euphrates at Al-Nasiriyah, suggested the Iraqis weren't prepared to put up much of a fight. Either that, or Saddam had other plans.

In the first Gulf War the ground offensive was over within a hundred hours and there was a widespread suspicion amongst the SCOTS DG Battle Group that, after two months of whirlwind preparations to get ready to fight, there would be little for them to do once they finally arrived in theatre. Or, as one of the troopers, put it: 'Six months of handing out fucking Rothmans to POWs and Fruit Pastilles to kids in fifty-degree heat! Newsagents in the desert, that's all we are – only sweatier and not as well paid.'

The men of the SCOTS DG Battle Group may have represented less than 5 per cent of the total 28,000 troops – and 15 per cent of its combat fighting power – from over ninety British Army units committed to Operation TELIC, but they still cut an impressive sight as their 150 vehicles filed out in a column stretching over five miles and swung north onto Highway 80. It was difficult for the men to picture the carnage that had been visited along this tidy stretch of motorway – now renovated and resurfaced – in 1991, when most of them were still in the first years of primary school learning to read and write. Known ever since as the 'Highway of Death', the road was the scene of the devastating assault by US aircraft that laid waste to the Iraqi troops as they made an armed retreat out of Kuwait laden with local hostages and booty. The images of 2,000 burnt-out vehicles littering the sides of the road were so powerful that President Bush was forced to call an end to the fighting, allowing Saddam Hussein to remain in power. And those images were the very reason why, over a decade on, Scotland's only cavalry regiment and the infantrymen of the Irish Guards were now lining up, Challenger after Challenger, Warrior after Warrior, leading a convoy of trucks and other support vehicles, on that very same section of road, engines revving, tracks grinding and clattering as they slowly began to move northwards towards the Demilitarized Zone (DMZ). Same war, new generation. The last entry in Major Brannigan's field notebook from the first Gulf War read:

'Prepare to head North to secure Basra.' The first entry in his field notebook twelve years later read: 'Prepare to head North to secure Basra.'

Captain Will Leek, the Recce troop leader, was the first through the breach, an insignificant opening in a ten-foot-high earth berm that led into the DMZ. The buffer between the two countries was empty but for three long rolls of barbed wire stretching way into the distance in both directions. Those expecting a dramatic entry into enemy territory were disappointed. The only signs of life were a few stray dogs sniffing and scratching at the sand. Staff Sergeant Jamie 'Dodger' Gardiner, 3rd troop leader of 'B' Squadron was given the honour of taking the first tank of the battle group into Iraq. He was one of the few men of the regiment still serving to have fought in the First Gulf War, as a gunner fresh out of basic training. The weather was cooler than the previous few days and a brisk wind whipped from west to east, bending the few shrubs dotted across the landscape and stirring up mists of fine sand that gave the blue sky above them a slightly unreal quality. The 200 UN observers were long gone.

As the column passed through the second berm and into Iraq, they were greeted by a sign at the side of the road reading: 'First Fusiliers Welcome You To Iraq,' triggering equal measures of laughter and abuse from each vehicle that passed it. The SCOTS DG shared a garrison with the Fusiliers in Germany and, though they had enjoyed their fair share of bar-room punch-ups over the years, there was a great deal of affection and respect between two of Britain's most celebrated regiments. It was galling, though, to be reminded that theirs was the last major British combat unit to cross the border and they all felt the sting of the joke.

As the first few vehicles passed through the DMZ, 'C'

Squadron's radio net fell silent as the men absorbed the significance of what they were doing – only for it to burst into life again moments later to the sound of Jim Morrison of The Doors, hammering out 'Break on Through to the Other Side.' One of the NCOs had linked his MP3 player into the system and played the song for a joke, but it failed to amuse 'C' Squadron leader, Major Biggart. 'This is Zero Alpha. Whoever's playing that music, turn it off now and show some respect, will you?' The Major saw the funny side of the prank, but he wanted to keep his men focused.

The mere act of crossing from Kuwaiti to Iraqi sand was enough to send the adrenaline coursing through the veins of the battle group as the vehicles filled with nervous, excitable banter. Thoughts of home and images of loved ones were put to the back of the mind. To a man, they were exhausted after days of frenetic activity, punctuated by endless fixing of gas masks and jumping in and out of shell scrapes at the sound of Scud alarms, but a palpable energy now ran through the column as one vehicle after another rolled into Iraq. In the previous twenty-four hours alone there had been over a dozen alerts as Saddam launched two Al-Samoud missiles and five Scuds towards the Coalition forces in northern Kuwait. All of them had landed harmlessly in the desert or been shot down by US Patriots, but if part of the plan had been to unsettle the invading forces and deprive them of much-needed sleep, then he had certainly succeeded. The latest rumour sweeping the Brigade was that US forces crossing the Euphrates at Al-Nasiriyah were likely to be the trigger for the Iraqis launching a chemical attack. But for the time being, that fear, as well as the deep fatigue from which they were all suffering, was washed away in the excitement of crossing from the relative safety and comfort of a friendly nation and into a war zone. Barely a dozen of the 1,200 men in the convoy had ever fired a shot in anger, and the tanks in which they were riding had never been tested in combat. They were passing into unknown territory in more than a geographical sense.

The convoy passed by the small, ghostly town of Safwan, a quarter of a mile over the border, where General Norman Schwarzkopf, the Coalition Commander, had held ceasefire negotiations with an Iraqi delegation twelve years earlier. A once-prosperous community full of shops and cafés serving day-trippers and tradesmen passing back and forth between the two countries, it looked now as if it had been visited by the Apocalypse. All but a few of its inhabitants who hadn't already abandoned the town had fled in recent days at the approach of yet another invading army. Its derelict buildings were riddled with bullet and shell holes; rusting cars without wheels slumped forlornly on the roadside. The strong winds picked up debris from rubbish piles and sent it dancing through the air. Graffiti on the ruins of a breeze-block wall read: 'Yes for Bleer and Bush. No for Sadam.' Three young children in dirty T-shirts, their thick black hair matted with dust and dirt, stood at the side watching the convoy without expression.

'Shit, we've invaded Airdrie by mistake,' someone wise-cracked.

The head of the convoy reached a network of slip roads and flyovers. This was where Route Tampa and Route Topeka, as the Americans had dubbed the two main supply routes through southern Iraq, merged in an otherwise empty expanse of arid scrub to form a bizarrely urban spectacle. A blue and white road sign, pockmarked with fresh bullet rounds, hanging over the carriageway, pointed the vehicles in the direction of Basra and Az Zubayr.

The 'B' Squadron radio crackled into life. 'Zero Alpha, this is Three Two. Er, just a thought – what side of the road do we drive on?'

'Three Two, this is Zero Alpha. You've just invaded the country in a tank. Drive on whichever side of the road you bloody well like!'

The maps issued to the tank commanders revealed the emptiness and the flatness of the landscape in southern Iraq, but what they didn't show was the eerie desolation of the place. Route Topeka followed a virtually straight line north from Safwan, bypassing Az Zubayr after twenty-odd miles and continuing a further ten over the Shatt Al Basra waterway, through the sprawling Shia slums and into the heart of old Basra. Closed down in tanks and armoured personnel carriers, only some of the battle group were able to take in the miserable scene outside as the convoy sped north. There were no towns or even villages on the road to Az Zubayr, just the occasional mud and breeze-block smallholding or hovel, installations related to the oil industry, strings of pylons, overground pipelines and the occasional ruin or war cemetery. No trees, no grass, no flowers grew in the baked, salty earth, just the odd hunchbacked shrub, bent over by the strong winds that blast across the flat barren terrain. Whichever way they looked, the land was studded with defensive positions, barbed wire and ditches and littered with the debris of conflicts, past and present. The burnt-out, rusting hulls of tanks, troop carriers and other military vehicles stood as wretched monuments to the dead of the eight-year conflict with Iran in the 1980s and the first Gulf War that followed just three years later. Years of rubbish, tipped and thrown from passing cars, choked the roadside. The air was filled with a fetid stench from the saline mudflats and stretches of lifeless brackish water.

The motorway was virtually deserted in both directions, but

every now and then a civilian car swept by, its occupants craning their necks as they stared at the column of armour heading the other way. Dusty, dazed civilians stood in small groups at the edge of the route, their belongings at their side in an assortment of boxes and bags. The further north the convoy travelled, the busier the road became and after twenty minutes the traffic, both human and vehicular, began to thicken significantly. They passed dozens of pick-up trucks, mostly containing men in civilian clothes waving makeshift white flags or white T-shirts, grinning as hard as they could. To the left of the road, three British soldiers stood guard over a dozen Iraqi POWs, sitting on their haunches in the dirt. The prisoners were wearing white, body-length dishdash robes and grey shemaghs on their heads. Their confiscated AK-47s were leaning up against the side of a Land Rover. A little further up, the remains of a large brown dog lay in the middle of the road, flattened by an earlier tank, no thicker than a doormat now but retaining its basic dog shape despite being pressed into the tarmac by 75 tons of metal.

The traffic on the radio networks became busier as the column began to pick up the frequencies of the other battle groups and Coalition units. As the commanders and radio operators flicked through the channels, they could hear reports of contact and even the rattle of automatic and machine-gun fire in the background. The view in front began to change too. The realization sunk in that what looked like gathering rain clouds on the horizon were in fact a series of giant oil fires that grew taller and taller with every mile they advanced. The orange flares licking the base of the billowing black smoke were just visible through the magnification sights of the tanks. The blackened, twisted wrecks of military vehicles littered the landscape on either side of the road.

'Welcome to Basra,' came an unidentifiable voice over the net.

One sight was more arresting than all the other grim spectacles combined – the wreck of an American M1 Abrams, the main battle tank of the US Army. A ripple of muttering passed along the vehicles as the convoy slowed down and rubbernecked the twisted, charred remains. The same uncomfortable question was passing through the mind of every tank crew member that saw it: *Blue-on-blue, T-72 or anti-tank weapon?* Further down the road, a handful of other US vehicles, Humvees and supply trucks, sat in the dust at the side of the road, riddled with bullet holes. Positioned at crazy angles, the scene suggested that the vehicles had been abandoned in haste. As they approached Az Zubayr, the air filled with the sound of rotor blades, American Apaches and Cobras mainly but also some British Lynx and Gazelle, swooping low and fast over the ground, flicking the convoy with their shadows as they rushed northwards towards the mountains of thick oil smoke dominating the skyline around Basra. The turrets of the Challengers hummed as the commanders scanned the terrain on either side of the road, swinging the barrels of the main armament back and forth.

The battle group turned off Route Topeka and headed west, away from Basra and Az Zubayr, and continued for a further ten miles into an area of open, uninhabited scrubland where the only sign of human activity was the occasional car passing the other way, a collection of flare pipes, some obsolete industrial units and warehouses, and the odd pillbox and watchtower. The sun, enormous and orange, was sinking towards the horizon ahead of them as the convoy ground to a halt, pulled off the road and prepared to 'go firm'. With a view for miles in all directions, this designated forward assembly area (FAA),

known as 'MORPETH', was as safe a place as any in the war
zone to spend the night. The three tanks of each of the eight
troops formed a circular hide with their guns facing outwards
while the Irish Guards picketed the route, each platoon divid-
ing into sections as they strung themselves out a mile or so in
each direction in amongst the tanks. The wind was still strong
and the telegraph wires along the road danced from side to
side as the men dismounted, stretching their stiff limbs as they
emerged from their hatches and doors and set about organ-
izing themselves for the night as fast as possible while there
was still light. Each troop put men on stag while the others
bolted bacon and beans from their silver foil ration packs,
downed mugs of tea and lay out their sleeping bags on the
back decks of the tanks. For the smokers, a cigarette was the
first priority. For many, it was nature that exercised a greater
call and several dozen men, as one, jogged a short distance
out into the desert to relieve themselves after five hours closed
down. Almost immediately, the men from the Quartermaster's
departments brought up the UBRE fuel tankers from the rear
and began the laborious task of refuelling every single one of
the 150 vehicles in the battle group. The three tanks of each
troop then took up defensive positions as best they could
along the side of the road.

Night fell quickly to reveal a sky streaked with tracer fire
and a horizon throbbing with orange and yellow flashes as
artillery and jets set about their targets. At some point in the
night, when most of the men were asleep, the air filled with
the familiar, wretched din of Land Rover horns – for the
umpteenth time in a fortnight. Brigade HQ was reporting
that the entire Area of Operations (AOR) was on red alert
for a chemical attack; it was a Dress State 4 alert demanding
that protective suits as well as gas masks were donned. A

collective groan greeted the alarm and, wearily and roboti-
cally, most of the men stood up and climbed into the ungainly
suits and pulled the cumbersome rubber masks over their
heads. Many didn't wait for the all-clear and quickly fell back
to sleep in their suits. The guardsmen lay by the side of the
road, the troopers on the backs of the tanks, making the most
of the heat from the huge 1,200bhp Perkins engines in the
cool night air.

An hour later, a column of vehicles from the US Marine
Expeditionary Force thundered through the battle group's
position at speed, the wheels of some of the more erratically
driven vehicles coming within a foot or two of the sleeping
guardsmen, forcing them to take quick evasive action. Dozens
of men jumped from the ground, some in rubber suits and
masks like zombies back from the dead, gesticulating wildly
at the passing convoy, their shouts of protest muffled by the
respirators.

The crown of the sun had yet to appear over the eastern
horizon but the stars were fading into a dirty grey when the
news swept along the battle group lines like a current of electricity: 'Brigade are sending us north of Basra, deep behind
enemy lines!'

2. Nick 104

The senior officers and NCOs of the battle group squeezed to the front of the canvas awning to get a better look at the map that Lieutenant Colonel Blackman held up in the diffuse light from the open rear door of Command troop's vehicle. Inside the cramped Sultan, the mobile Operations room of the battle group, the powerful figure of Captain Macmillan pressed the telephone receiver harder to the side of his head and crouched towards the narrow shelf that served as his desk to take down the finer details of the orders from Brigade HQ. Behind him, partially obscured by an entanglement of wires, radios and other equipment, Warrant Officer Class 2 Brotherton was nodding impatiently as he adjusted his headset with one hand and rubbed the sleep from his eye with the other. It was 5.30 in the morning, the sun had yet to make an appearance and every man in the 'O' group, including the Commanding Officer himself, was straining to resist the impulse to yawn. Major Brannigan rolled an unlit Marlboro through his fingers behind his back as he tried to remember the last time he had enjoyed more than three hours sleep in a night. It was 5 March, eighteen days ago, he worked out. *What is the expression my troopers use? 'Hanging out', that's it.* They were *hanging out* – and they hadn't even been in Iraq for a full day yet.

Even a Boy Scout with the most basic map-reading skills could have seen the difficulties of the proposed march as Lieutenant Colonel Blackman ran the butt of his pencil along the route they had been given by Brigade. The first part was straightforward enough: north along a metalled road past the former RAF base of Shaibah airfield and round the western perimeter of Basrah International Airport. It was what followed that turned the sleepy faces of his audience into a cartoon gallery of frowns and raised eyebrows. Crossing over the northern end of the Shatt Al Basra, the brown road on the map gave way to a candy-stick line of brown and white, denoting a dirt track, passing through a haze of green dots, which, according to the map's standardized legend at the foot, denoted 'vineyards or orchards' but in all probability meant date palm plantations or tomato farms. Iraq has more date palm plantations than any other country in the world, most of them hugging the fertile areas along the Tigris and Euphrates and their tributaries. The nature of the vegetation was unimportant; the point was that it provided cover for the enemy: armour, infantry and irregulars. Of even greater concern was the myriad of waterways that spread out like blue veins across the area through which they would be passing – and these were just the canals and tributaries significant enough to be given a blue line of representation on a 1:100,000 scale map. This indicated two potential problems for an armoured column: bridges and boggy terrain.

The mission they had been given by Brigade was simple: to put in a block to prevent enemy armour entering or leaving Basra to and from the north. The move was part of the wider strategy to isolate Iraq's second city, squeeze the enemy and stoke up the pressure amongst the largely Shia population to rise up against the Sunni-dominated regime, allowing the British to take control of the city with a minimum of casualties. The battle group was to secure two major road junctions, ten miles north of central Basra, both running roughly parallel with the Shatt Al Arab. One of the routes, Highway 6, was the main road to Baghdad and the other bent round on a westerly direction after about six miles towards the oil fields of Al-Rumaylah.

The Commanding Officer barely needed to point out to his senior officers that the location to which they were heading was completely cut off from the rest of the Coalition forces. To the west of these positions, there was nothing but desert; to the south, nothing but Basra and its suburbs; to the east there was the Shatt Al Arab. The north was not an option either, because they would be even more remote from supplies and would quickly run out of fuel, rations, water and ammo. Separated from the rest of Brigade, the SCOTS DG were to be the most northerly based regular British forces, by some distance. The Intelligence, explained Blackman, was patchy and it was anyone's guess what resistance they might encounter. They would have to be especially vigilant. Points on the map along the routes of southern Iraq had been given numbers by the planners known as 'Nicks'. The SCOTS DG Battle Group was heading to Nick 104: a small pinprick in a large map, but a place that many of them would never forget.

The light was starting to fade by the time the SCOTS DG had completed their advance through the area held by the Fusiliers Battle Group and slowed to a halt on the southern side of Bridge One, the most northerly of the five structures spanning the Shatt Al Basra on routes into Basra. On the approach, the SCOTS DG troops had their first encounter with friendly tanks inside Iraq when they passed close to a squadron of Queen's Royal Lancers (QRL) attached to the Fusiliers. The commanders from each regiment acknowledged one another with a wave from the hatches of their Challengers. There was a decent chance that they were waving to old mates from Sandhurst or Bovington, but in their helmets, headsets and body armour it was difficult to distinguish one man from another. Although it was reassuring to encounter 'friendlies' in the field, the sight of so much British armour in one area was also unsettling for the crews because it brought home quite how close the coalition units were going to be operating to one another other over the coming days and weeks. As they set off for Nick 104, this brush with the QRL was a timely reminder that all 120 British tanks in theatre were going to have to be especially careful when it came to identifying enemy targets, particularly at night when a tank became no more than a green shape on a black or white fuzzy background on a thermal-imaging screen. Their eyes alone were not going to tell them the difference between a T-72, T-55 and a Challenger; cool heads and clear communication were needed to avoid blue-on-blue incidents.

They continued on their way north with 'C' Squadron passing through 'B' Squadron to lead the advance across the broad canal, accompanied by the muffled boom of the 155mm guns of the Royal Horse Artillery drifting up from the south. The rounds, passing somewhere overhead, were landing with distant thuds in the outskirts of Basra. Captain Jameson's 4th troop, supporting the eight Scimitars of the battle group Recce troop, had already crossed and they were several miles up country when the rest of the column began to snake its way out of the Coalition areas of operation and into enemy territory, passing from wide tarmac carriageway to narrow dirt track on the northern side of the bridge.

After pausing for the entire battle group to assemble, the drivers of the twenty-eight Challengers ran up their engines, sending clouds of JP-8 diesel smoke into the atmosphere as the heavy caterpillar tracks tensed around the six double roadwheels on each side and dug their teeth into the earth below. Inside the crews could hear nothing, but outside the tanks roared and growled as the armoured convoy, elongated by twenty-eight Warriors, the infantry fighting vehicles of the Irish Guards, began the push into a world strikingly different from the arid scrubland they were leaving. Irrigated by a network of ditches, canals and natural waterways, this was fertile land dominated by thick groves of date palms, interspersed with expanses of drained marshland and patches of swamp. A haze hung over the water between the trees, giving the area a sub-tropical, prehistoric quality. 'I thought this was a desert war, not bloody Vietnam' was the comment in one turret as the column wound its way into the increasingly lush vegetation.

The sixty vehicles passed over tributaries of the Shatt Al Arab, the confluence of the Euphrates and Tigris, towards the ancient land of Mesopotamia. Progress was painfully slow along the narrow earth levees and single-lane country tracks as the convoy tentatively creaked its way through a string of small, scruffy hamlets of dilapidated houses, outbuildings and rusting farm machinery. If there were any locals in residence, it seemed that they had retreated indoors at the sight of the dust trail on the horizon moving their way. After twenty minutes they reached a village where two young boys ran out of a house at the sound of the approaching column and stood gawping as it rolled through in a cloud of powdery dust. A black goat chewed at its tether, and a sleepy donkey tied to a telegraph pole paid no attention to the stream of armoured vehicles clattering past, just a few feet from where it stood. An elderly man sat under a tree fidgeting with a string of worry beads. The thought running through minds of the troopers and guardsmen was: *Where the hell is everyone?* There was barely any sign of human activity, let alone any enemy. From time to time, a jet screeched overhead, to or from a bombing raid to the north, but that was the only indication that they were in the middle of a war zone.

The banter of the crews faded away as the column crept into enemy territory. Small bridges of uncertain structural quality punctuated the route, forcing the entire battle group to grind to a halt each time it reached one. The vehicles crossed one at a time so as to exert as little pressure as possible on the jerry-built structures. The reconnaissance troops of the Queen's Dragoon Guards (QDG), also known as the 'Welsh Cavalry', had travelled the route in their Scimitars earlier in the day, but at eight tons their lightly armoured vehicles, designed with speed rather than protection in mind, weighed just over one tenth of the Challengers with their extra armour. There was no telling whether a crossing could withstand the accumulated stress of a column passing over it. One by one, painstakingly, the tanks crossed, and it was the crews at the rear that let out the loudest sighs of relief on reaching the other side.

The column crept its way forward towards its objectives at no more than a trot. Each vehicle was doing its best to put a bit of distance between itself and the one in front so as not to drive through the clouds of fine dust that each was spewing up to its rear. No vehicle in the desert likes to 'eat dust' and a slow advance in a narrow line is not how the tank chooses to travel; tanks want to spread out and range over the terrain at pace. Mobility is one of the tank's three great assets and without it, as they were now, its other great strengths – firepower and protection – were automatically compromised. The tank prefers to fight on the move, facing its enemy with its thickest armour to the fore; sitting still or crawling slowly it will attract fire like a magnet, with its less protected areas to the side and rear exposed and vulnerable. Here, the soft ground and 'complex terrain' of ditches and vegetation severely restricted their room to manoeuvre. The narrowness of the tracks, the 'single vehicle frontage' they had been forced to adopt and the weakness of the bridges meant that speed was a problem too.

But this was their only route in. More worryingly, it was their only route out.

Six miles in from Bridge One, the column passed through the village of Qaryat al Hillat, the first settlement of any significance that they'd encountered since receiving orders to start the road move in the early afternoon. The late-afternoon sun was squinting through the files of date palms that bordered the road on both sides and the air was completely still as the tracks of the leading tanks crunched towards the first houses. Washing hung on lines between trees and dogs roamed the street but there were few signs of human activity. Outside one home, an Iraqi army uniform had been folded neatly over a fence post above a pair of boots and a helmet. A further hundred yards along the road another uniform had been laid out in exactly the same way. Was this a sign to the invaders that the men of this area had renounced their regime? The column advanced with the men keeping silence in the turrets. Towards the far end of the village, a thickly bearded man wearing a flowing white dishdash with a red and white checked scarf wrapped around his head leant against a telegraph pole, an AK-47 slung over his shoulder and a bullet belt around his waist. He smiled as the column passed by, revealing a set of crazily cragged teeth.

The intercoms and radio nets of the column crackled into life as the loaders, standing out of their hatches manning the turret-mounted gimpys, gripped the machine guns that little bit tighter.

There were half a dozen more men a little further up the road, some in the traditional Arab garb, others in T-shirts, trousers and open-toed sandals or trainers. All of them were armed with automatic rifles. Some smiled at the passing vehicles, others just stared. The men on the gimpys glared back from under their helmets, training the gun sights over the heads of the locals as they passed.

On the wider stretches of the road, the Warriors and Challengers overtook each other and dropped back as they scanned the terrain. In the to-ing and fro-ing the vehicles of 'B' Squadron and No. 1 Company had become entangled and the vehicles were forced to stop and rearrange themselves before making the final leg of the march.

'C' Squadron, with No. 2 Company Irish Guards to the rear, continued the advance towards Nick 104. They had pressed on for ten minutes when the voice of Captain Leek, the Recce troop leader, burst over the Brigade radio net.

'Zero, this is Mike Two One. Contact! Wait! Out!'

Contact, wait, out! Three words charged with a power and significance only a soldier can understand.

Thirty miles to the south, across the other side of Basra, on the outskirts of the town of Az Zubayr, the three tanks of 3rd troop 'A' Squadron, commanded by Staff Sergeant Hanson, were pulling up close to a small farmstead bordering a tomato field. Down a rutted old track, far from the main roads but with a good 360-degree view of the terrain, it was as safe as any place to park up, yet no more than a ten-minute drive from the munitions store where they had spent the afternoon on overwatch. Not that the troop was retreating from harm's way; it had been an uneventful first full day since 'A' Squadron of the SCOTS DG had crossed the border with the rest of the Black Watch Battle Group. Commanded by Major Tim Brown, 'A' Squadron was the third SCOTS DG squadron to deploy to Iraq, but with only two armoured squadrons per battle group, they had been reassigned to support the infantrymen of the Black Watch along with Egypt Squadron of the 2nd Royal Tank Regiment.

If there was a war going on in Iraq, no one it seemed had told the people of Az Zubayr. Streams of curious locals had come and gone along the main road close to the munitions store, but the only inkling of trouble they had encountered was a minor fracas involving a young man they caught sneaking out of the compound with an armful of assault rifles and an RPG. He claimed he wanted the weapons to protect his family in the event of civil unrest – and he may well have been telling the truth – but he was promptly sent on his way empty-handed as one of the tanks reversed over the weapons, flattening and mangling them beyond use. That had been the highlight of the day. For the rest of the time, the most taxing challenge for the men was to stay awake.

Eight hours on, the shadows were starting to lengthen as the men heaved themselves from their hatches. Stretching, yawning and grumbling, they lowered their leaden limbs down the side of the Challengers and prepared to go firm for the night.

Like their counterparts in 'C' Squadron, the troops of 'A' Squadron were in fine working order after the luxury of a full training year. In the words of the Squadron leader, Major Brown, the only Briton to have commanded a tank in both Gulf wars, they were 'as battle-ready as you can get an armoured force to be in this day and age'. But since storming across the border thirty-six hours earlier, as part of the spearhead of the invasion, they had come across nothing to suggest that that finely honed battle-readiness was going to be put to a significant test. The only Iraqi armour they'd encountered so far had come in the form of the burnt-out wrecks of past conflicts. Privately, most of the men were resigning themselves to a long, hot tour of overwatch and vehicle checkpoint (VCP) duties.

When the battle group had pulled up outside Az Zubayr the day before after a rapid march from the border, there was barely any sign of the 7 Regimental Combat Team of 1st US Marine Expeditionary Force that they'd been tasked to relieve. Back in Kuwait, the two groups had rock-drilled the 'relief in place' exercise until they could almost carry it out in their sleep, but in the event itself, there was only a handful of US vehicles there to greet them.

'We've not actually been into A-Zed but it seems real quiet down here,' the captain had shouted in a southern drawl over his shoulder, jumping back into his vehicle to catch up with his compatriots on their headlong charge for the Iraqi capital. 'Baghdad's where the shit's gonna be goin' down! Y'all have fun down here now.' Thus, the tank crews of the Royal Scots Dragoon Guards and the infantrymen of the Black Watch watched the rearguard of the US Marines disappear into the distance in a column of dust, took out their maps and set about pinpointing the key junctions they needed to hold to block the routes in and out of the town.

With an estimated population of 400,000, 'A-Zed' was home to more inhabitants than the populations of Newcastle on Tyne and Sunderland combined: the perfect place for defenders to hide, but a nightmare for a small offensive force to dominate and secure. It was considered a potential hornets' nest and the plan was for the Black Watch Battle Group to sit on the outside and give it a prod with some aggressive patrols, then wait and see what nasties, if any, swarmed out to sting them. Ten miles south of Basra and by far the largest town between there and the border, the Shia town with a significant Sunni minority was the Iraqis' first line of defence. But being smack in the middle of the Coalition forces' main AOR and under constant surveillance from the air, what resistance was lurking in there was highly unlikely to venture out to meet the opposition. Only when Scotland's most famous infantry regiment, supported by the twenty-eight Challenger 2s of the SCOTS DG and the 2RTR, set foot inside the town would they know if they had a proper fight on their hands.

The battle group's first objective on their arrival had been to secure three key installations to the south of the town: an oil pumping station, a chemical plant and, right next to it, a military complex housing a large store of munitions. The planners had dubbed the facilities the 'Crown Jewels' to stress their strategic importance. The pumping station was a key economic asset while the chemical plant housed large quantities of chlorine which, if blown up, would cause mayhem among the local populace and the British forces operating in the area. 'B' Company Black Watch, under Major Lindsay MacDuff, secured the military complex and chemical factory while Major Dougie Hay's 'D' Company seized the oil station, each taking a troop of tanks in support. Neither unit set eyes on an enemy soldier, let alone met any resistance. With the sites safely in Coalition hands, the battle group positioned itself along the arterial roads to the south and west of the town in a belt of VCPs at key junctions.

Since then, Major Brown's four troops had been rotated in overwatch shifts at the various locations, with the commanders and gunners taking it in turns to scan the terrain with the sights, traversing the turrets back and forth, for hour after exhausting hour. Only a few of the hundred men had managed to snatch more than an hour's sleep since arriving in Iraq, as they had been busy securing the area and establishing the lie of the land. Fatigue, and the accidents it causes, was starting to emerge as a greater threat to life and limb than enemy fire. Bombardments rumbled all day along to the north but 'A' Squadron were yet to fire a shot in anger.

3rd troop had arranged their hide in a classic troop triangle giving them 360-degree cover as well as an area in the middle to congregate under the desert camouflage nets, or 'camnets', for the men to talk, eat and unwind. The last beams of the dying sun were filtering through the tomato plants in the field beyond when a tall elderly man emerged from the tumbledown mud and breeze-block farmhouse 200 yards away and slowly walked towards them carrying a shallow basket at his side.

The troopers stopped what they were doing as the man, his face dark and leathered after decades of life under a baking sun, hobbled towards Corporal Dean Gibbs, commander of call sign Three Two. The man handed over the basket and bowed his head in greeting. The basket, woven with thick reeds, contained dozens of beautifully ripe tomatoes and a dozen flatbreads, still warm to the touch. The young commander's eyes lit up and a smile broke across his face as he thanked the old man effusively. They shook hands as the rest of the troop gathered around and began helping themselves to the fresh produce. It doesn't take many bacon and baked bean boil-in-the-bags before the human body begins to crave real food.

'Well, this war business could be a lot worse, couldn't it, lads?' said Corporal Gibbs.

Thirty miles to the north, the rounds fell in rapid succession on the advance units of the SCOTS DG Battle Group. Captain

Leek's Recce troop and Captain Jameson's 4th troop were in mid-handover with the QDG, all of them spread out around the crossroads at Nick 104, when the mortar bombs began to rain down amongst the assembled Scimitars, hurling geysers of powdery earth high into the air. Jameson's driver Trooper Thorburn was sound asleep, closed down at the front of the tank, when the explosions hit their location and it was only a sharp word from his commander that managed to stir the young trooper out of his slumber and into sudden action. Thorburn was in the reclining position with his hatch down when Jameson barked at him down the intercom, making him crash his helmet on the ceiling of his compartment when he sat bolt upright.

All the vehicles had spread out so as not to offer the enemy a single large target, but the incoming shells were close enough to shower a number of them with grit. It was just a matter of luck that none of them had received a direct hit. As the rounds crashed around them, the guardsmen and troopers swore in astonishment, tossing away their cigarettes and disappearing into their hatches like rabbits down their holes. No one in the troop had ever experienced a bombardment and it was difficult for them to work out in that heart-stopping instant whether the incoming was mortar fire or a payload from the dreaded BM-21 truck-mounted rocket launcher. Either way, the accuracy of the shelling indicated that whoever was in charge of the firing knew exactly what they were doing, and within seconds all dozen vehicles of the handover party were on the move to avoid being bracketed. This was no place for the light vehicles of Recce troop and the QDG and, barely before the dust from the first shells had settled, the order for them to extract was given. The three heavily armoured tanks of 4th troop were to stay behind to face down the threat before the rest of 'C' Squadron, now no more than ten minutes behind them, arrived on the scene.

4th troop was considered to be one of the strongest in the regiment and Jameson one of its coolest, most capable commanders. This was the first time he had ever been shot at, but the 25-year-old Scotsman, the son of a former Commanding Officer of the regiment, showed no sign of panic as the second wave of rounds crashed into the open scrubland behind them.

Yes, we are definitely being bracketed here, he thought as he stubbed out his Marlboro in an old tin and ordered his troop to shake out and keep moving. There was no point in returning fire for the simple reason that they didn't have the first clue who was engaging them – let alone from where. As the three drivers floored their accelerators, the Challengers' giant engines let out a collective roar and the tanks sped away from the falling rounds. The troop headed due east towards the second objective, the next main junction two miles down the road, close to the suburban sprawl that hugs the western bank of the Shatt Al Arab. As his 75-ton tank jolted forward, Captain Jameson cursed when the hot coffee from his commuter mug, passed to him by his loader just a moment earlier, sloshed onto his combat trousers. Through the rear periscopes he could see fountains of earth and smoke bursting out of the ground as the last of the Scimitars raced away in the opposite direction, leaving a billowing trail of dust in their wake.

The ground either side of the two-mile stretch of road between the two junctions was much firmer and slightly flatter than what they had driven through so far and the troop needed no invitation to pull off the road and range across the terrain, riding the undulations like boats in a heavy swell. Open country is the tank's habitat of choice. Roads are for cars. The Challenger 2 can hit speeds of 45 mph but its optimum speed, in terms of comfort for the crew, is around 15–20mph, when the hydrogas suspension system is able to absorb almost all the uneven movement beneath the tracks. For the first time since crossing the border, the twelve men of the troop experienced that peculiar sensation of sitting inside 75 tons of solid metal and armour, bouncing over hummocks and hollows, and yet somehow floating on air.

As they ranged over the terrain, Troop Sergeant Larry Lamb, commanding call sign Four One, scanning the area to the south, brought the traversing turret to a sudden halt. A white Hilux flatbed, sitting at the top of a road at the edge of the suburbs, filled his sights. A dozen men in civilian clothes leaning on RPGs and AK-47s were perched on the sides at the back of the vehicle. Civilians were milling around in the street behind. Among them were a number of small children, reminding him it was 23 March, his daughter's birthday. He pictured the joyful noise and chaos of her party back in the barracks in Germany, then quickly shook the image from his mind, and flicked the sights to full magnification to get a close-up on the irregulars in the truck. They were men in their late twenties – just like him – some of them clean-shaven, some bearded, but all of them armed and all of them with a mixture of trepidation and exhilaration etched into their faces – just like him. He immediately reported the sighting over the Squadron radio net, with details of the location and the armed men.

The rest of the column, now more tightly compressed into a three-mile chain, had crossed the final bridge of the march and were advancing as fast as the narrow track would allow them. On hearing Captain Leek's electrifying contact report, one thought had been wriggling in the mind of every man in the battle group: *If the enemy blow one of those bridges behind us, we are well and truly stuffed.* The entire column of twenty-eight tanks, twenty-eight Warriors and 400 men would be trapped. At every point of the compass, their route was blocked. The soft, boggy terrain flanking most of the route meant they were unable even to venture from the track along which they were edging towards Nick 104.

Afternoon was fading into evening when the various troops and platoons set about securing the route on a three-mile frontage. Rolling dunes of earth and scrub flanked both sides of the route that led towards the residential area at its eastern end. The closest buildings were no more 200 yards from where 4th troop had taken up position and the crews didn't need their magnification sights to see that hundreds of locals were going about their business barely a five-minute stroll from where they sat. Cars and pedestrians were meandering up and down the streets, mothers shopped, men sat outside cafés and restaurants drinking coffee, passengers boarded and disembarked from buses, children, back from school, played at the side of the road. It was an ordinary, busy day in northern Basra – and it was strange to be sitting on the edge of it, looking in, from the cramped interior of a Challenger 2 tank. It was even stranger that no one appeared to be paying a blind bit of attention to them.

Captain Le Sueur's 2nd troop were no more than half a mile from 4th troop, halfway between the two strategic junctions that were their objectives, when they were ordered south down a track passing through the barren scrubland and towards the communities spilling out of Basra. Their task was to investigate the suspicious white Hilux reported by Larry. The troop was without call sign Two One, which had been kept back for essential maintenance, so Zero Charlie, commanded by the squadron 2iC, Captain Cattermole, joined Le Sueur and Corporal Craig Dougal in Two Two to make up the three-tank packet. The commanders and gunners of each kept their faces glued to the sights, scanning the terrain, trying to distinguish foe from friend in the confusion of everyday life. They had been in Iraq for the better part of twenty-four hours but they were yet to see an Iraqi in uniform.

They had advanced only a few hundred yards from the main road when a white Toyota Hilux turned the corner, accelerating towards them before the driver slammed on the brakes. There were two men in the driving compartment and two men sitting in the open compartment at the rear; all of them had red and white shemaghs wrapped around their heads. The four men leapt from the vehicle and stood facing the Challengers. They were wearing long white dishdash robes, the classic Arab attire, and they stood grim-faced by the side of the vehicle with their hands buried deep inside their clothes. The tanks ground to a halt.

Captain Le Sueur in call sign Two Zero switched the sights to full ×11.5 magnification and the four men appeared to leap towards him as he zoomed in. His gunner, who could see the same image through his sights, gripped the firing mechanism. The troop leader realized that he was breathing a little bit faster. The loader checked the breech of the coax machine gun was clear. They had been closed down for over four hours now and the turret felt stuffier and more claustrophobic than ever.

'That must be them, boss,' said the gunner. 'Shall I fire?' A three-second squeeze on the trigger and all four of them would be dead.

Captain Le Sueur paused for a moment. 'Let's not get ahead of ourselves,' he replied coolly. 'Fire at them only if they fire at us. They could be armed to protect themselves against anyone . . . Let's press on, but keep it slow,' he added to his driver.

The grit crackled beneath the grinding tracks as the tanks edged forward. The four men stood poker-faced by their vehicle. The tanks pulled alongside them. The Iraqis, as one, immediately pulled their hands from their robe pockets and began frantically waving white strips of cloth. Wreathed in broad smiles, they flagged the Challengers through with their improvised gestures of peace.

Le Sueur let out a sigh of relief, but he was still troubled. *How the hell are we going to distinguish the enemy from the innocent? And are the enemy going to be irregulars or regulars disguised as civilians?* The tanks continued further south, deeper into the increasingly dense suburbs. After two miles, the same distance short of central Basra itself, the small packet of Challengers swung a sharp left into the light traffic of a broad metalled road. The locals stared at the spectacle of the three British tanks, their main armaments sweeping back and forth like prehistoric animals seeking out their prey.

Dougal's tank clipped a kerbstone and sent it spinning into the air. A man leading a donkey weighed down with ceramic pots threw his arms into the air in remonstration and yelled an insult in their direction. At the end of the mile-long road, the signal on the radio began to break up and fade, cutting out altogether for periods. In silence, the three Challengers turned left again onto a dual carriageway running parallel with the Shatt Al Arab and headed up towards the junction where Jameson's 4th troop had taken up position.

Dusk was descending fast and lights were starting to come on amongst the palms on the far bank of the waterway as they turned a shallow bend in the broad dual carriageway. The darkening sky up ahead of them was smeared with green tracer.

The radio net began to splutter back into life. The three commanders, pressing the headsets to their ears, caught only snatches of the traffic as the signal cut in and out. Two words, though, came through loud and clear: 'multiple' and 'dismounts'. With a roar of exhausts, the three Challengers sped north.

Back on the outskirts of Az Zubayr, 'A' Squadron and the Black Watch were being swept up in a rapidly escalating drama of their own. Major Brown, and the Squadron Sergeant Major, Ross Anderson, stood at the rear of the Sultan command vehicle listening anxiously to the radio as two tanks of 4th troop, call signs Four Zero and Four One, attempted to clear the route into the town for 'D' Company Black Watch. Over the voices of the commanders' updates, they could hear the rattle and phut of the coax chain gun and the shouts of their men inside the turrets. The two most experienced men of the squadron gnawed at their thumbnails as they tried to picture the running fight erupting across the town. There is only one scenario worse than being shot at and that is listening to your comrades and friends being shot at – and it was even worse if they were men under your command. As a unit of the Black Watch Battle Group, they were not masters of their own operational destiny. They could do nothing but sit and wait for orders. They were effectively a guest of the Black Watch and it was not their position to call the shots. It was, as Major Brown put it to his troop leaders, a little like walking into another regiment's officers' mess for dinner. You kept your distance, waited to be offered a drink and let the hosts decide when it was time to sit down to eat. They were part of the entertainment but it wasn't up to the guests to set out the programme.

An hour earlier, the two men had been enjoying a brew and reminiscing about their experiences together in the first Gulf War when Brown was a young troop leader, recently out of Sandhurst and Anderson his fresh-faced radio operator and loader. Now their faces were furrowed with apprehension as they listened, with increasing discomfort, to the sitreps (situation reports) from a search party as it raced through the streets of Az Zubayr in a desperate search for two missing soldiers from a Royal Engineers specialist bomb disposal unit.

Details were sketchy but what they had been able to fathom was that the engineers, attached to the Fusiliers Battle Group, had got lost and were passing through the northern outskirts of Az Zubayr in two Land Rovers when they were ambushed by Fedayeen soldiers. Dressed head to foot in black uniforms, the attackers strafed the vehicles with automatic fire as they swarmed into the road. One of the Land Rovers managed to escape but the other was not so fortunate. The two engineers, a young sapper and an experienced Staff Sergeant, both bleeding heavily, had been dragged from the vehicle and, watched by a mob, driven away at speed by Saddam's notorious henchmen. Immediately, Lieutenant Colonel Mike Riddell-Webster, Commanding Officer of the Black Watch, dispatched 'D' Company, supported by the two Challengers of 4th troop leader Ed O'Brien and his Troop Sergeant Jock McKelvie to find the men.

Making the deepest incursion into the town so far, the small armoured column was encountering intense, co-ordinated fire from units of heavily armed, well-organized fighters. Most of them were wearing civilian clothes, but there was nothing amateur about their combat skills. Emerging from underpasses and side streets, the main tactic was to wait until the tanks and Warriors had passed before bringing not just their automatic weapons but RPGs to bear on the more vulnerable rear and sides of their vehicles. Listening to the contact reports, it was plain to the 'A' Squadron leader and his Sergeant Major that their comrades were being engaged by professionals who had planned the ambush and anticipated the immediate deployment of a rescue party. The Fedayeen were the most feared and loyal of Saddam's troops and the Intel was that they were going to fight to the bitter end – not least because if they failed to beat off the invaders, the men of the predominantly Sunni unit would more than likely be strung up from the nearest lamp post by a Shi'ite mob.

Brown and Anderson blew out their cheeks and shook their heads in disbelief as the contact reports buzzed over the radio. The search party was taking multiple hits and, after such a quiet couple of days with barely a hint of enemy activity or civil disquiet, the intensity of the fighting was a shock to them. Aside from the immediate crisis of hunting for two injured British soldiers and their captors, they were now facing the inescapable fact that the enemy had regrouped and was prepared to mount a tenacious defence of the town. A-Zed was a hornets' nest after all.

Thirty minutes later, the raiding party roared back to Battle Group Headquarters. They had found the Land Rover, burnt out up a side road, but with no sign of the two engineers they withdrew under intense fire. The adrenaline from the engagement was still coursing through them as the men dismounted from the vehicles, wild-eyed and grim-faced.

'It's the fucking Wild West in there!' said one of them, emerging from the light at the back of a Warrior. Call sign Three Three Alpha, the Sergeant Major's wagon, had an unexploded RPG stuck in the vehicle's side armour.

As the men prepared to get their heads down, and the

guards on stag took up their positions, the news from Intel filtered through the battle group. The two engineers were almost certainly dead. They had been refused treatment for their injuries and then executed by their captors.

'Zero Bravo, this is Four Zero. Contact wait out ... Zero Bravo, Four One, we are engaging RPG team to south ... Zero Bravo, Two Two, engaging four enemy pax to north ... Zero Bravo, Four Two. Engaging multiple dismounts ...'

The traffic over the radio was near-continuous as the fighting erupted north of Basra. The SCOTS DG Battle Group, stretched out over its thin three-mile front, was under attack from north and south, but the most ferocious engagements were taking place on the eastern flank, around the Nick 104 crossroads itself, where 'C' Squadron's 4th troop had been joined by 2nd troop and the tanks of Squadron leader Biggart and his 2iC Captain Cattermole. Major Brannigan's 'B' Squadron were at the western end of the line with the Commanding Officer, Lieutenant Colonel Blackman, positioned in the heart of his battle group.

Rocket-propelled grenades and small arms fizzed and whistled between the tanks of 2nd and 4th troops while mortar rounds crashed around them. The tanks stayed on the move, back and forth over the route between the two junctions, to avoid being bracketed.

Corporal Dougal commanding Two Two was scanning the short stretch of scrubland to his south when four men ran into the road on the edge of the town and dropped a large mortar plate to the ground. Adrenaline burst into his body and his heart hammered against his ribcage as he tried to steady his grips on the control handles. Civilians poked their heads from doorways behind the mortar team, but most had retreated indoors. The air was cool now, but sweat ran down from under his helmet. In among the shrubs and tall, dry grass over to the right two other men sprinted across the undulating terrain, disappearing from sight behind the earth embankments every few seconds. One was carrying an RPG launcher, the other its grenades.

The Geordie tank commander ran his right thumb over the touch control button, moving the sights rapidly from left to right and back again. A minute ago, it was no man's land; now it was crawling with enemy dismounts, weaving their way through the hollows towards the tanks. In the streets behind, men leapt from the back of technicals, the open-backed pickups troops used as improvised fighting vehicles. With night descending fast, he flicked the sights to thermal-imaging mode to reveal a world of ghoulish green figures. Dougal had been in the Army for almost twelve years, serving in Kosovo and Bosnia, but he had never been in combat; he'd never shot another man, and he'd never been shot at. It was the same story for every other man in 'C' Squadron taking the brunt of the assault at the eastern flank of the battle group. The squadron had basked in praise at the end of a highly successful training year and they were as well prepared as any armoured unit that the British Army could put into the field. But there was just one problem: they had never trained for urban operations such as this. *Never take a tank into a town or operate against dismounted infantry without your own close infantry support*: one of the golden rules of armoured combat. Recruits learn that on their first day. Tanks simply aren't designed to fight infantry at close quarters – and this was extremely close quarters.

Thousands of rounds of small-arms fire, mostly from AK-47s, streaked into the tanks, but against the two-foot thick Dorchester armour it was no more effective than dried peas against a brick wall. If anything, it was a help because it revealed the bunkers from which the fire was coming; what's more, the phosphor-tipped tracer fire of the enemy was green, distinguishing it from the red used by British troops, thereby reducing the chances of a blue-on-blue incident with the Irish Guards, picketing the routes in between the tanks. Small-arms fire may be no more of a threat to a Challenger than a shower of confetti but RPGs, fired into its softer spots, are capable of causing some serious damage. A very good shot, or a lucky one, into the exposed sprockets or tracks at the back of the tracks may even immobilize the tank. The Challenger 2 is widely considered to be the best protected main battle tank in the world, but no tank is entirely invulnerable to smaller weapons.

It was difficult to know which target to hit first but with civilians moving about right behind them, going for the mortar team was out of the question. Dougal switched his focus to the two-man RPG team. They were now about a hundred yards away, scurrying through the gloom, barely making any effort to crouch or duck from view. It was as if they thought that nobody could see them in the darkness. Clearly, they had no idea that through the thermal-imaging night sights they were an even more distinct target than they were in broad daylight. More worryingly, maybe they were fanatics who didn't care whether they died. Switching to the higher magnification, Dougal saw one of the two kneel down and load a grenade, just like an archer of old might have laced an arrow in his bow.

Remarkably similar to a Sony PlayStation, the Challenger's firing and sights controller has two handles and half a dozen buttons and switches operated by the thumbs. It is very easy to work – especially for the more recent recruits brought up on computer games – and it is also extremely reliable and accurate to within inches even over the longest distances for all three types of ammunition: HESH, FIN and 7.62mm coax. Nine times out of ten the target will be destroyed in the first instance. The days of bracketing are long over.

Dougal was aware he was gripping the fire control mechanism too tensely and tried to relax his hands. His gunner, Trooper Todd, sitting two feet below him and clutching a replica of the commander's controller, leant into the sights and waited for the order to fire. The commander has two options in an engagement: identify the target, then release the control grip to allow the gunner to fire while he gets on with scanning for new targets on his independent panoramic sights. This system is known as 'hunter–killer'. The commander hunts, the gunner kills. But the commander can also keep control of the gun and destroy the target himself. And Dougal wanted to destroy this particular target himself. Every soldier needs to know if he has got what it takes.

He fired the laser at the target with the aiming mark that appeared in his sights as a small red dot. In the blink of an eye, the computer calculated the exact distance to the target, taking into account the contours of the land as well as the prevailing wind and weather conditions. The turret automatically drove onto the target with a short hum of its electric motor. Dougal flicked the weapons switch in the centre of the controls from Off to Coax, pushed open the keyhole catch behind the left-hand handle and placed his shaking index finger on the firing button. The entire procedure from identifying the target to preparing to shoot had taken just three seconds, but to Dougal, the most nervous he'd been since entering the Army twelve years earlier, it felt like minutes. He could hear his breathing over the humming of the turret. Corporal Chris Reid, commander of call sign Four Two to Dougal's left, also had the men in his sights and was going through exactly the same procedure and emotions as his friend a hundred yards way. A stone's throw from them both, the kneeling man steadied the launcher over his shoulder and aimed for the front of the cupola around Dougal's turret. He wanted to take out the primary sights and blind the tank. No Challenger tank had ever been hit by the latest generation of RPG and Dougal was in no hurry to find out how much damage it might cause.

All three men fired at once.

Several hundred rounds of 7.62mm spat out of the chain guns to the left of the main armament of the two tanks, their streaking trajectories lit up by the red tracer in amongst them. It was only a short distance but the rounds appeared to arc as they scythed into the two men, shredding their clothing and sending them spiralling to the earth in a dusty, lifeless heap. It was as if the pair had been picked up by a violent gust of wind and dumped two yards backwards. Simultaneously, the rocket-propelled grenade streaked away in the opposite direction, bounced on the bank in front of call sign Two Two and careered over the turret and harmlessly into the open land behind.

Dougal exhaled loudly and leant back in his seat, his helmet brushing the hatch above his head. Cramp attacked his left calf muscle and he grimaced as he stretched it out over the shoulder of his gunner. It had been over ten hours since they had mounted up and he felt the ache in his lower back as he put his face back into the sights and started feverishly scanning again. This was no time to reflect on what he had just done, but he noticed that he was breathing easier than he had been a few seconds earlier. Up and down the line, the guns of the Challengers were returning the fire of their attackers – with interest – pouring hundreds of rounds into the scrubland before them. The phosphor from the tracer had ignited patches of the long grass and flames began to lick the darkness; tendrils of smoke hung over the battleground. Half a dozen corpses lay draped over the baked dunes, their heat signature slowly fading away through the thermal imaging. Dark silhouettes crawled and dashed across the infernal landscape.

No matter how much fire the Challengers pumped into their positions, the enemy kept coming. Seconds after the RPG pair were taken out, two others ran forward to take up the weapon only be to be chopped down in a hail of coax. Moments later, another tried to retrieve the launcher, but he too was dispatched with a short depression of the fire button. Inside the tanks, there was no questioning the bravery of their opposition or, as the gunner in one turret put it: 'These guys are madder than a shithouse full of rats!' Nor, they worked out fairly quickly, were they facing a bunch of irregulars and have-a-go-heroes that their civilian clothing had at first suggested. These men were well-armed and organized enough to join forces, communicate with each other and launch co-ordinated attacks. There was no doubt in the mind of any of the commanders that they were up against a company-size unit of regular forces, who had dressed up as irregulars to make life more complicated for their opponents. Besides, as Captain Jameson was pointing out to his troop, if a man is firing a rocket-propelled grenade or mortar at you, what does it matter if he's wearing combat fatigues or a dressing gown?

Having worked out that darkness provided no cover from the all-seeing Challengers, yet another RPG team had taken up position behind a dune in front of 4th troop, to the left of 2nd troop and the rest of 'C' Squadron, looking down into Basra. But the two men soon discovered they weren't much safer there either as all three call signs began chain-gunning the bank of earth into non-existence. Dirt flew into the air as streams of 7.62mm bullets hammered into the berm like an invisible pneumatic drill. Within minutes, three foot of baked earth had disappeared to reveal the two prostrate figures. Running away was pointless and they took their punishment where they lay. One of the men, badly injured, managed to crawl away over the next berm. To see a man missing parts of his body was a shocking sight for the young tank crews, especially in high magnification, and one gunner was so appalled by the effect of the coax on the attacker that he sat back in his seat in shock, unable to fire. A row erupted in the turret. 'Put the poor bugger out of his misery, will you?' his commander snapped over the intercom, while kneeing him in the back of the helmet. 'Go on! You'll be doing the lad a favour. Don't let him bleed to death.' All three tanks pumped rounds into the desperately injured man as he rolled and groped his way in and out of the ditches. And they did it not to inflict more pain on the man, but to put an end to it.

The situation was quieter at the western end of the battle group's line where, but for the odd mortar round and potshot from a Kalashnikov, they received no significant incoming, or at least nothing on the scale raining down on half of 'C' Squadron. After an hour and a half, the shelling appeared to have stopped altogether as the Iraqi forces concentrated their efforts on the eastern flank. For the most part, the four troops of 'B' Squadron and 1st and 3rd troops of 'C' Squadron could only sit, watch and listen to the battle taking place a mile or two up the road. Some even felt confident enough to get out of their tanks to stretch their legs and relieve themselves in the open, rather than in the empty water bottles that they kept for that purpose inside the Challengers. Sergeant 'Dodger' Gardiner, 'B' Squadron's 3rd troop leader and not a man to be unduly worried by falling ordnance, considered it safe enough to get into his sleeping bag under the tank and grab a couple of hours' sleep. But he was the only one opting for that arrangement.

Major Brannigan and his 2iC, Captain Alex Matheson, were standing between their tanks in the centre of the Squadron HQ circle, watching the tracer fire lighting up the horizon further up the road. The Squadron Sergeant Major, WO2 Tam Spence, had all but ordered his Officer Commanding and right-hand man to get some sleep and leave him in control of the Squadron HQ. Above them, the bright stars studded the pitch-black sky and in the distance, straight ahead of them, the lights of Basra and the burning oil fires beyond created a hazy glow above the city, interrupted from time to time by the bright plume of an artillery shell or an air strike.

'Look at those rockets,' said Brannigan, pointing to the north-west.

'Are they ours, do you think?'

Barely had Captain Matheson asked the question when one of the rounds landed a hundred yards behind them with a thud.

'Well, I think we have our answer.'

There is no sedative for fear quite like deep fatigue. A minute later, both men had climbed into their sleeping bags on the back decks of their call signs and were sound asleep.

They were among a handful of men who chose to sleep on their tank's deck. But most opted to stay inside the vehicles. They could still see shadowy figures moving around on the edge of the town in front of them, close enough to hear them shouting. 'B' Squadron had a platoon of Irish Guards providing local security around their hide as well as one man per troop in the loader's hatch on the mounted GPMG, with its 360-degree arc of fire. It was not only safer up there, but there was also a better chance of getting eyes on any enemy crawling across the terrain. All the same, most of the men in the other two tanks of each troop were taking no chances. It wouldn't take the brains of an archbishop for the enemy to work out how to approach the tanks – they simply had to look in which direction the turret was pointing and then slip up the side. When the tank is closed down, the crew cannot see the area immediately around the vehicle. As one trooper put it, securing the hatch, above him: 'This is a grand place to have your throat cut in your sleep. Think I'll brush my teeth in the morning.'

This wasn't tank country whichever way you looked at it. Never in all their training had the men of the Royal Scots Dragoon Guards run through an exercise in which they practised going firm for the night within little more than a grenade's lob from a built-up area bristling with heavily armed enemy. This was infantry country through and through but, strung out over such a broad frontage, two companies of Irish Guards, 300 men in total, simply weren't enough to protect the entire armoured column. They picketed the route as best they could, but some were also needed over in the east to engage bunker positions. At the Commanding Officer's order, Major Ben Farrell, Officer Commanding No. 2 Company, pushed his No. 4 platoon right out on the eastern flank to seek out an unidentified bunker position that was peppering Captain Jameson's men with constant harassing fire. As they moved forward through the dark, the platoon, led by Lieutenant Thomas Orde-Powlett and Sergeant Perry, identified two bunker positions in close proximity. Anti-tank weapons were fired into both bunkers before the platoon launched a successful assault. As the infantrymen withdrew to their Warriors, four enemy launched a counter-attack with RPGs only to be cut to ribbons with strafing fire from the 7.62mm mounted GPMGs.

As the Warriors extracted, the fighting was flaring to the south of the position. The brushfire had spread into other areas of the battleground and a blanket of smoke, heavy and sinister, hung in the still night air. The smell of searing flesh, mingled with cordite, seeped into the tanks. A group of men carrying RPGs jumped from the back of a technical at the top of one of the streets and sprinted into a crumbling, abandoned two-storey building, slightly detached from the rest of the town. Seconds later, the men appeared on the roof. Sergeant Lamb in Four One and Dougal in Two Two, a few hundred yards to his right, had them in their sights. It was obvious to the young NCOs what was going on: the enemy were trying to get some height over the Challengers in order to target the more vulnerable upper side of the tank. *These guys know their stuff*, muttered Lamb under his breath.

His loader, Trooper Gillon, lifted the heavy black HESH round from the storage area below the turret ring and, plastic yellow tip first, slid it into the barrel, put the charge up behind it, slammed the breech shut and closed the shield, shouting: 'Loaded!' The British had always preferred manual loading to automatic: they believed it was a more reliable system, less prone to jamming and time-consuming repairs and, with a good operator like Gillon, it was just as fast. In one of the Challengers' first firing tests in the mid-nineties, it was a SCOTS DG crew that demonstrated the tank's fearsome capability by destroying eight targets in under a minute.

Lamb lased the top of the building and heard the turret buzz round from the left. The 120mm main armament elevated about a foot. Three hundred yards away to his right, Corporal Dougal was doing exactly the same.

'HESH, building!' Lamb screamed, identifying the target for the gunner.

'ON!' came the reply from his gunner below him, indicating he had the target covered.

Lamb released his finger from the controller, handing over the firing system to the gunner below him.

'Fir-ING!' yelled the gunner. On the '-ING', he pressed the red firing switch and the shell tore out of the barrel in a flash of orange and blue flame. The mighty gun recoiled into the belly of the turret and a blast of warm air swept around the fighting compartment. Inside, the crew could hear virtually nothing, but outside the noise was ear-splitting as 24 mega-joules of sound energy rent the air. A Challenger can fire a HESH round up to five miles, but in this instance, with the target no more than a hundred yards away, the impact was almost instantaneous. The thin metal shell squashed on impact with the breeze-block wall and, all in a fraction of a second, the plastic explosive spread out into a pat and was detonated by the base fuse. The effect was instant devastation. Masonry flew in all directions as the HESH round punched a hole into the building, a body arced high into the air out of the flash of the explosion, flames poured from the windows below. Almost immediately, a second round, from Two Two, crashed into the target with equally shattering results. Smoke floated out of the fume extractors halfway along the barrels but a small amount of cordite drifted back into the turrets of the two tanks.

Fire quickly took hold of the abandoned building and threatened to spread to the neighbouring houses. Within minutes, the sound of wailing sirens grew louder and louder and revolving blue lights headed up the streets towards the fighting. Two fire engines parked up on the edge of the town and the crews jumped out, unravelled hoses from the rear of the vehicles and calmly set about dousing the flames. Either side of them, tracer fire whipped back and forth. It was as if the battle wasn't there.

Sergeant Lamb put his head back and took a deep draught from his plastic water bottle. *This is getting weirder and weirder*, he thought.

Captain Roger Macmillan was sitting in the rear of his Sultan command vehicle on the southern side of Bridge One when the order from Brigade came through. It was short, clear and unequivocal: get the SCOTS DG Battle Group out of there – and fast. The sky to the east was revealing the first shades of grey when the call from 7th Armoured Brigade HQ, at a secret location in the south of Iraq, startled the Operations Officer from a semi-stupor induced by yet another sleepless night. Within seconds, he had relayed the message up the line, signing off: 'Just get the hell out of there!' Within minutes, the entire column was heading westward, extracting at speed.

The Intel Officer, Captain Paddy Trueman, from the neighbouring command vehicle inside BGHQ poked his head into the back of the Sultan with more details. Brigade had received information from the most reliable sources available to the Coalition forces on the ground that a very large armoured force was on the move towards Nick 104 and that Iraqi Special Forces were infiltrating the area to blow the bridges and trap the British battle group. He did not need to spell out the significance of this to Macmillan. Setting aside the propaganda and political implications, such a scenario would be nothing short of an operational disaster. *If the Iraqis were to blow one of the smaller bridges over the shorter stretches of water, there would be a small chance the Royal Engineers might be able to lay M3 rigs – pontoons*

– and lead the tanks across, but what if they blow two of them? In that case the battle group, now running low on fuel and ammo, would face the nightmare scenario: they would have to try and fight their way back through Basra . . . Or what if they trapped the battle group on one of the many single-track stretches of road by destroying one tank at the head of the column and one at the rear with only marshland to the north and south? The possibilities were too grim to consider. Macmillan flicked a cigarette into his mouth and stepped out of the back of the vehicle to fire it up.

By two o'clock in the morning, the fighting had died down enough for one tank out of three in each hide to stay on watch while the exhausted crews of the others tried to salvage some sleep from the wreckage of the night. When the order to extract came through over the radio, many of them were nodding and snoring in their seats, but to a man they sat bolt upright and wide-eyed when they heard the urgency of the order. The troops further to the west, out sleeping on their decks, stuffed their sleeping bags and boots into the hatches and jumped in after them. Cigarettes were flicked from hatches, drivers gunned the engines and the heavy rubber and metal tracks, squealing and clanking, tightened around the road wheels beneath the armoured dust skirts as the Challengers spun round to the west and waited for the order to move.

Major Brannigan was almost comatose with his head inside his sleeping bag when Captain Matheson thumped him on the shoulder, yelling 'Chris! Chris! We're leaving NOW!' The Squadron leader's gunner, Lance Corporal Nick Brown, was leaning over the commander's hatch when the cigarette he had lit moments earlier fell from his mouth into the turret. Half his body had disappeared below the hatch as he looked for it when a mortar round dropped out of the sky and exploded at the front of the tank. It wasn't so much the shockwave as the noise that made Brannigan almost lose his balance. He pushed his gunner into the tank with his foot and leapt in after him. The rounds were falling all along the column and the crackle of small-arms fire erupted once again, the green tracer still clearly visible in the gloom of early morning.

The two Squadron leaders, Brannigan and Biggart, took up position at the rear of their men and with Matheson's tank on point, 'B' Squadron led the fighting withdrawal. The vehicles of the BGHQ and the Warriors of the Irish Guards were spread out in the middle as the three-mile column squealed and clanked into life and began to retrace its steps down the dusty track. Coax spat from the Challengers and the guards-men pumped off rounds from their mounted machine guns as they disappeared up the road, away from the rising sun, in a cloud of pale dust. Trails of tracer followed them until they disappeared from view.

The senior officers and troop leaders did their best to play down the urgency of the situation, but it was impossible for the other ranks not to notice the hasty, chaotic manner of their departure.

'Is this a retreat, boss?' came a voice over the intercom inside Zero Charlie, the call sign of 'C' Squadron's 2iC. The tracer streaked around the turret and a mortar round threw up a spout of earth just to the front of them.

'Well, it's not exactly a bloody advance, is it?' replied Captain Cattermole.

The crown of the sun had appeared over the horizon behind them by the time the head of the crawling column reached the first of the many bridges they had to cross. When Captain Matheson brought his tank to a halt, Major Biggart, the last vehicle in the line, had only just set off from Nick 104, three miles behind. This was the most difficult and potentially hazardous leg of the journey: the road took the form of a narrow raised dirt levee with steep banks on either side rolling down to marshland. If a vehicle was to break down it would block all the others behind it. The column was ten miles shy of Coalition territory and it would take other ground units, or reinforcements, two hours' march along this difficult route to come to their support. It was, in short, the perfect location for the enemy to trap the battle group – as well as their only realistic chance. Once all the vehicles had crossed, it was unlikely the Iraqis would risk their own annihilation, from the air, by following them down the narrow track.

The cracked edifice of the ageing concrete bridge did not inspire confidence, even in men untrained in structural engineering and architecture. The knowledge that several thousand tons of solid armour were about to pass over it for a second time in twenty-fours hours made the prospect of crossing all the more worrying. To the north of the bridge lay an abandoned canal and to the south there was a steeper, fifty-foot drop into a deep tributary that flowed into the Shatt Al Arab in central Basra. As the vehicles lined up to cross, there wasn't a man in the column who didn't wonder whether it had been mined.

The temptation was to speed across the precarious structure and get to the other side as fast as possible but the laws of physics state that slower progress is the safest approach because less pressure is exerted. And so it was at a crawling pace, as painful to watch as it was to experience, that one by one, starting with Captain Matheson's Challenger, twenty-eight 75-ton Challengers and twenty-eight 27-ton Warriors edged their way to the other side and, with a sense of release flooding each vehicle, accelerated away down the road. It took almost half an hour for all the armoured vehicles to cross the hundred-yard span to the relative safety that awaited them.

When Major Biggart, holding up the rear with the main gun pointing back down the road towards Nick 104, reached the firm ground on the other side, he lifted the hatch so that it was slightly ajar, into the 'umbrella' position, and breathed in the fresh air, like a man enjoying his first taste of freedom after a spell in captivity.

The balmy spring sun was high in the sky when the long dusty column pulled up alongside the perimeter fence of Shaibah airfield, the former Second World War RAF base that was to become the battle group's base over the coming weeks. Stiff as the armour they climbed out of, having been closed down in the claustrophobic, cramped interior of their vehicles for over a day, the men emerged from their hatches, gulped the fresh air and shook out their limbs. A handful of the young troopers, some of them teenagers, who had been involved in the sharpest fighting, were visibly shattered and shaken. Some crouched on the ground, or leant against their tank, with their heads in their hands trying to gather themselves and hide their fatigue-fuelled emotions. Immediately, their commanders and troop leaders took them to one side. They slapped them on the back, they congratulated them on their performance, they talked them up, cracked weak jokes, handed them cigarettes, reminded them that war was not meant to be easy, that it was OK to be freaked out or scared sometimes, that their families would be proud of the way they had conducted themselves, that they, their commanders, were even more proud of them . . .

Soldiers will tell you that the scale and importance of an operation or action is not always an accurate measure of its unpleasantness for the people tasked to carry it out; a huge operation can be a waltz in the park, while a routine foot patrol, a shift on overwatch, can be a trying, traumatic, even tragic experience. It wasn't exactly the evacuation at Dunkirk, and military history will record Nick 104 as a relatively trifling encounter, but for those at the sharp end of it, experiencing the terror and exhilaration of combat for the first time, killing to avoid being killed, the events during the night of 23 and 24 March 2003 burnt deep into the soul.

3. A-Zed

It is impossible for a newly recruited trooper or young subaltern in the Royal Scots Dragoon Guards not to feel the weight of the regiment's illustrious history on his arrival at the Regimental headquarters in Fallingbostel, northern Germany. The corridors and rooms are festooned with plaques, medals, battle honours, statues, guidons, memorials, portraits of distinguished officers and troopers, pictures of famous battles, commemorative silver and Rolls of Honour remembering those who lost their lives serving in the regiment. Formed in 1971 from the union of the 3rd Carabiniers and the Royal Scots Greys, the SCOTS DG can trace their history back to 1678, making them the oldest surviving Cavalry of the Line regiment in the British Army. Everywhere the new arrival turns there is evidence of the regiment's glorious role in the great campaigns and actions over the years: from Blenheim, the celebrated charge of the Greys at Waterloo – '*Les terribles Chevaux Gris*' as Napoleon cursed at the time – to the charge of the Heavy Brigade at Balaclava where two squadrons of Scots Greys surged uphill and routed 3,000 Russian cavalry in a ferocious engagement. This latter was one of the great episodes in British military history, but, overshadowed by the Light Brigade's ill-fated charge shortly afterwards, it is now largely forgotten beyond military circles. And then there are the battle honours of more recent bloody campaigns, including the Second Afghan War, the Second Boer War, most of the notable actions of the First World War, El Alamein, Normandy . . .

In amongst the memorabilia, providing a more intimate and personal insight into the life of the regiment, are the informal records of its history, including scrapbooks of newspaper reports, cartoons, letters of condolence and congratulation, amusing or poignant internal memos and photographs. In one of these scrapbooks inside 'C' Squadron's headquarters is a newspaper photograph from the mid-1970s, yellowed and frayed with age, showing a proud father in uniform sitting on a Chieftain tank, holding a toddler in one arm and a baby son in the other. The man is Trooper Tam Gardiner, back from his fourth tour of Northern Ireland – and how his face would have beamed even brighter had he known at the time that his two lads were going to follow him into the regiment and serve in Iraq thirty years later. It is difficult to imagine now that the same cute toddler is the burly, no-nonsense figure of Sergeant Jamie 'Dodger' Gardiner, 3rd troop leader 'B' Squadron, and the tiny tot, his brother Corporal Ali Gardiner, tank commander call-sign Four Two, 'A' Squadron.

It is a source of great pride to the brothers that at least one member from each generation of their family has served in the British Army since the Boer War. The SCOTS DG have always been a strong family regiment, a tradition passed on from both the Greys and the Carabiniers, and in Iraq in 2003 there were six pairs of brothers and cousins on the frontline. But for a serving member, going to war for the first time, there was the inescapable fact that the pride he felt so keenly in his family and regiment brought with it a heavy burden – of living up to the deeds of those who had gone before him.

And it was precisely that pressure of expectation that was bearing down on Corporal Ali Gardiner of 'A' Squadron as he sat in the commander's hatch at the front of the armoured column heading into Az Zubayr, his heart battering against his ribcage, breathing as if he had just been pulled from an icy sea.

Jamie had seen action in the first Gulf War, but this was Ali's first experience of a war zone and as the order to advance from 'D' Company commander Dougie Hay came over the radio, he tried not to let his voice betray the tension that gripped him. To his crew, Gardiner sounded completely normal: focused, determined, calm; but inside, his stomach was churning and his mind was racing. He did not want to embarrass himself or compromise his mates through a failure of nerve or character at the critical, defining moment in his career as a soldier. His father and those before him had all proved themselves as soldiers and he didn't want to be the first in the family line to be found wanting. Nor was he the only one wondering whether he had what it takes. There wasn't a heart in those three tanks that was beating in less than double time.

4th troop's task was to clear the route into town with the infantrymen of the Black Watch following behind in their Warriors. Following the ambush of the Royal Engineers, the policy of the battle group towards Az Zubayr had changed overnight from a softly, softly wait-and-see approach to an altogether more aggressive stance. There was anger, sadness and anxiety in equal measure within the battle group following the brutal deaths of the men they'd been working alongside, and the Commanding Officers were keen to send a message to Saddam's henchmen as quickly as possible that the actions of the Fedayeen would not go unpunished. Or, as one of the troopers, pulling down his hatch, put it more colourfully: 'Let's get in there and give the fuckers a bastard good hiding.'

It was a peculiar feeling for the crews of the three tanks of 4th troop to be leading the advance. If this was a routine joint training exercise, the tanks would sit back in a ring of steel on the edge of the town, ready to hit targets when requested, while the infantry went in and cleared the area or seized their objective. What they were tasked to do was an exact reversal of all the doctrine they had been taught over the years. For the twelve men of 4th troop the new tactic was an unsettling, counter-intuitive prospect that dislocated all their expectations of combat, just as it had done for 'B' and 'C' Squadrons a few hours earlier, thirty miles up the road. They had never done it in training, and now they were being asked to carry it out for real. The week before, they had spent the two allocated training days – their only experience of desert training – sweeping across the Kuwaiti sands running through traditional armour/infantry field exercises. Little did the troops imagine at the time that just a few days later, far from executing similar manoeuvres across the border, they would be heading into the heart of a hostile town.

It was vital that they stuck to the main roads and open squares wherever possible, but entering a town the size of Leeds without a map of its layout meant that was going to be difficult. The Challenger's firepower is less effective when fighting at very close quarters because the coax machine gun, mounted to the left of the main gun, cannot depress low enough to find targets in the thirty yards around the tank. And sticking the loader up in the hatch on the gimpy was out of the question in a built-up area where any sniper worth his pay packet would have little trouble in taking him out. Only a mad man, or an extremely courageous one, would be prepared to stick his head into a meteor shower of small-arms and RPG fire. Moreover, in narrow streets the Challenger runs the risk of striking its five-yard-long barrel against a building or telegraph pole when traversing the main gun.

All these concerns were running through the minds of the

three tank commanders as the column crossed over the railway tracks on the western outskirts and pushed towards the centre of town on both sides of a well-maintained dual carriageway. Corporal Gardiner was on point over to the right, Sergeant McKelvie to the left and Lieutenant Ed O'Brien one bound back. The formation enabled them to cover each other with overlapping arcs of fire.

Thousands of flags and banners in black, green or white were draped across the streets and hanging from windows of the two- and three-storey buildings, vestiges of the festival of Muharram, the first lunar month of the Islamic calendar that had begun ten days earlier. Advertising boards in Arabic lined the streets and telegraph wires hung limply between listing poles on both sides.

It was mid-morning and, looking straight up the broad mile-long street, the crews could see crowds of people going about their daily business. But at the sight of the Challengers appearing over the horizon, the entire route, longer and busier than Oxford Street, emptied in an instant; thousands of human beings just vanished, as if someone had pulled a giant plug and the ground had swallowed them up. The disappearing act could mean only one thing: there was going to be trouble. The quickly unfolding scene reminded Corporal Gardiner of the Westerns he used to watch when a posse of guys ride into town, the locals stare in horror and then quickly sneak inside and hide under the tables, waiting for the shooting to erupt. He was half expecting a ball of tumbleweed to blow across the street.

As the advance quickened, the driver stepped on the gas and the crew felt the power of the engines surge beneath them. It was unnaturally quiet, inside and outside the turret. The radio traffic had faded away too, leaving nothing but the fizzing of white noise in the earphones. There was nothing to report. Looking down the side streets, the commanders could see vehicles flashing past the junction, but, no more than a blur of white or red, they were impossible to identify positively as they sped along the smaller streets running parallel with the main route. *Is this the enemy mobilizing itself or just innocent civilians fleeing the scene?* The fact that the whole country seemed to drive a white or red Toyota Hilux flatbed, or technical, made identification of targets that much more difficult. What they could be certain of scanning down the side streets was the sight of shopkeepers hastily pulling down the metal shutters at the front of their outlets, café owners rushing their tables and chairs inside, women and children scampering across the street and shooting into a maze of alleys and stairwells.

On the main street, there was still nothing, just the odd face at a window and a shadow on a rooftop. A stray dog sniffed in the gutters, unaware of the emptiness and the silence, oblivious to the tension.

Several hundred yards behind the tanks, the infantrymen of the Black Watch were crouched on the benches in the Warriors in full combat gear, leaning on their assault rifles, waiting for the order to pour out of the back to clear a house or take up position along the route.

Corporal Gardiner and 'Wee' Gary, his gunner, moved their independent sights back and forth across the street. A blur of white outside a shop a hundred yards up on the left-hand side of the road appeared in the commander's peripheral vision. Adrenaline burst through his body. Immediately he swung the sights round. Nothing. He could have sworn he saw someone. *Maybe the nerves are getting to me*, thought Corporal Gardiner. *Maybe my imagination's playing tricks on me*. He took two deep gulps of air to calm his breathing, and flicking the sights to high magnification, he kept them trained on the spot. The minute details of the shop zoomed into view. It was a general provisions store with tables and sacks of produce stacked up outside, selling everything from vegetables to plastic footballs. Colourful rubber dinghies hung in a bunch outside the entrance to the shop. *Weird*, he thought. *Where's the beach?* Through the open door, he could see shelves heavy with tins and boxes. He could almost read the labels. It was as silent outside the tank as it was in the turret. Only the metallic clanking of the tracks and the throaty growl of the engine disturbed the peace.

Suddenly, a man in a white dishdash jumped from the door of the shop holding a loaded RPG launcher and went down on one knee. Half of him was obscured by a pillar, but it was clear that he was taking aim at Sergeant McKelvie's tank on the left-hand side of the street. Like Corporal Gardiner, McKelvie had the armour-piercing FIN round up the barrel of his tank, which was unsuitable for bunker-busting or buildings. The only way of getting it out was to fire it. The coax had jammed so the main armament was the only option.

'Enemy dismount with RPG one hundred yards on left. Permission to engage,' Sergeant McKelvie came over the net to ask Major Hay. 'We have FIN loaded.'

Barely had the 'D' Company commander given his permission when Corporal Gardiner saw a flash from the end of call sign Four One's barrel and the main gun recoil into the turret like a horizontal piston. Even in the virtually soundproof world of the Challenger's fighting compartment, he could hear a muffled boom as the tungsten dart shed its plastic casing, shot from the barrel and – generating enough energy to pass through twenty yards of sand or earth and still penetrate a T-72 tank – streaked towards the shop. Travelling at over 1,000 yards a second, the impact was almost instantaneous. The human eye and brain do not work fast enough to register any time lag between firing and impact at such close range. Even though its speed decreases the further it travels, a FIN round can be deadly at ranges up to three or four miles. Into a target just 200 yards away, the effect was catastrophic. Corporal Gardiner recoiled from his sights in astonishment at the devastation it wrought. The entire contents of the shop, together with glass and masonry, as well as the insides of the two shops beyond, burst across the street in one monstrous violent wave of debris.

And then there was nothing. Just a cloud of dust and some red and blue plastic footballs bouncing into the gutter on the other side of the street.

Corporal Gardiner had only ever seen a FIN round fired into a distant wreck on a training range. To see its full force being brought to bear on a building so close to where he sat left him momentarily stunned. The only time he had seen anything like it was in news reports of the massive IRA bombs used to such a lethal effect on high streets in the 1970s and 1980s. He felt his shoulders rocking up and down and he let out a loud guffaw. His loader looked up from behind the breech of the gun and furrowed his brow in surprise. He was laughing uncontrollably and his eyes welled up. Not because he was happy or amused or even relieved. It was just his body unloading the nervous equivalent of the kinetic energy in that FIN round. All his anxiety came spewing out into the turret, like the debris into the street. Then it was gone. He was breathing hard still but he was calmer now.

He put his eye sockets back to the sights. A militiaman was standing in the middle of the road right in front of him, frantically loading a grenade into his launcher. At the same time, a technical with a 'Dushka' heavy machine gun mounted on the back appeared from a side street on the left and shot across the road. As it did so, a Fedayeen soldier in black uniform, sitting with his feet either side of the gun's tripod, poured streams of 12.7mm rounds towards the advancing tanks, while his comrade fed the ammo belt into the side of the weapon. The rounds, almost twice as powerful as the Challenger's coax, bounced harmlessly off the frontal armour in a shower of sparks. To the commanders' relief, they also missed the tanks' primary sights and the barbette protecting the thermal-imaging sight above the mantlet of the barrel.

Before the tanks had a chance to react, the technical had shot down an alley opposite. The street was now alive with enemy fighters, none of them in uniform. They appeared from doors, in windows, on rooftops and from the back of vehicles. It was an all-out bid to halt the troop of Challengers rolling and grinding towards them spitting fire in all directions. The enemy knew they had only to disable one tank to claim a resounding victory and cause a major crisis for the Coalition. Having to abandon the tank was a scenario too hideous for the crews to contemplate.

Corporal Gardiner was desperate to get shot of the FIN round up his barrel so he could start loading the more appropriate bunker-busting HESH. In ordinary circumstances, he would never dream of using an armour-piercing round on a dismount, but he had no choice. The coax had jammed and the loader was waiting for it to cool off so he could clear out the obstructing round. An RPG was pointing straight at him, the point of it almost touching him on the nose, or so it seemed looking through the high mags. Dabbing the man with the red dot of the laser rangefinder, he shouted: 'FIN! RPG attack! Mine! Load HESH!' He depressed the firing button and felt the tank rock gently back on its heels. Instantly, the breech of the gun flew open, releasing a blast of air and a powerful whiff of cordite from the bag charge around the turret. Out of the corner of his eye, he saw the loader slam a HESH round up the barrel. There was no sign of the RPG man. One second he was there, a fully functioning sentient human being, the next he was gone. He had effectively been vaporized. 'God Almighty,' Corporal Gardiner heard himself mutter.

The fighting was everywhere now. All three tanks were pumping out streams of coax as they continued their remorseless, irresistible advance up the street. Showers of glass fell onto the pavements, fruit and vegetable stalls erupted in fountains of colourful pulp and puffs of dust appeared in streaks along the walls of buildings as the 7.62mm rounds ripped into the stonework. A misdirected RPG tore through a canvas shop awning. A sniper fell from a distant rooftop, riddled with chain gun fire. Behind the Challengers, the men of the Black Watch poured from the back of the Warriors and rushed into buildings and doorways. But, concentrating on their task of clearing the route forward for the infantry as best they could, the three commanders were only half taking in the chat on the 'D' Company net. They had very little idea of what was unfolding behind them.

The enemy – an alliance of Fedayeen and army regulars in civilian clothes – were putting on a valiant show considering the firepower ranged against them. Clearly they understood the propaganda value of disabling a mighty Challenger, the best-protected tank in the world – or what many would argue is the best tank in the world, full stop. It didn't seem to matter how many hundreds and thousands of rounds the Challengers sprayed into their midst. Still, they kept coming, hoping to get lucky. Corporal Gardiner shook his head in disbelief.

His gunner squeezed a burst of coax into a Fedayeen soldier, sending him cartwheeling over a shop stall into the doorway behind. Immediately he shouted: 'RPG next corner on left!' Gardiner swung his sights round and, sure enough, there were the tips of a bunch of the long grenades slung over a man's back, like a quiver full of arrows. The man, no more than seventy-five yards away, was hiding round the corner and clearly had no idea his weapons were sticking out in full view of the tanks rolling up the street. RPG units usually worked in teams of two, one firing the weapon, the other carrying the grenades. From the way this character was standing, with his back to the main street, it was likely that he was in consultation with his other half, the man with the launcher.

No RPG had found its target since the engagement had begun, so the tank crews still had no idea what damage a direct hit in the right spot would cause. As the tank rolled forward, Gardiner flicked the switch from 'Main Gun' to 'Coax' and tried to lase the corner of the building – but the computer failed to respond. He tried again, but still nothing. The target was too close, the computer was flashing. It couldn't get a range on the target because it fell under the reach of the coax. *If you can't lase it, you can't shoot it.* The gunnery maxim they were all taught as recruits ran through Gardiner's head like a stuck record. For what seemed like an eternity, commander and gunner tried to get a fix on the target, but the computer stood its ground. There was only one option: Corporal Gardiner turned the switch back to 'main gun'.

The HESH round exploded into the wall in a mighty flash, sending debris bursting in all directions, and when the smoke and dust cleared a great chunk of the street corner had disappeared.

Half a dozen men ran into the street from the corner of the damaged building, pouring fire into the tank that was now no more than thirty yards away from them. A shower of rounds engulfed call sign Four Two but, inside, the crew could feel and hear nothing. It might just as well have been a shower of sleet for all the bother it was causing Britain's main battle tank. The advancing column was almost at the end of the street, approaching a wide stretch of open land up on the left. The last of the dismounts were running right in front of the tanks, kneeling down every fifty yards or so and shouldering their AK-47s and RPGs. They had been bright enough to work out that the closer they got to the tanks the safer they were – unless they got too close and found themselves being flattened into a human blanket by 75 tons of armour.

Call sign Four Two kept up a steady stream of harassing fire with the coax chain gun in an effort to see them off but, as the trajectory of the fire could not be lowered any further, the rounds and tracer were flying straight over their heads. One of the dismounts foolishly ran too far ahead, putting himself within the range of the scything machine gun. A burst of rounds hit him in the bottom of the spine, passed straight through and sent his AK-47 spiralling up into the air. Immediately, a group of four ran out into the middle of the road as a pack from the right. Two were firing Kalashnikovs on the run and the other two were an RPG team. Just out of range of the coax, the two men took their time to get eyes onto Four Two as it rumbled towards them.

'HESH! GUN TEAM!' shouted Gardiner. There was no need to shout over the intercom in the quiet of the tank's turret, but this was a battle and it was difficult not to with more adrenaline than blood pumping round his heart.

'ON!' shouted the young gunner and with that his commander released his control over the gun.

A split second later, the earth erupted in front of the fighters in a giant white flash. For a few seconds the crew could see nothing except a cloud of dust and smoke. When it cleared, there was nothing but a crater where the four men had been standing.

The three tanks surged out of the heavily built-up stretch of the route, as if out of a tunnel, and pulled onto the complex of sports pitches over to their left. Like ducks drawn to water, the three Challengers sought the natural habitat of the open ground without even conferring. There was a row of three-storey buildings running north on the street alongside the pitches a hundred yards away. The three tanks went into a roughly circular formation to cover all angles of attack. Sodden with sweat, the twelve men of the troop drank hard from their water bottles and tried to recover their breath. The turrets fell silent as the men tried to absorb the enormity of what had just happened. Lying close to a set of football goalposts on a neighbouring pitch was a downed Phoenix, one of the unmanned drones used by the Coalition; millions of dollars of state-of-the-art technology sitting mangled in the dirt. Two young boys were running towards it from the other direction.

'Are we stopping for a brew, boss?' asked the loader.

Gardiner didn't have time to reply before Gary blurted: 'Sniper, on the verandah, two o'clock!' All the men, as one, stubbed out their cigarettes and dropped the water bottles between their legs as the man opened fire. Within seconds the turret was traversing around and the gun elevated to the position pinpointed by the computer. With his first burst, no more than a two-second squeeze, Gary hit the gunman square on, shredding his clothes in a hail of fire. The man slumped forward and tipped over the balcony, hitting the ground below with a heavy thump. As he did so, half a dozen more fighters appeared on the verandah and opened up on the tanks with a range of small arms. Coax strafed the building, puncturing the walls and sending glass and shrapnel flying in all directions. Undaunted, the paramilitaries kept up their fire and when one of their number fell, another appeared from indoors to continue the fight.

The Warriors of the Black Watch appeared around the corner at the very moment that a HESH round tore into the balcony, sending it falling to earth in a pile of rubble and dust. Dozens of fighters, marshalled by the Fedayeen, were swarming from alleyways and clambering over rooftops as Major Dougie Hay gave the order to extract. With the Challengers covering their withdrawal, the Warriors disappeared up the road. Under a canopy of tracer fire, the three tanks began to follow them, reversing slowly and returning fire as they went. Four Two's coax stopped firing. They had run out of ammunition for it; all 4,400 rounds were gone. Ten seconds later, the troop was out of effective range of enemy fire and the commanders gave the order to turn. The drivers rammed their vehicles into first gear, the Challengers pivoted on the spot and roared away in cloud of diesel fumes, the tracer fire fading behind them.

'Crazy! Absolutely fucking crazy!' said Wee Gary. 'And I thought we're meant to be handing out the sweets by now.'

Corporal Gardiner didn't reply. He was miles away, wondering what his father would have made of it all.

The soldiers of 31 Armoured Engineer Squadron, supporting SCOTS DG, finished clearing the last of the mines from the abandoned runways and hangars and began bulldozing the earth to form squares of protective berms. As they did so, the twenty-eight Challengers of the battle group, followed by the Warriors of the Irish Guards, rolled through the main entrance of Shaibah airfield and set up their Battle Group Headquarters. They lined up in a long row, unpacked the desert camnets for protection from a sun that was growing hotter by the day and, sitting on thirty minutes' notice to move, waited for their next set of orders. Ten miles south-west of Basra and seven north-west of Az Zubayr, the airbase, built in the 1920s and the inspiration for the song the 'Shaibah Blues', was close to the frontline, yet safe from most forms of attack. It was within range of enemy mortars and artillery fire but in a war zone no location was ever going to be entirely invulnerable. As the reserve battle group, the SCOTS DG were well placed to provide support for the Desert Rats. Operating around Basra and Az Zubayr, the other three battle groups of 7th Armoured Brigade were drawing increasingly intense and co-ordinated fire at their vehicle checkpoints and their positions on the southern side of the five bridges spanning the Shatt Al Basra shipping canal.

Following their gruelling foray up north to Nick 104, the main priority for the Royal Scots Dragoon Guards was for the men and their machines to get some much-needed rest and maintenance. Both were hungry and thirsty: the men were craving a proper meal to eat and something more appetizing than warm water to drink; the Challengers were groaning for fuel, ammo, fresh air filters and other spare parts. Both needed to strip down to their bare essentials and enjoy a good scrub down too: the men were filthy and unshaven, in pressing need of a shower and a razor; the wagons were clogged and caked with dust, crying out for the balm of a thorough oiling and greasing. The men of the two squadrons' SQMS packets, who had remained behind listening anxiously to the contact reports, were quick to attend to their comrades. They 'replenned' the tanks with diesel and whatever supplies they already had in store. Next, they took a shopping list of needs from the Troop Sergeants before heading back to Kuwait to pick up provisions, parts and post from the Royal Logistics Corps.

Once they had got their breath back, the consensus at that evening's 'O' group with Lieutenant Colonel Blackman was that Nick 104 had been an invaluable experience for them all, from senior officers and hardened NCOs down to the youngest, most impressionable troopers. Nick 104 was their blooding. It had given them a taste of combat as well as an insight into their enemy and his strategy. This much was now clear: this was going to be no rerun of Gulf One; they were in for an irregular war. If, as they had imagined back in Germany, it was going to be a straight scrap between British regular forces and Iraqi regular forces, armour on armour, then it was never going to be a fair contest. But, up against determined irregulars in amongst the civilian populace with the media watching their every move, they were now facing an altogether more awkward challenge.

The planners had estimated that by now the British would have taken upwards of 6,000 prisoners of war. In fact, they had taken just 200. Many army regulars had deserted and melted back into civilian life, but many others, some of their own free will, some under duress from the Fedayeen, were taking the fight to the British all along the front south of Basra. Pre-invasion, the best-case scenario had been that the Brigade would already be in the heart of the sprawling city by now, soft hats on and helmets stowed, with the SCOTS DG mopping up the POWs behind. This was not meant to be a drawn-out affair, let alone a bloody siege of a massive city. Interesting days lay ahead – but if interesting days were to turn into interesting weeks, then the Coalition forces, and the politicians who had sent them here to fight this war, had a major problem on their hands.

Proof, were it necessary, of the challenges that lay ahead came in the form of the dramatic skyline as the troops settled down on the back decks of the Challengers to try and snatch their first decent night's sleep since arriving in theatre. Explosions and tracer lit up the skyline as the air rumbled and shook with ordnance. What no one in the SCOTS DG knew as they climbed into their sleeping bags and got their heads down was that one of those bright yellow flashes on the horizon, a few miles to their north, had just destroyed a Challenger tank, killing two of the crew outright and seriously injuring two others standing nearby.

When war in the Gulf began to loom, Lance Corporal Barry 'Baz' Stephen of the Black Watch was back in Scotland working with the regimental recruiting team based in Perth. Black Watch to the tips of his boots, Baz couldn't bear the idea of his mates going into battle while he sat at home watching television. To his great relief, he soon received a call to rejoin the mortar platoon of the 1st Battalion at their garrison in northern Germany. In the late evening of 24 March his mortar platoon section came under ferocious attack in Az Zubayr. With the AFV 432 vehicle pinned down by the hail of fire and the enemy closing in, Baz Stephen broke out of the escape hatch to man the mounted GPMG. He was returning fire, enabling the raiding party to extract, when an RPG round him hit him square on the body armour protecting his chest. The force of the strike knocked him clean out of the vehicle. In the mad scramble to withdraw and regroup it wasn't until they were a mile or so down the road that his comrades realized the 31-year-old Lance Corporal was missing.

Immediately the news came over the radio, Lieutenant Colonel Mike Riddell-Webster, the battle group's Commanding Officer, ordered a search party of three Warriors and an 'A' Squadron Challenger to go and find their comrade. Emotions were running high amongst the men and such was the sense of urgency to rescue Baz, one of the most popular men in the regiment, that the Colonel decided to lead the search himself. It was unusual for a Commanding Officer to risk himself but Riddell-Webster wanted to lead his men from the front. One of his boys was missing and he was as eager as anyone in the battalion to get him back. There was no time to lose. Nobody wanted a repeat of what had happened to the engineers twenty-four hours earlier.

As the raiding party was assembling, Sergeant Will 'Monty' Montgomery, commander of call sign Three One, was coming to the end of a gruelling ten-hour shift on overwatch at one of the many VCPs the battle group had strung around the town. Each call sign had been putting in far longer stints than the crews would have liked because there was such a large area for the Challengers of 'A' Squadron SCOTS DG and Egypt Squadron 2 RTR to cover. The tanks had been tasked to provide local protection for the infantry manning the checkpoints and it was vital they kept eyes on the surrounding terrain. With their high-magnification sights and thermal-imaging capability, the tanks had become indispensable to the task. They acted as the eyes for the men on the ground – as well as the muscle if it came to a major engagement. It was especially important that the crews remained vigilant at night when the men outside could barely see beyond the end of their assault rifles. Like the rest of the battle group, the crews had had no sleep since crossing the border two and a half days earlier. For the commanders and gunners, taking it in turns to do the scanning, overwatch duty was especially punishing. Scanning was fine for half an hour or so, but even in training exercises when the men have slept better and are less stressed, the concentration involved makes it an exhausting ordeal over long periods. After three nights without sleep, it starts to feel like torture, made all the worse by the knowledge that if they were to nod off, they would put the lives of their comrades at risk.

Sergeant Montgomery was furiously rubbing his face with his open hands, snapping at himself to stay awake, when the contact reports burst over the net, making him jump in his seat. From the urgency of the voices and the background rattle of machine-gun fire, he could tell it was a ferocious engagement. There was no question of falling asleep now as he pressed the headsets tighter to his ears and listened with a mixture of horror and exhilaration to the fighting. *This town is turning into a fucking nightmare*, he thought. Earlier in the day, Sergeant Steven Roberts of the 2nd Royal Tank Regiment became the first British soldier killed in action in Iraq, in an ugly incident just a three-minute drive along the road from where Montgomery was sitting now.

Roberts had climbed out of his Challenger to try and quell a riot at a checkpoint. He had given up his enhanced body armour due to temporary shortages in the infantry. He was attacked by the mob, his pistol failed and, in the escalating chaos, he was shot by a comrade trying to protect him. The saddest aspect of it all was that Sergeant Roberts would have survived if he had still had his body armour. His death had affected

Montgomery deeply; he didn't know the man personally but the two had so much in common it was uncanny. They were both Challenger commanders, both sergeants, both from northern England originally, both married with children, both in their early thirties, both had given up their body armour, both were on overwatch duties around Az Zubayr at the time . . . It could just as easily have been his mugshot that was going to appear in all tomorrow morning's newspapers back home. *Why him, not me?* He wasn't the first serviceman to ask himself that question.

Sergeant Montgomery looked at the map resting on his knees and through the Sellotaped fold above Az Zubayr he could see that his call sign was the closest to the rescue party that was being hastily assembled. He sat and waited for Major Brown to come over the net. Sure enough, seconds later, the crisp, well-spoken voice of his Squadron leader crackled into his earphones and informed him that Colonel Riddell-Webster and his three Warriors were minutes away from his location. His heart sank; but instantly he thought of Baz Stephen, lying injured or crawling in the street, or captured, or dead – and a sense of purpose ran through his exhausted body and mind like an electric shock.

As the most experienced tank commander in the squadron after Major Brown, Sergeant Montgomery had been given the least experienced crew. This was standard practice but now, heading into a killing zone, it didn't seem such a great idea. His driver Stu and his gunner Daz had both recently turned eighteen. Just a few months earlier they weren't old enough to buy alcohol in a shop. Daz had been drafted into the crew at the last minute after the original gunner had gone AWOL in Germany. His loader operator, Andy, was talented and efficient but he was not the most experienced by any means.

They were all troopers. There wasn't a stripe between them. When Montgomery went over the intercom to explain that they were going to be leading the rescue party into the heart of Az Zubayr, the turret filled with a grim, edgy silence. It would have been no consolation to the young crew to know that their commander, in his own words, was 'virtually shitting' himself as well.

As the Warriors lined up behind the Challenger, the Commanding Officer came over the infantry net and gave him a grid reference to head to. Baz Stephen could have fallen from the vehicle anywhere along a mile-long stretch as they withdrew in contact, and they were going to retrace their steps back to where the fighting had erupted, into the heart of the hornets' nest. Two facts struck Sergeant Montgomery as the four-vehicle column roared into the night with their tracks clattering and chewing up the tarmac surface. The first was that he had never been into Az Zubayr. He was going to have to navigate at night through a maze of unknown streets with only his handheld GPS to guide him if they got lost. The other, even more unsettling realization, was that his was the only tank in the packet.

In over twelve years in the Royal Armoured Corps, he and his colleagues had always worked and trained in numbers, sometimes as pairs, but usually as a troop or as a squadron. Tanks, like wolves, work in packs. As he led the column into the unlit streets of a town overrun with enemy fighters, Montgomery was suddenly aware that there was no one covering or looking out for him. The Warriors didn't have night vision, only an image-intensifier that was effectively useless for a night operation of this nature. It was up to him and Daz alone to spot enemy threats – and, with luck, the heat source of Baz Stephen's body. It was alarming enough for a tank to find itself heading into a hostile town; it was more alarming still to be doing it at night through unknown territory with a crew of boys, two of whom could still be doing their 'A' Levels. Then there was the big question that had been nagging away at every crew of the 120 Challengers in theatre: how will the armour bear up against the RPGs and anti-tank weapons?

The plan was no more than a rough one – how could a frantic hunt in the dark for a fallen comrade through unknown streets of a killing zone be anything else? The four vehicles were to get into the area where Baz was likely to have fallen, the Black Watch were to debus and conduct a search on foot while call sign Three One stood off, scouring the area and providing covering fire.

The crews didn't lay eyes on a single human being or moving car as they advanced. A town of one third of a million people had fallen completely still. There were no lights in the streets or in the buildings. Either there had been a power failure or someone had deliberately turned off the grid. Rival Sunni and Shia factions were known to be roaming the streets, battling to fill the vacuum of power that was opening up, but that was not the only reason behind the unnatural silence. In a town on the brink of civil pandemonium, word spreads fast of any event that might light the blue touchpaper. News of the attack on Baz Stephen's section had spread faster than the advancing column of armoured vehicles sent to rescue him. They knew the Brits would come – and they knew that they weren't coming to make peace. The Black Watch were coming to rescue their brother soldier and they were going to fight tooth and claw to bring him back, dead or alive.

Sergeant Montgomery and Daz were scanning the street and alleyways for signs, the two of them covering one side of the route each with their independent sights. They were deep into the town when the humming of the turret stopped, the lights flickered and half the electrical equipment inside the tank went blank.

'Shit! Shit! Shit!' muttered Sergeant Montgomery, his mild Geordie accent now suddenly sounding much stronger. 'This is just what we don't bloody need right now!' Daz and Andy added their own volley of expletives to the darkness before an uneasy silence filled the fighting compartment. Their commander turned off the GUE – the secondary auxiliary engine which powers the turret and other electricals and runs independently of the twelve-cylinder, 1,200bhp Perkins main engine. The GUE had been playing up since they'd crossed the border but there had been no time to have it repaired. Until now, this had been more an inconvenience than a fatal problem because the electrics can run off the power of the main engine to some degree.

The Challenger 2 has been cleverly wired so that it will never experience a full system failure, and the thermal-imaging capability has a battery back-up with enough life to allow the crew to get back to safety. But, in the dim, quivering light, this was little consolation to the young crew, knowing that if they were to come under attack they would be unable to move the guns and defend themselves or the infantrymen following behind. And, if the smaller engine could fail, why not the main engine? The Challenger 2 may have been hailed as the most reliable tank in the world, but no vehicle is ever completely immune from breaking down from time to time. All day they had been relying on the main engine to compensate for the GUE's stuttering but as soon as the revs ran down, lowering the power, the electricals immediately started playing up and the turret stopped traversing. Without the ability to fight, the tank was no more than a well-armoured minibus, asking to be disabled.

They waited in silence for the system to reboot and Montgomery's mind at once wandered back to thoughts of Baz Stephen. *Where is the poor lad? Is he in pain? Has he been captured? Is he holed up somewhere trying to work out an escape route?* He didn't know the man on a personal level and he could only imagine what his Black Watch comrades must have been thinking right then. If it was one of the SCOTS DG boys he had worked alongside over the years, he knew the anxiety would be almost overwhelming. *And what about the man's wife back home in Scotland, sound asleep probably by now, without the faintest idea about the ordeal unfolding 3,000 miles away?*

It was only thirty seconds that he waited before starting the GUE again but it was as if half the night had passed by the time the sound of the turret's hum filled the fighting compartment once again and the flickering lights returned to full power. Thoughts of the soldier's fate made him shudder violently and he crouched forward again, put his eyes back into the sights and started scanning furiously. The task of finding the missing man had come to feel like an almost physical urgency. Without any words being exchanged, Montgomery sensed the anxiety of his young crew as the GPS led them to the grid reference the Colonel had given him. It was open ground, like a deserted car park, perhaps the site of the town's main market, surrounded by shops and other buildings. There was the dark outline of a mosque's dome over to one corner of the square. Through the TI sights, it was difficult to work out the finer details of the location. Staring into the optics, half-hallucinating with exhaustion, the world outside was a strange kaleidoscope of white and green shapes against a black background. Az Zubayr was just a bad trip.

'Spooky or what, boss?' muttered Daz from the seat below as he clutched the controls and turned his head, buried in the sights, first one way and then the other, like a submariner running his eyes along the horizon through a periscope.

Sergeant Montgomery didn't reply. He was too busy zooming in on the movement he thought he'd noticed on the far right of the square. He bit hard on his lip and flicked his sights to high mag. The shock of the adrenaline into his exhausted body took his breath away. There they were, clear as the boots on his feet: roughly fifteen enemy dismounts, about 250 yards away, taking up position in doorways and up alleys. By the way they walked and stood, he could tell they didn't think they could be seen by the packet of British vehicles. He made a conscious effort to inhale as he grappled with the controls on the radio system hanging round his neck. The Black Watch were debussing from the back of the Warriors and spreading out. He flicked to the infantry frequency and, trying to sound as cool as his thumping heart would allow, he informed the Colonel of what he had seen and finished: 'Permission to engage, sir.' The Colonel put it more formally, but the upshot was clear: if they're armed and taking up positions, then get amongst them and keep their heads down with plenty of repressive fire while his men combed the area for their fallen comrade.

Montgomery traversed the turret onto a small pocket of the fighters gathered in the entrance of a three-storey building. Some were loading their RPGs and AK-47s, others knelt and pointed their weapons in the direction of the British vehicles. It was clear that they were waiting to try and draw them a little closer before opening up. Throughout his career, he had often heard the soldier's expression 'The training just kicked in' and he was aware that right then, in spite of the emotional tumult he was experiencing, he was methodically going through the procedure drilled into him by years of practice exercises. It was as if the tank was on automatic pilot. He brought the turret to rest on the enemy packet, lased them with the rangefinder, released control of the firing mechanism and told the gunner to engage them while he set about identifying a new target. But for the hammering of his heart, he may as well have been in the simulator back at the training centre in Sennelager.

'It's not firing!' Daz shouted.

'Come off it, man!' shouted Monty from above him, resisting the temptation to knee the young gunner in the back of the helmet. 'Of course, it's bloody firing!'

As he spoke, through the sights he could see the shadowy figures spread out along the doorways, facing the Challenger.

'I'm trying, boss, but it's not bloody working! It's the GUE playing up again.'

'No, it bloody isn't! Right, let me take over,' said Montgomery. Pressing the override switch behind the controls with his right hand he gave the coax a long squeeze with his left. Dozens of tracer rounds squirted from the left of the tank, lighting up the darkness as they streaked, in a very shallow arc, towards the target. The enemy had no warning before the first of the 7.62mm bullets tore into them, scything one of them to the ground in a motionless heap. The others scattered in all directions, scampering into the shadows and down the alleys behind. Montgomery stayed glued to his sights, his chest rising and falling rapidly.

Ten, twenty, thirty minutes – it was difficult to say how long they sat on overwatch as the Black Watch boys searched high and low for their comrade. With so many friendlies now out in the open, the Challenger crew had to be especially careful in identifying targets. A blue-on-blue incident now would turn a full-blown crisis into a tragedy. They scanned the shadows and waited. The Black Watch weren't going home without their man. They were going to have sit this out for as long as it took. The only noise inside the fighting compartment was the humming of the turret. The occasional burst of small-arms fire shot through the darkness outside. Every now and then a shadowy figure appeared from a doorway or a back street and then melted back into the darkness. Sergeant Montgomery splashed water on his face and looked at his watch. Back at the Battle Group Headquarters and the VCPs on the edge of the town, the rest of 1st Battalion and 'A' Squadron sat in their vehicles, waiting anxiously for news.

The voice of the Colonel crackled through the headsets. Those listening in sat bolt upright.

'This is Zero Alpha,' he said. 'We have found the body of Lance Corporal Stephen. We are extracting immediately.' He tried to sound dispassionate, but there was some powerful feeling in his voice.

As his comrades lifted his lifeless body into the back of the Warrior, the news of his death was met with silence and a collective slump of the shoulders two miles away.

No sooner had the raiding party begun to manoeuvre to withdraw, when the darkness burst with incoming fire, as if someone had just flicked a switch and the lights had come on. Tracer fire poured out of the surrounding buildings at the Challenger and the Warriors. Bullets rang against the metal hulls of the vehicles and skidded off the concrete in a shower of sparks. With a roar of exhausts and a squeal and clatter of tracks the four vehicles swung into action, all of them returning fire with devastating bursts of their own. Such was the suddenness, scale and ferocity of the assault that it can only have been a co-ordinated action, designed to disable one of the armoured vehicles and force the others to stay and fight it out. Pockets of enemy appeared from balconies, windows and doorways, and sprinted to take up positions closer to the British column. Muzzles and barrels blazed in both directions in two minutes of frenzied violence. RPGs ripped through the air, exploding on the ground and against the surrounding buildings. Leaving the Challenger to cover them, the Warriors extracted first. Gunner Daz, perhaps galvanized and upset by the news of the Lance Corporal's death, had recovered himself and was spraying the enemy positions with coax, pumping off hundreds of rounds while his commander guided Stu in reversing the Challenger to safety. Not until they were out of effective range of the enemy weapons could he risk exposing the fuel drums and the engine, especially given the weight of fire to which they were being subjected. *Never turn round!* Another of the golden rules of tank warfare. And never was it more apposite than now with the enemy closing in on them. Two thuds rang the armour in quick succession.

'What the hell was that?' someone shouted over the inter-com. The Challenger leapt backwards as Stu slammed the Challenger into reverse.

The shouted orders and instructions grew even louder.

'You're getting hit by RPGs!' hollered Colonel Riddell-Webster over the radio.

'I know! I know!' replied Montgomery, praying that the grenades skidding off the sloping frontal armour didn't take out his thermal imaging, primary sights, the coax or the tracks.

In less trying circumstances, reversing a Challenger tank is a reasonably straightforward business. The commander leans out of his hatch and guides the driver back over the intercom with a series of simple instructions. But this was an altogether more taxing challenge, even for a commander of Montgomery's experience: in the dark, under intense fire, bedlam in the turret, the weapons system and control of the tank in the hands of boys young enough to be his children, no other call signs to cover him, unsighted Warriors manoeuvring behind and only a small sight embedded in the cupola for visuals – and all the while trying to take in the shocking news of a comrade's death. Montgomery was keeping his cool – well, at least that's how it came across to his young crew.

'That's it, Stu, left stick, right stick, bit more left, keep her straight, keep going, step on the gas, right now swing her round and let's get the hell out of here . . .'

Stu slipped the Challenger out of reverse and into first gear to put her into a neutral turn, and 75 tons of armour spun on the spot like a ballerina and accelerated up the nearest road with a roar of its mighty engine. A shower of rocket-propelled grenades fell and streaked around them; sparks from machine-gun rounds sprayed off lamp posts.

There was no sign of the Warriors. Montgomery looked at the map on his knees. He didn't have a clue which road they were on. There were three main roads coming off the square and they could have been on any one of them.

'Just keep driving, Stu,' he said over the intercom. 'The only place we're going is out of this hellhole.'

Stu stepped on the accelerator and quickly moved up the gears into sixth. Within seconds, they were doing 40mph down the dual carriageway. Five minutes later, they bounced over the railway tracks on the edge of town and were hammering along the main orbital route.

Back at the battle group camp, the men of the Black Watch raiding party, shoulders slumped, heads down, climbed silently from the back of the Warriors. The body of Lance Corporal Barry Stephen was taken away by the medics. Moments later, the plaintive strains of a lament, played by a lone piper, drifted across the night air.

Baz Stephen was dead, but he was back among his mates. The mates he had been trying to save.

4. Special Assignment

At Shaibah five miles to the north-west, the SCOTS DG Battle Group, unaware of the night's dramas, woke to the rousing sound of bagpipes as Corporal Jimmy Johnson and Lance Corporal Davie Dodds played reveille. The men had enjoyed their best night's sleep in weeks and the sun was poking its head over the distant mountains of neighbouring Iran as they climbed down off the back decks to wash and make the first brew of the day. But the quiet of the morning was quickly blown away by the shocking news that a Challenger of the QRL, attached to the Fusiliers Battle Group, had been destroyed by a high-explosive round overnight, just a ten-minute drive from where they had been sleeping. The round, the second of two, was believed to have passed straight through one of the hatches. The force of the explosion caused by the HESH rounds cooking off inside was such that it lifted the turret onto the back deck of the tank. The commander, Corporal Stephen John Allbutt, a thirty-five-year-old married father of two, and Trooper David Clarke, a nineteen-year-old, engaged to be married on his return from Iraq, were killed outright. The body of Trooper Clarke was never found. Two others were severely injured, including the driver, who suffered severe burns, and the gunner, who had been asleep on the back deck.

The fact that the round was fired by another British Challenger, an RTR tank in the Black Watch Battle Group, into Coalition-held territory, only made the event more shocking.

Details were sketchy, and wild rumours were mingling with the facts as reports of the incident spread around the camp like brushfire. When the broad truth came to be known anger joined grief and bewilderment in the cauldron of strong feelings that had been stirred up among the crews of the SCOTS DG. The question everyone was asking was: *How could one Challenger, on overwatch at Bridge Four on the Shatt Al Basra, have fired across the fire boundary separating two battle groups, onto a friendly tank at Bridge Three just a couple of miles to the north-west? The restricted firing lines (RFLs) had been changed as the two battle groups had moved forward to the bridges – but surely someone had passed that on to the tank commanders?*

Only forty-eight hours earlier the SCOTS DG Battle Group had passed through the QRL squadron on their march to Nick 104 and the commanders had acknowledged each other from their hatches. The exchange of greetings had been an uncomfortable reminder of the very intimate proximity in which the different units of the Brigade were operating. But the most unsettling fact of all was that the blue-on-blue incident had happened before the Coalition forces had even laid eyes on any enemy armour. The big question now sitting in the forefront every man's mind was: *What kind of confusion is there going to be when the proper fighting starts?*

The humidity had been thickening all day. The temperature climbed into the low thirties. The men donned their shades, doubled their water intake, sought out the shade of the hangars and the camnets and tried to put thoughts of Baz Stephen and the blue-on-blue incident to the back of their minds. When the storm came, it was like no storm any of them had ever experienced. Watching it build on the southern horizon, growing ever higher and darker and dispatching increasingly powerful winds in its van, toying with the colours in the sky, only made the event that much more spectacular and humbling. The turbulent mass rolled slowly, relentlessly, across the desert on a front stretching from one end of the skyline to the other. By the time it broke over them, it had become a giant wall of black reaching from earth to heaven. First came the sand, twisting and churning through the air, lacerating skin, stinging eyes and choking mouths. It is said that under Bedouin law a man may kill his wife after five days of such conditions.

All Coalition operations were halted. All activity on the ground stopped. And then the sky erupted with nature's heaviest artillery. Slabs of lightning burst through the darkness, thunder bellowed and cracked. The rain fell not in drops but in sheets, instantly turning the hard surfaces into running streams and the baked earth into a quagmire of pale mud that enveloped the guards on stag as they lay over the berms. The wind ripped at the camnets and tarpaulins slung over the vehicles, and the men clung to the guy ropes to stop them from somersaulting into the sky and away into the desert.

The message from nature to the men fighting below – and it did feel like a message to those who experienced it – was this: you can light up the sky with your guns and your bombs all day long, but *this* is real power.

The following morning, crawling as quietly as 150 tons of armour can, it was barely light when the two Challengers pulled up fifty yards short of the Az Zubayr police headquarters. Tanks bring many invaluable assets to an army's capability but sneaking up on inner-city targets unnoticed isn't usually found on a conventional list of its battlefield strengths. It will take quite some shift in military thinking, or a spectacular leap forward in design and engineering, before Special Forces and other covert operatives start creeping around hostile towns in a main battle tank. The tracks of the SCOTS DG tanks creaked and ground to a halt and the throaty growl of the engines faded away to a menacing rumble. Sitting at a crossroads before a set of traffic lights in the centre of one of Iraq's biggest towns, the Challengers were about as inconspicuous as a pair of rhinos at a bus stop.

'A' Squadron leader Brown, in call sign Zero Bravo, took up position on the right-hand side of the road facing the three-storey concrete building, with his 2iC, Charlie MacDermot-Roe, in Zero Charlie, on the left. The Warriors of Dougie Hay's 'D' Company stood off to the rear waiting for the word to debus. The black, white and red flag of Iraq hung limply from a pole sticking out halfway up the building's facade. The two commanders told their operators to prepare to load more HESH. Major Brown was surprised to hear himself almost whispering the order over the intercom, as though by speaking a little quieter he might succeed in not alerting the enemy to their presence.

Neither of them, nor even Major Hay, who was commanding the operation, had the faintest clue what enemy or asset lurked inside. They had simply received orders from Brigade that night, following an Intelligence tip-off, to go in and destroy the target. Since the fighting had erupted two days earlier, most of the Black Watch raids into A-Zed had been launched under the cover of darkness to give them the element of surprise. The soldiers on the ground were also able to exploit the advantages of their night vision goggles. The battle group had been quick to find excellent sources of information inside A-Zed and, based on the Intel, the Jocks had mounted a series of raids and become embroiled in some ferocious encounters. In the glaring absence of a visible regular army, it had become clear to the British that the Iraqi strategy was to lure Coalition forces into the 'complex terrain' of urban areas to blunt their superior firepower. Fighting them in the streets, infantry against infantry, with the civilian population as a shield, would be a more even contest, likely to inflict heavy casualties. Clever thinking, great theory. But there was just one problem in the enemy planning, a 75-ton problem: the Challenger 2 main battle tank.

Zero Bravo and Zero Charlie had just rolled through town like they owned the place. They were poised to strike one of the main hubs of the resistance in what Command were hoping would prove to be a spectacular show of strength and bravado. If a tank can survive in a town, its firepower is lethal and thus far no weapon the enemy had brought to bear against the Challenger had succeeded in stopping it in its tracks. Tank raids, against specific targets identified by Intelligence, had the capacity to destroy the Fedayeen and Ba'ath party infrastructure, thereby ripping out the heart of the enemy resistance – and, crucially, tanks could do it quickly. Left to unsupported infantry, such a task would take weeks and cost dozens of lives.

Night was giving way to the dull gloom of first light when Major Brown saw two armed men in khaki uniforms walk from the front of the building. They took one look at the awesome bulk of the two Challengers, stared down the black muzzles of the giant 120mm guns pointing straight at them, dropped their weapons and fled back inside.

Brown immediately reported to Hay that he had identified the target and was ready to engage, aware that any element of surprise they had managed to bring was about to disappear. There was no hesitation in the reply: 'Destroy the target!'

Brown immediately swung the turret round and lased the building. The information bouncing back from the laser beam called for a readjustment and automatically the computer elevated the gun by a barely appreciable inch or two.

'HESH! Building!' ordered the Squadron leader.

'ON!' replied Sergeant 'Vince' McLeod, a veteran who had served in Brown's troop in the first Gulf War and acknowledged as one of the best gunners in the regiment. Not that his ability to post a round through a letterbox from two miles away would be needed now. He had to do little more than make sure the turret was pointing in roughly the right direction, then press a button.

The major had just released control over the gun to him when Vince piped up: 'Hang on a tick, boss, there's a fella crossing the road.'

Sure enough, a late-middle-aged man in a jacket and shirt was standing over to the right, poised to cross. He checked to his left for traffic, then to his right, and without an obvious care in the world he stepped off the pavement and began to walk straight in front of the tanks. He held a leather bag in his right hand and looked every bit the commuter setting off for a day's work in the office. As he approached the Challengers, his head just a few feet below Zero Bravo's muzzle, he looked up at the tank, nodded and smiled.

Major Brown was nonplussed. He was as tense and focused in the turret of his tank as he had been at any time since 1991, the last time he fired a shot in anger. His heart and mind were racing in double-quick time and there, standing a few feet away from him, was a man calmly wishing him and his tank crew a pleasant morning and politely thanking them for giving him the right of way to cross the road. 'How very extraordinary,' the Squadron leader muttered to himself, gripping the firing controls tightly and sweating with concentration. If he fired now, he wouldn't just burst the man's eardrums – he would probably kill him with the shockwave or with a piece of flying shrapnel.

'Shall I fire, sir?' asked Vince, the uncertainty evident in his voice.

A man of impeccable manners and personal charm himself, Major Brown was the last character to reward such a bold display of civility and trust by blowing the courteous pedestrian to Kingdom Come.

'No, let the gentleman cross the road – then let rip.'

The man had reached the safety of the other side of the street when Vince pressed the fire button and unleashed a local version of Armageddon. Neither commander or gunner, with twenty-five years' service between them, had ever seen anything quite like it. They had fired live rounds at distant targets on the ranges of Germany and prairies of Canada and they had fired them at T-72s when they galloped and charged across the Kuwaiti desert twelve years earlier. But this was the first time they had fired a main armament round in a built-up area – or anywhere at such short range – and neither of them had given any prior thought as to the impact it was going to have. Both now sat rooted to their seats, almost winded by the shock of what they witnessed in the blink of an eye that it took the HESH to burst from the barrel and smash into the building. It wasn't so much the explosion, although that was impressive enough; it was more the effect of the round's shockwave as it sped at high velocity over the fifty yards of open ground. Every bin, every scrap of litter, every item of loose material in the vicinity, together with a great pile of dust, was scooped up and swirled round in front of them like a giant tornado. One moment the world was completely still and quiet, the next it was the Apocalypse. They could see nothing except swirling debris.

'Christ, what the hell's happened?' shouted Vince. 'What have we hit? An ammo dump?'

'I haven't got a bloody clue,' replied Brown, as a hint of cordite filled the fighting compartment.

Bunker-busting HESH, a thin metal shell filled with plastic explosive and a delayed-action base fuse, needs a reasonably hard surface for the explosion to have maximum effect. If the target surface is too soft or the round is fired at too high a velocity, fragmenting or dispersing the pat of explosive too thinly, the force of the explosion will be reduced. Though it is not fired at the very high velocity of a FIN round, a HESH has enough speed and power to pass through the front room of a house, destroying everything in its wake, but leaving everyone in the kitchen next door largely unscathed – so long as the building doesn't come down. Judging by the immense eruption before them, this particular HESH round had found plenty of purchase on its target. There was no question of it having passed through the building.

Through the billowing cloud of smoke and dust, the tank crews could see the police HQ spewing flames through a gaping hole at its centre. The dust from the first round was still settling when both Challengers, almost simultaneously, fired more HESH into the maelstrom. The double impact was cataclysmic. Once again, the air outside filled with a pall of twisting debris and dirt, higher and wider than the building itself, bursting in all directions and enveloping the tanks. Looking through the sights, it was as if they had driven into an erupting volcano.

It took over a minute for the atmosphere to clear and it did so from top to bottom as the dust and debris began to fall. Where there was once a concrete facade with windows and a door there was now only a grey sky. When the full picture of the scene was revealed, there was a giant pile of smouldering rubble and men in khaki uniforms wandering around, dazed and dusty. The Black Watch sections streamed past them in the gloom to round up prisoners and take the injured away for treatment. From the sound-proof interior of the Challenger it was like watching a silent black-and white movie.

Major Brown swung his sights over to the left and there, on the corner of the road, just as he had been twenty seconds earlier, was the commuter, frozen to the spot, his briefcase on the ground at his side. His hair, matted in dust, had been blown into an unruly mop. He was staring, open-mouthed, at the scene of devastation. He turned towards Zero Bravo, nodded and walked away.

There were four distinct noises in rapid succession: the rumble and growl of armoured personnel carriers, the rattle of heavy-machine-gun fire, a howl of pain and shouts of 'Medic! Medic! Medic!'

At the sound of gunfire and the sight of tracer fire skidding off the concrete into the gathering darkness, hundreds of infantrymen dropped what they were doing and seized their assault rifles, tank crews leapt onto Challengers and mounted up. Those closest to the gunfire instinctively threw themselves to the ground or crouched and put their arms over their helmets. It was dusk and the Black Watch Battle Group was a hive of activity. Patrols were coming and going, crews carried out maintenance on tanks, weapons were being cleaned, rations being scoffed and plans drawn up for that night's raids into town. Within seconds, a Charlie Charlie call, the message to all call signs, was put over the radio with the news that there had been a blue-on-blue incident.

It was a fact of military life that since the Falklands War twenty-one years earlier a soldier was far more likely to die or sustain a serious injury in an accident than by enemy action. Accidents happen in all workplaces but when a man works with massive pieces of equipment like a tank or armoured personnel carrier, surrounded by all manner of weapons and live ammunition, gruesome accidents become an occupational hazard, especially in the stress of a war zone when troops are deprived of sleep and rattled by combat stress.

And this *was* a gruesome accident – involving two highly experienced and respected Sergeant Majors that left one on the cusp of death. A column of Warriors was returning to camp after a raid into Az Zubayr. As was standard practice, a colour sergeant from the Royal Highland Fusiliers, who had been lent to the Black Watch for the tour, was on foot leading the vehicles safely into the camp through the gloom. As the front Warrior was being guided into its parking position, it lurched over a ridge and the driver instinctively slammed on the brakes. The safety catch for the 7.62 mm coaxial chain gun was still off following the raid and as the vehicle stopped dead in its tracks everyone inside lunged forward. The other Sergeant Major, sitting in the gunner's position, quickly put out his hands and feet to break his fall. His boot hit the firing pedal and a stream of coax tore across the legs of the Colour Sergeant a few yards away, almost severing them and bursting both main arteries. The blood rushed from his body and he only had minutes to live. The medics were on the scene immediately and battled to save him. If it hadn't been for their prompt action and skill he would have lost his life. As it was, the negligent discharge cost him one of his legs and his career in the Army. One moment he was a soldier doing the job he loved, the next he was a man fighting for his life.

At first light, a few hours after the casualty was casevac'd away for emergency surgery, the Black Watch Battle Group was on the move to a new location. The convoy of 'A' Squadron tanks and support vehicles rolled through the gates of the abandoned Iraqi marine camp and immediately spread out to form the squadron hide with a troop on each corner and Squadron HQ and the vehicles of the Quartermaster department in the middle. Naval equipment was strewn across the compound: rusting patrol boats on their sides, decommissioned artillery pieces, anchors, ropes, chains, road vehicles . . . The road leading up to Bridge Four, the main route into Basra, was no more than a hundred yards away from where the most forward troops set up their positions and already the locals were starting to appear in great numbers on the other side of the perimeter fence.

The situation in Az Zubayr had changed dramatically in the previous twenty-four hours. After four days of armoured raids and furious street fighting, the town had suddenly fallen quiet. The Black Watch Battle Group had smashed the operating bases of the resistance and the infrastructure of the regime. The Fedayeen and other paramilitaries had melted back into the population and headed into Basra, where the resistance was stiffening as the British closed in. Lieutenant Colonel Riddell-Webster moved quickly to win the 'hearts and minds' of the local populace, calling for as much humanitarian aid to be poured into A-Zed as they could get their hands on. The Black Watch tossed away their helmets and donned their Tam O'Shanter soft hats. Tanks were regarded as a menacing, unsettling presence that sent out all the wrong messages in a campaign to reassure the civilians, so Brigade dispatched them three miles up the road to the old marine base to await orders for more specific tasks. The Black Watch were manning VCPs along the routes in the surrounding area and, for the time being, the tanks were assigned to overwatch duties to provide assistance if needed.

Word had reached Basra the night before that Az Zubayr had been subdued and, seeing that the next phase of their fighting was set to take place on their own doorsteps, thousands of Baswaris started heading south over the bridges at first light to keep out of harm's way. Many of them had children and elderly relations in tow, with donkeys carrying their personal belongings.

Major Tim Brown and his squadron Sergeant Major, Ross Anderson, stood, hands on hips, watching the mob of people and donkeys jostling for space beyond the wire mesh perimeter fence, no more than a grenade's throw away.

'I'm not entirely sure that this is the safest place for us to be setting up home,' said the Squadron leader drily.

'No, nor me,' replied Anderson. 'I shouldn't be surprised if we'd been dicked already . . . probably by that shifty-looking character on his mobile phone over there.'

'Oi, wake up!'

'No, bugger off! I've only just gone to sleep.'

'"C" Squadron's been put on immediate notice to move.'

'Pull the other one. Where we off to? Blackpool pleasure beach?'

'The other side of the Al Faw peninsula, you muppet.'

'You're taking the mick. Why the f . . . ?'

'To team up with 40 Commando, the Royal Marines.'

'You're having me on!' He sits bolt upright in his sleeping bag. 'Why? They don't work with tanks and it's bloody miles away . . .'

'The Marines are completely cut off down there with no

armour to protect them – and the Iraqis have just worked that out and are preparing a major attack – with a regiment's worth of armour!'

'Jeez, this could be lively.' He leaps from his sleeping bag. 'You certainly don't sit around on your backsides with the Marines, do you? We'll be like the cavalry riding to the rescue!'

'Aye, but we *are* the cavalry, brains. And before you get too excited, there's just one problem. We have to get there first.'

The order that came down from 1st (UK) Armoured Division, via Brigade, was not detailed or complicated. In so many words it said: 'Mount up, you're off, there's no time to discuss it now, we'll explain it to you on the way down.' And it was probably just as well that, in the ordered chaos of their departure in the dark from Shaibah, no one in 'C' Squadron had time to dwell on the entirely unprecedented task that they had been asked to carry out.

It was an extraordinary assignment on so many levels. For the Squadron leader, Major Johnny Biggart, it was by a long stretch the most daunting challenge of his twelve years in the SCOTS DG and one that might well define his future career – although that was the very last thing on his mind when the orders came through and he absorbed the size of the challenge that lay ahead. Biggart was a man tipped for high office in the Army and if he pulled off this operation, codenamed 'Panzer', which was going to be watched with great interest at the very highest levels, his stock would rise even more sharply. But if the operation came to grief . . . well, there would be a great deal more than a stalled career to worry about.

To the squadron Second-in-Command, Captain Ben Cattermole, or 'Captain Two Brains' as the subalterns and troopers liked to call him, the task was so mind-bogglingly complex and fraught with potential disasters that it might just as well have been dreamt up as an outrageous exercise by a mischievous or spiteful, possibly insane, staff college examiner to fox his upstart students. The conundrum that had been set for the squadron went like this: you are one formation in the west of the military theatre, a squadron of fourteen Challengers from 7th Armoured Brigade, augmented by the Warrior of the Forward Observation Officer (FOO) from the Royal Horse Artillery, two Challenger armoured repair and recovery vehicles (CRARRVs), manned by a REME fitter section, and an AVF 430 ambulance. Your task is to move through fifty miles of enemy-held territory, to the eastern end, where you will team up with a formation from the Royal Navy, the Marines, who haven't worked with armour since the Second World War. You will have no infantry to offer you intimate support as you pass through enemy territory.

But this isn't even half your challenge.

Your march will begin at night with a road journey around Az Zubayr, the scene of ferocious fighting and a series of lethal ambushes in recent days. You will continue through an area of operation controlled by a separate battle group that has just been involved in a blue-on-blue incident with another squadron of tanks from a neighbouring area of operation. You will then cross the Khawr Abd Allah, at the southern end of the Shatt Al Basra, on a motorized aluminium pontoon, where the waterway is no longer a canal but a fast-flowing tidal estuary. We don't have the tide timetable, I'm afraid. Again, you will be doing this in the dark. Once across, you will be advancing through marshy salt flats entirely unsuitable for a donkey and cart, let alone a 75-ton main battle tank. There are no roads, so you must stick to the earth levees covering the pipelines running to the Al Faw's two huge oil installations, which the Marines had secured a week earlier.

What about the logistic supply chain, you are wondering? Obviously, there is no way your SQMS packets can follow the tanks in their thin-skinned vehicles through an area of unknown threat levels but said to be crawling with enemy tanks, armoured personnel carriers and infantry dug into well-established bunker positions. The Royal Marines can't resupply your logistically hungry, fuel-guzzling tanks, so there's no choice but to leave your own supplies a day's journey to the rear through unsecured territory. So, you'll just have to work that out when you get there. Be resourceful. That's what you're paid for.

Just to make life a little more challenging, you will have completely different radio frequencies to the Marines – and, whoops, almost forgot, I'm afraid we don't have any maps of the Al Faw to give you. We've run out, so you'll just have to get hold of some from the Marines after you have arrived. That's assuming you can find them, of course. But be sure to ask nicely, because they are going to be jolly tired after a week fighting and roughing it in the open. In the meantime, use your hand-held GPS. And don't forget to warn the Marines that it's you that's coming down the road to their position and not that increasingly cocksure Iraqi column that has been harassing and probing them over the last couple of days. That's assuming you can get them on the radio, of course. We don't want any more bloody blue-on-blue incidents; you don't want one of those jet pilots mistaking you for a T-72. Oh yes, and mind the barbed wire and the mines – it would be a real bore if your lead tank was disabled and blocked your route on one of those wretchedly narrow dirt causeways . . .

For a staff planner, Operation Panzer was as easy as pushing a plastic model of a tank across a map on a table. For the men of 'C' Squadron, Royal Scots Dragoon Guards, it was going to be the greatest challenge of their lives. Was it a raid, an advance to contact, an attack, a provision of reinforcements or a rescue mission? It wasn't for 'C' Squadron to reason why they had been asked to carry out an assignment that bordered on the impossible, but clearly the planners weren't playing games. There was a grave urgency behind their highly ambitious plan. Only one thing was for sure: if Biggart and his men could pull this off and reach 40 Commando in time then the message it sent to the increasingly bold Iraqi resistance was loud and unequivocal: there's simply no way you can beat us.

The troops quickly stowed their sleeping bags and other personal belongings in the storage bins at the back of the tanks, strapped on their helmets, threw on their body armour and jumped through the hatches of the Challengers. The excitement and trepidation of the men was palpable, manifesting itself in barked orders, shouts of encouragement and streams of abuse and banter as the crews mounted up and ran through the routine checks on the operating control systems in their turrets. Within minutes, led by 1st troop and moving out in ascending numerical order, with Biggart's Zero Bravo and Cattermole's Zero Charlie in the middle, 'C' Squadron were off. Their war was about to begin in earnest. Under the envious eye of the 'B' Squadron troops, they pulled out of the giant airfield and turned right, or south, onto the metalled road towards Az Zubayr in a squeal and clatter of tracks and a throaty bellow of exhausts – and then promptly ground to a shuddering halt with the rear vehicles of the column still stuck inside the perimeter fence. In other circumstances, it would have been funny.

A call sign from 1st troop had become entangled in a roll of barbed wire they hadn't spotted in the darkness. After the mad dash to depart and the adrenaline rush that news of their assignment had unleashed, to be stopped in their tracks by a measly roll of barbed wire was to say the least something of an anti-climax – and it triggered a rollocking from Major Biggart, anxious that any delays might compromise the operation. While the rest of the column sat and waited, the unfortunate crew were forced to dismount and spend thirty minutes frantically trying to cut themselves free from the yards and yards of wire that had wrapped itself around the running gear and strangled the tracks. Major Biggart may have been as affable and good-natured a man as you could you hope to meet outside a war zone – but in the words of one of his Troop Sergeants: 'You don't want to go pissing him off.' Likewise, the Challenger may be one of the most sophisticated 'user-friendly' fighting vehicles in the military world, but, like all main battle tanks, it remains vulnerable to being ensnared in plain old barbed wire.

The tank had come into being in the First World War, almost ninety years earlier, as a machine that could crush its way through infantry-shredding wire, a sort of bullet-proof mobile trench; and that was an irony not lost on the commanders as they sat in their hatches at their state-of-the-art control panels, surveying the night skyline and waiting for the order to resume their advance. Over the radio net, if they found the right frequency, they could hear the Black Watch and their comrades from 'A' Squadron, just a mile or two down the road, setting off and returning from raids into Az Zubayr. One of the parties had just led in a humanitarian aid convoy, the first 'raid and aid' mission to distribute food and water for the increasingly hungry and thirsty inhabitants. They were met by a large restive mob and as the men of 23 Pioneer Regiment RLC handed out boxes of provisions and filled containers of water brought by the locals, the mood turned ugly. Soon they came under attack from RPGs and small arms and were forced to pull back. The hornets' nest of A-Zed was still buzzing with enemy activity, just a mile or so down the road from where they sat.

'C' Squadron's march could be broken down into four distinct phases, beginning with a twenty-mile road journey around the north of Az Zubayr. From there they turned south along a highway that runs parallel with the Shatt Al Basra and leads eventually to the port of Umm Qasr on the Kuwaiti border, where the river flows into the Persian Gulf. The second phase was to negotiate the estuary, the third a cross-country journey along the manmade berms latticing the salt flats of the drained marshland. That took them back north towards the southern suburbs of Basra, and the march ended with an advance eastwards, through the layered defences of the enemy positions, along the main arterial route to the Al Faw peninsula to link up with the stranded Marines.

Usually a troop leader would lead the Squadron, but given the circumstances of the recent blue-on-blue and that they were conducting a forward passage of lines through a different battle group and into a different Brigade AOR at night and without the benefit of any close recce in support, Major Biggart felt it his duty to lead his men.

The column slowed to a walking pace as it approached the border between the Fusiliers' area of operation and that of the Black Watch. Radio contact was made to clear their passage through their positions. It was a peculiar sensation for the crews to feel as nervous passing through 'friendly' territory as they had done advancing through the bandit country towards Nick 104. But barely thirty-six hours had passed since the tragic accident and emotions in all the Brigade's tank squadrons were still running high. Fears of a repeat were uppermost in the minds of all crews. The blackened, twisted wreck of the QRL call sign remained in situ at Bridge Three as the accident investigators pieced together the evidence. Poor communication was partly responsible for the deaths of the two crewmen and as 'C' Squadron passed within a mile of the location from where the RTR tank had engaged the other Challenger, Biggart was at pains to make sure the radio contact was crisp, clear and constant as the column completed its forward passage of lines. Otherwise, the turrets were silent.

To the north, explosions lit up the skyline around Basra. The column headed south with the Shatt Al Basra somewhere in the darkness over to the left and Az Zubayr over to their right. From within the virtually soundproof, hermetically sealed world of the Challenger's interior, the town's twinkling lights created the illusion of a community at peace with itself turning in for the night. But in amongst the streets and alleys, the rounds ripped back and forth as rival factions of Shia and Sunni gangs fought each other. All fourteen tanks scanned both sides of the road, scouring the shadows for signs of an ambush.

Twenty-five miles to the east, close to the Shatt Al Arab, and with the border with Iran no more than a HESH round away, the Royal Marines of Lieutenant Colonel Gordon Messenger's 40 Commando and the Brigade Recce Force, together with elements of the QDG attached to 3 Commando Brigade, were digging into the drained marshes and building up their defensive positions for the night, waiting for the enemy's armoured thrust out of their base in the leafy suburbs around Abu Al Khasib. There are few enemy threats that can ruffle the composure of the Navy's infantry, but taking on a regiment of tanks may have been asking a little too much of their superhuman reputation. There was a handful of

Scimitars of the QDG Recce troop but these lightly armoured reconnaissance vehicles are no match for a main battle tank. The extra firepower and protection brought by one of the British Army's finest cavalry squadrons was certainly a heart-lifting prospect.

Passing the barracks and munitions complex south of A-Zed, part of the Crown Jewels being zealously guarded by the Black Watch units, 'C' Squadron pulled over and went into all-round defence at the side of a road. A hundred yards to the west lay the tracks of Iraq's main railway line, running from Umm Qasr via Basra and Baghdad to Kirkuk and Mosul in the north and beyond to the Syrian border. It was not long ago that British travellers had travelled on those very tracks on the Orient Express and Baghdad Railway to and from London. The hulking silhouettes of the engines and wagons now sat motionless on the tracks, barely visible through the gloom. Beyond the railway line lay an industrial complex and an arrangement of oil reservoirs and water towers. To the left, or east, they could see nothing but the impenetrable darkness hanging over the marshland of the Al Faw.

Troop by troop, 'C' Squadron went forward to the packet of SQMS vehicles that had accompanied for a final 'replen'. It was the last time they'd see Staff Sergeants Tam McVey and Mick Lillie and the rest of the SQMS boys who attended to every need of man and machine for . . . Christ, who could say? From the hatch of Zero Bravo, Major Biggart watched the three UBRE fuel tankers, each carrying 6,300 litres of diesel, fill the tanks of the Challengers, squeezing in every last drop to the maximum capacity of 1,600 litres. The Squadron leader tried not to dwell on the logistical nightmare of carrying out the *next* replen. The Challenger 2 has a range on a single tank of fuel of up to 280 miles by road, but over rough terrain, where the engine has to work that much harder, the range is between 120 and 150 miles – barely enough, in other words, for a round trip to base with no diversions from the route. But it wasn't just a shortage of diesel that was a worry. A tank cannot live on fuel alone – and although the Challenger 2 is acknowledged as the most reliable main battle tank in service, it still doesn't want to travel too far from its supply of lubricants, oils, filters and other spare parts. The men had enough food for three days and water for two, but if needs must, they could beg and borrow from 3 Commando Brigade.

The cloud that had started to form earlier in the night was descending ever lower, shrouding the area in a thin cool mist as the Challengers stocked up on provisions from the three Bedford trucks. The ammunition of all the tanks had already been replenished following their return from Nick 104, each call sign carrying 30 rounds of armour-piercing Fin, 15 bunker-busting HESH and five smoke for masking movement from the enemy, together with 4,400 rounds of 7.62mm for the coax and the mounted gimpy. Using a hose from the tanker trailer at the back of one of the Bedfords, the men of the SQMS filled each of the tanks' internal water containers to the brim and handed up boxes of rations, tea bags and coffee to the loaders, who squeezed them into the ration bin below the water boiling vessel. Forget the guns and the ammunition – the 'BV', used for making brews and rations, together with their personal mugs, were considered by the crews to be the most important items of equipment in the tank. Packets of cigarettes and a few Mars bars were gratefully stowed away in the small pockets and storage areas around each of the crew's cramped positions. Each crew member has his own little hideaways to keep small personal effects and items of comfort. Some commanders frowned upon the practice of having pictures of loved ones inside the turret, for fear that they softened and distracted the men, but most of the troops found a discreet place to store them to look at in the quieter moments. The tank was effectively their second home. They worked in it, ate in it and slept on it.

'It'll be cases of champagne and boxes of cigars next time we see you boys!' shouted one of the SQMS boys as he humped the last of the boxes from the back of the truck as fast as the laws of physics would allow. As he did so, two giant explosions in rapid succession rocked the skyline to the north, brief brilliant flashes of yellow through the haze followed a second later by a thud and a rumble. Then darkness and silence once again.

The squadron bade a hurried farewell to the SQMS echelon and, lined up in a single long column, turned down a dirt track leading to the location of the river crossing they had been given by the Liaison Officer from 3 Commando Brigade. The lights of Az Zubayr and its satellite industrial plants grew ever dimmer behind them as the caterpillar tracks crunched and crackled over the grit surface. The commanders sat out of their hatches and let the cool damp air flow over them as the column rumbled through the darkness along the western side of the glinting Shatt Al Basra.

A tank commander is at his happiest with his head sticking out of the turret, wind tugging at his combats and a full 360-degree view of the landscape around him. If nothing else, it was a pleasant change from the fetid, confined atmosphere below. Even with the efficiency of the air conditioning system in a modern battle tank – the fighting compartment somehow still always smelt of old sweat, diesel, bacon and beans ration packs, broken wind and coffee breath. If the tank was closed down for long periods and the crew forced to urinate into water bottles, the stench could become even more exotic . . . And if there was an outbreak of D&V in the ranks, the 'tankie' begins to wish he'd joined the infantry after all. A tank crew lives together and fights together. And smells together.

5. Operation Panzer

'Welcome to Romney fucking Marshes,' grinned the cammed-up engineer from under his helmet as he stepped from the misty shadows waving a glowstick in each hand. Undeniably, crossing point 'Anna' did look more like the wetlands of south-east England than somewhere in the Middle East. The air was cold and a dense mist hung over the water and the flat landscape of the Al Faw beyond the far bank. The moon, no more than a diffuse glow behind the haze, was just bright enough to add a shiny gloss to the mudflats revealed by the rapidly retreating tide.

It was one minute to midnight Zulu time – three o'clock in the morning to the locals – when 'C' Squadron reached the landing craft site and were greeted by 3 troop, 23 Amphibious Engineer Squadron, Royal Engineers – all of them territorials who had dropped their lives back home to contribute to the war effort.

'So how's this going to work?' asked Major Biggart, leaning out of his hatch, to make himself heard over the rumbling engines of the Challengers.

'We're just working that out!' came the reply. 'This is the first time we have ever done this operationally.'

'Well, that makes two of us. We haven't even done one in training!'

Both men forced out a laugh.

The amphibious squadron provides the only wide-water-crossing capability in the British Army but news that this was the first occasion they had ever used the aluminium pontoons, known as M3 rigs, outside a training exercise on the Rhine was not exactly what the exhausted young tank crews wanted to hear. They stared at the 250-yard stretch of fast-moving water and said nothing.

Tankies are used to bouncing and churning over rough terrain, crashing over steep banks and ditches and getting bogged down in thick mud, and the Challenger 2, with its hydrogas suspension system, hydraulic track tensioner and powerful engine, is designed to cope with the most taxing of conditions. But what they were about to embark upon was an adventure of an entirely different order and magnitude.

One by one, each call sign was to be ferried the 250 yards across the estuary. The engineering behind the operation was reasonably straightforward – in fact, not much more complicated than the wooden rafts used for carrying the cavalry horses of the Union and Confederate armies across the Mississippi and other mighty rivers during the American Civil War. So long as you don't overload the craft, it floats, and so long as there is a force propelling it that is stronger than the flow of water beneath it, and provided it doesn't get shot up on the way across, then there is no reason why the floating platform shouldn't reach the landing site on the other side.

The difficulty facing the Challengers was getting on to the rig in the first place.

To do that, the tank had to tip, unsighted, over the lip of a bank so steep it that it looked almost sheer from a distance, and then slide down a mud slope and onto a rig that was only a foot wider than the vehicle itself. In normal circumstances, the squadron would be given two or three days' training with a team of experts, starting with lectures and instructional videos and, after a series of dry runs, ending with an attempt on a far less daunting challenge than the one they faced here.

When the instructions from the engineers were passed down the chain of command, they triggered the same reaction inside every turret: a deep breath followed by 'Right, so we're fag-packeting it, are we?' The instructions from the engineers were clear and concise, and they were demystified and simplified still further by Major Biggart, but no one in the squadron believed for a second that what they were about to attempt was going to be a straightforward operation. The mood was summed up by a request to the commander over the intercom inside one of the tank turrets: 'Sir, permission to soil myself.' The fact that the waterway was tidal only made the task that much more complicated and hazardous. The tide was going out, and the lower the water level fell, the steeper the drop for the tanks. They had to hurry.

'Right, so who's up for the first splash?' laughed one of the engineers. The banter was designed to relieve the tension, but it earned no more than a muted chuckle from those within earshot.

Zero Bravo was to be the first to cross. Major Biggart wanted to lead from the front to inject some confidence in the crews behind, and he was also under pressure of time to rendezvous with the Liaison Officer of the QDG Recce troop who was to hand him his orders from 3 Commando Brigade. They were to meet at a prearranged grid reference at 0300 Zulu hours somewhere in the middle of the Great Nowhere that is the Al Faw peninsula. Finding it without a map was likely to be a time-consuming task.

The driver was at the controls of the tank, but it was up to the commander, guided by the engineers on the ground, to steer the tank into the right position by talking him on. The helmets disappeared below the hatches as Zero Bravo went closed down. With a risk of the tank rolling, this was not a manoeuvre to be carried out sitting in the hatch. Troop leaders Le Sueur, Jameson and McLeman needed no reminding of the dangers involved. Just two years earlier, a friend in the RTR who had passed out of Sandhurst with them had been killed when his tank rolled on exercise on Salisbury Plain.

Negotiating a steep bank and getting the tank to balance on the cusp is something of an art that the Royal Armoured Corps instructors at Bovington try and drill into all new recruits. It's a question of getting the speed right: too fast and the tank will career over the edge; too slow and it will stall and slide back down the way it came or get bogged. The Challenger 2 is semi-automatic with six forward gears and two reverse, but first was all that was required for this delicate manoeuvre. One Zero's driver revved the engine, and slowly edged the tank ever closer to the edge of the drop. Biggart offered his driver quiet words of encouragement; outside, the engineers waved their glowsticks and torches and bawled instructions, although there was little chance of making themselves heard through two feet of armour. The commanders and loaders, sitting up in the hatches of the call signs behind, could barely watch as the Challenger balanced precariously on the lip of the bank. One false manoeuvre and the tank would roll; one false move on the water and they would sink like a boulder.

The tank teetered back and forth for what seemed like minutes to those inside or waiting their turn in the queue: the equivalent weight of ten Routemaster double-decker buses balancing like a tightrope walker at the top of a mud chute. And then it plunged over, disappearing from view in the blink of an eye. It was just as well the onlookers didn't hear the noise inside Zero Bravo's turret. The sensation for the crew was similar to that experienced when a rollercoaster plummets over the edge after the slow steep climb. They all knew it was coming but still let out an involuntary yell. The front of the tank lurched weightlessly through thin air for a couple of seconds, then slapped into the mud with an almighty jolt. Very slowly, almost perpendicular at first, it began to slide headlong towards the rig on the edge of the water. The temptation for the driver was to slam on the brakes but that was the very last course of action to take as the tank might veer to the side and roll over down into the estuary. It was counter-instinctive to sit doing nothing but Zero Bravo's driver kept his cool.

With the Challenger now back in the horizontal position, the crew looked through the sights to see two engineers standing on the ramps of the rig urging them forwards with their hand-held lights. To manoeuvre the 75 tons of metal out of the bog of soft glutinous mud and onto the narrow metal ramps that were shaking under the force of the fast receding water was no less demanding a challenge than it had been taking it over the edge of a near-vertical drop. Inch by inch, the tank nudged forward in a din of revving engines and a cloud of diesel exhaust fumes as the tracks tried to find some purchase in the unwilling conditions. The grunting Challenger slipped and slithered for several minutes until finally the front of the tracks gripped the solid metal surface of the rig with a satisfying clatter. The driver gingerly steered the full nine yards of its hull aboard the pontoon and the crew and engineers blew out their cheeks in relief.

The weight of the vehicle pressed the floating pontoon deep into the water as the engineers fired up the motor and pushed out into the estuary. The tide was tugging hard and the water lapped at the portside as the rig moved out of the shallows. Inside, it felt as if they were gliding through the air, wobbled from time to time by a blast of turbulence. On the bank behind them the crews looked on anxiously as the dark hulk of the Challenger vanished silently into the mist. The same logic that tells the nervous passenger of a Jumbo Jet that the aircraft is simply too heavy to stay airborne was now telling the anxious crew that a sheet of floating aluminium was far too light to hold the fully loaded main battle tank.

The M3 rig has a top speed of 9mph but its progress was considerably slower on this the first occasion it had ever been used in a real operation, but the crew could do nothing but sit in their cramped compartment, feeling the powerful water yanking beneath them – and pray. The knowledge that were it to succumb to the tide, the plummeting tank would take at least a minute to fill with water and start drowning the crew only made the crossing feel that much longer. It took five nerve-shredding minutes to reach the other side, and the crew made no attempt to disguise their relief when the rig slid with a gentle jolt and pinpoint precision onto the metal ramps the engineers had laid out on the mudflats. The bank on the eastern side was not as steep as the other but Zero Bravo still had to negotiate it in first gear with a screech of revs before bringing the bow of the tank back down to earth with a heavy thump on the harder ground of the gravelled area above.

Grunting, growling and spewing fumes, rocking back and forth on its tracks, dripping water and mud from its flanks and swinging its barrel back and forth through the mist, the dark menacing silhouette of the Challenger was every inch the reptilian beast emerging from the deep to wreak havoc on the land.

As the driver manoeuvred the Challenger into position, the drive sprockets at the rear of the tracks became ensnared in a jungle of barbed wire that the engineers had laid out to protect themselves from a possible attack. Realizing the irony, following the earlier entanglement, Biggart cut over the Squadron net: 'Well, that's poetic justice for me, I suppose!' In different circumstances, the crews of the other call signs would have been amused by the the Squadron's leader mishap, but lined up, one after another, braced for a nerve-shredding river crossing, there was little laughter in the turrets.

After the Squadron leader, the troops were to go over in numerical order so call sign One Zero, commanded by Lieutenant Alex Marjoribanks (pronounced Marchbanks), the youngest officer in the battle group, went to the head of the queue. As Zero Bravo's crew dismounted to start cutting their tank free of the barbed wire, they watched the rig set off back across the water. Through a break in the mist they were able to make out the silhouette of One Zero moving into the tipping position at the top of the bank. Twenty minutes later, Marjoribanks's tank roared up the bank to join them on the Al Faw. One by one the Challengers pushed out into the mist, but progress was painfully slow and fraught with difficulty. Three vehicles an hour were brought over, each of them facing an ever more hazardous descent on the start bank. It wasn't just that the drop grew lower as the water level fell; it also grew steeper and more difficult as each call sign ploughed and chewed up the soft mud at the embarkation site. By the time 4th troop went over the top, the glistening mudflats had been transformed into a crazily rutted quagmire that made precise manoeuvring almost impossible.

Four hours after their arrival at the launching site, the first grey streaks of morning were appearing on the eastern skyline when the last call sign, Four Two, appeared through the fog and thundered ashore to complete the leaguer of muddied tanks. The crew needed no second invitation to clamber out of their hatches and join the rest of the squadron in stretching their legs and enjoying a hot brew. There was relief in the tired, drawn faces of the men. Combat is not the only occupational hazard of a tank crew. The crossing was as challenging as any exercise or operation any of them had ever carried out.

Military honours are usually handed out for gallantry in battles but, in its own way, pulling off this most dangerous and complex water crossing was as impressive an achievement as a victory in combat. Just because the forces ranged against them weren't sitting in a tank or a bunker didn't make the struggle any less demanding . . . Not that any of the men were thinking about congratulations. Equally towering challenges lay ahead.

When half his squadron had crossed the estuary and with the first streaks of day appearing on the horizon, Major Biggart punched the grid reference of his rendezvous with the QDG into his GPS, climbed back into Zero Bravo and disappeared up the dirt track into the fog, leaving a trail of pale dust in his wake. 'C' Squadron was now in true enemy territory, thirty to forty miles to the south-west of 40 Commando's positions. Trapped by the waterway behind them, if they were attacked now, they would have to fight their way out to the north along tight causeways with no room for manoeuvre. In between the only two Coalition units on the peninsula there lay as lifeless and inhospitable an expanse of land as anywhere on the planet.

The Al Faw is a grey, pockmarked landscape almost completely devoid of any human activity or living eco-system; it's just dead, salty earth with not so much as a thorny shrub or a cactus growing out of it. Only along the irrigated shores of the Shatt Al Arab, the more formidable twin of the Shatt Al Basra, is there any evidence of natural life. There is a scattering of dwellings and industrial complexes near the river-bank, but the only community of any significance is the town of Al Faw, a small fishing port located down at the bottom of the peninsula where the Shatt Al Arab flows into the Persian Gulf. If it was to be twinned with another comparable place, Mars or Pluto would be the only contenders. Or as one of the troopers put it, laying eyes on the landscape for the first time: 'And I thought Maryhill was the worst place on earth.'

Zero Bravo criss-crossed the terrain, turning left, right, north, south, east and west along the narrow earth causeways to try and find a route through the flats to the RV location. Sitting up in the hatch of Zero Bravo, Major Biggart could see the bloody history of the peninsula etched into the terrain all around them: ditches, berms, oil trenches, bunkers, rusting barbed wire, the street grids of former army camps, derelict buildings, piles of rubble and the foundations of destroyed installations. In amongst them, the rusting wreckage of dozens of tanks and other military vehicles lay twisted and scorched across the moonscape – ugly sad monuments to Iraq's vicious eight-year war with Iran between 1980 and 1988 – sinking inch by inch into the soft earth. To the pilots of the aircraft flying overhead on a clear day, the faint outlines of the one-time military communities resembled the archaeological footprint of a lost civilization.

The RV was no more than six miles as the crow flies, but it took the better part of an hour for Zero Bravo to navigate its way through the hellish maze. The Liaison Officer of the QDG, a Sergeant Major attached to 3 Commando Brigade, was standing outside his Scimitar when Zero Bravo appeared through the fog. He greeted Major Biggart in a strong Welsh accent and handed him his orders on a crumpled scrap of paper no larger than a playing card.

Major Biggart ran his eyes down the action slip in mounting disbelief. It read:

> Orders for CH Sqn
> Route from Anne: North from 705591, NE To Scapati 725685
> NW to SAB up to Waterloo LD 671668
> Access assault is pipeline running ENE to Taku 780705
> LOE is 84E, no mov S of 67N
> PRIM QDG 32-050 ALT 40 UCN VHF 33100
> Multiple TTTs armour WH on levied track moving east to west
> All friendly c/s sth of 67N
> 721670
> request use c/s panzer
> Wo2 QDG LO to 3 Cdo Bde

It was not, to say the least, the most detailed set of orders Major Biggart had seen in his career. To a layman it may have looked comprehensive enough but to an experienced soldier it effectively translated as 'Head north, turn right, destroy any enemy you come across and mind out for the Marines at the other end.'

Over the years, the cavalry have become accustomed to receiving orders written in haste, short on details. The Light Brigade at Balaclava may be the most famous instance, but it was by no means the first or last cavalry unit to find itself handed confusing, sketchy or downright nonsensical battle instructions. It is the nature of their role on the battlefield for the cavalry to be sent into action on the spur of the moment with the briefest of briefs. Whether mounted on a horse or a tank, they bring speed, mobility and the capacity for delivering massive shock and firepower to an action at very short notice. Major Biggart resisted the temptation to enquire whether the orders had actually been written on the back of a cigarette packet – the Sergeant was only the messenger after all. Besides, there was a more pressing issue.

'We don't actually have any maps of the Al Faw. Is there any chance that I may have yours?'

The Sergeant Major looked surprised. 'Fine, yep, I think we know the way back,' he replied glancing over his shoulder into the grey haze clinging to the landscape. 'Er, well . . . All the best now on the way down to the Marines. Be on your toes, mind. There's been more armour by the day creeping out of Basra . . .'

The two men climbed back into their vehicles and, driving as fast as the narrow berms of the Al Faw allowed them, disappeared into the fog in opposite directions.

When Major Biggart arrived back at the leaguer, the eighty men under his command were standing outside their tanks or sitting up in their hatches and finishing their silver ration packs of bacon and baked beans. Usually the troops were given a variety of ration meals but following a mix-up with the logistical supply chain back in Kuwait, freeze-dried bacon and beans, brought to life by some hot water, was the only food they had tasted in over a week – three times a day. There were rumours in camp that the Army had had to destroy several years' worth of rations after two Iraqis, working in the factory, had been found contaminating the packs. But given all the other supply difficulties and equipment shortages they had experienced, it was far more likely that the rations had simply fallen by the wayside somewhere along the delivery chain. Too tired or too busy thinking about what fate lay in store for them over the coming hours, barely any of the men were talking.

One or two sneaked a glance at pictures of their loved ones back home or jotted thoughts into their diaries.

Major Biggart's first act on his return was to seek out the engineers and thank them for delivering his tanks and crews safely across the estuary. His men knew that the Squadron leader deserved some of the credit himself for his calm supervision of the operation and for the simplicity of the instructions he passed on to his men. That was one of the qualities that the men admired most about their boss: the ability to take a thorny stick of a problem and then pare and whittle it down to its bare, easy-to-grasp, essentials. Under Major Biggart's command, everyone was clear what they were meant to be doing.

He delivered the orders to his troop leaders, Troop Sergeants, 2iC and Sergeant Major at the back of Zero Bravo with the same no-frills clarity. There was no effort at rousing Churchillian oratory. There was no need. He only had to look at the taut faces of the young men staring out from under their helmets to see that the blood was pumping hard enough as it was. This is what they had trained for: armour-on-armour warfare. The bare facts of their task spoke for themselves. Cool heads and clear judgement were the order of the day, not feverish overwrought excitement.

During the first Gulf War, British armoured units, including the SCOTS DG – who were said to have fired the first shots of the ground offensive – did engage Iraqi tanks but, bombed from the air for weeks on end, the resistance was patchy, disorganized and half-hearted. It was, as 'A' Squadron leader, Major Tim Brown, recalls it, 'mainly a gallop across the Kuwaiti desert'. But, if the Intelligence was accurate, waiting for 'C' Squadron in the complex, well-defended terrain of the Basra suburbs just a few miles to the north was a challenge of an entirely different scale and nature.

Major Biggart gave the coordinates of 40 Commando's positions to the four troop leaders and laid out the plan of action. They were going to try and reach the Marines with a twenty-mile run east, through heavily defended enemy territory along the southern edge of Basra's suburbs, against an unknown quantity of armour – possibly as many as fifty tanks. All enemy armour was fair game, but there was to be strictly no engaging of positions across coalition firing lines without permission and, in a break with conventional practice, troop leaders rather than sergeants or corporals were to lead their units. The squadron was to split in two from the Line of Departure (LD) with 2nd and 3rd troops together with Major Biggart's Zero Bravo leading the main attack. They were to advance eastwards along a raised pipeline to a major road junction, codenamed 'Taku', and then along the wide metalled carriageway for eight miles to the next interchange, known as 'Coriano'. At the same time, 1st and 4th troops, led by Captain Cattermole in Zero Charlie, were to take an almost parallel route from the LD along a more complex off-road route running two miles or so to the south of the others. Their task was to provide fire support for Zero Bravo's group and prevent enemy 'leakage' at the eastern end. If all went to plan, the two halves of the squadron were to reunite at Coriano and then continue a few miles further to the east to team up with the Marines.

In a neat twist of fate, the LD was a point on the Coalition maps that had been given the codename 'Waterloo' by the war planners. It was at the Battle of Waterloo that the Royal Scots Dragoon Guards, in their earlier incarnation as the 2nd (Royal North British) Dragoons – but known to all as the 'Scots Greys' – achieved fame for a series of heroic charges that helped carry the day for Wellington's men. The first charge, 'the greatest thunderbolt ever launched by British cavalry', smashed through the lines of the leading French division. Led by Colonel Inglis Hamilton, who was last seen alive with both wrists slashed and holding the reins of his charger in his teeth, the Greys scythed through the ranks of the second division lined up behind. On reaching the hill above, they cut the gunners of the French artillery batteries to ribbons. Of the 416 Greys who began the day, 200 were killed or wounded and 240 horses also perished. During the charge Sergeant Charles Ewart captured the Standard of the French 45th Regiment of Infantry. The eagle on top of the standard became the regimental cap badge and is still worn today.

As the fourteen Challengers of 'C' Squadron began to rumble through the mist towards Waterloo almost 200 years later, it was difficult for the men not to feel that somehow they were facing their own moment of truth as cavalrymen.

The column pushed north to the LD for five miles along a rough track above the waterway. Major Biggart had ordered radio silence until he gave the word to advance; the commanders and operators of each crew could hear nothing but the faint fizz of white noise in their headsets. The intercoms in the turrets had fallen quiet too. H-hour, set at 0500 Zulu time, was just minutes away. The only sounds came from the engines ticking over in idle mode, the humming of the turret motors and the flicking of switches as the crews went through their final checks of the equipment. The tanks swung round to the east and lined up in formation. Behind them, water from the giant lock known as Bridge Five rushed from the canal into the estuary several dozen feet below. Just three miles to the north, obscured by the fog, the streets of densely populated southern Basra were starting to fill. Market stalls and shops opened for business, cars and carts jockeyed for space across the network of roads and alleys. It was far busier than normal for this time of the day and most of the traffic, pedestrian and vehicular, was streaming south over Bridge Four towards Az Zubayr.

Captain Fraser McLeman, 3rd troop leader, took up position at the head of the column as the tank 'on point'.

'Three, two, one . . . Move!' Major Biggart's voice came over the squadron net crisp and clear. The clocks on the walls of PJHQ back in London showed exactly five o'clock as 'C' Squadron launched the most important and daring British tank operation in living memory. Inside the turrets, the crews felt the tracks tense around the twelve road wheels and bite into the earth. Each driver released the brake, stepped on the accelerator and the two lines of seven tanks rolled across the line of departure and went their separate ways into the mist.

In a traditional cavalry advance into battle, the troops, lined abreast with swords raised, began in a trot, then accelerated into a gallop and finally into a thunderous charge that was timed to hit the enemy lines at full pelt to achieve the greatest effect of shock and power. In this instance, the call signs of 'C' Squadron, lined up one behind the other, were barely able to manage a trot over the soft crumbling soil of the narrow embankments that fell away to the salt flats on either side. Like chargers rearing and tugging at the reins, the Challengers expressed their disapproval of the sluggish, tentative progress by shuddering and vibrating – a sensation that only fuelled the steeply rising tension inside the turrets. The Challenger will give its mount a far smoother ride in the gallop than in the trot, but there was no chance of a rapid advance across open ground here. And the tight, restricted formation in which they were advancing along one of Iraq's main pipeline trails only intensified the edgy, claustrophobic atmosphere inside the tanks. They had no freedom of movement, nowhere to take cover. On the ranges, the Challengers flew over the open terrain at up to 45mph, using the contours of the land as protection, jumping between woods and copses, hills and hummocks to take up position and keep out of view. Here, they had no more licence to manoeuvre than a train on a railway track. Only the crew of a battleship leaving the open seas for the narrow confines of a canal would have been able to identify with the frustrations and fears of the two columns of armour as they crept through the clinging mist towards the enemy positions.

As Zero Bravo's half of the squadron edged ever closer towards the Taku road junction – on a two o'clock axis from the LD – breaks in the mist revealed snapshots of the area beyond. Running in a parallel line about 200 yards to their left was a string of giant electricity pylons; beyond that, the faint outline of an industrial complex. To the right, there was nothing but mud, mist and the ghostly silhouette of an abandoned watchtower, like a lighthouse on a hidden sandbank. Somewhere beyond it, the other seven Challengers of the squadron were trying to navigate their way across the empty expanse. Visibility had improved a little since daybreak but it was still down to 200 yards, and the commanders were using their thermal-imaging capability more than the day sights as they scanned the terrain for enemy.

Looking out across the desolate landscape, Captain McLeman recalled the images from Wilfred Thesiger's *The Marsh Arabs*, which he had read on the long boat journey out to the Gulf with the Challengers. It was difficult to imagine that for centuries these vast stretches of southern Iraq had been, until very recently, a thriving natural habitat, teeming with wildlife that included water buffalo, wild boar and all manner of exotic birds – as well as a home to one of the most ancient peoples on the planet who lived in ingeniously designed reed houses along the banks of the myriad of waterways. When Saddam drained the marshes as a punishment for the Shia uprising after the first Gulf War, the survivors of his violent crackdown were forced to seek refuge in the slums of Basra just three miles to the north of where the column was now passing.

The young troop leader shook his head and took a deep breath. The fatigue from the all-night crossing, combined with the silence and the hypnotic repetition of casting his eyes back and forth across the foggy, featureless world outside, had a soporific effect. He stared down the sights at the earth cause-way stretching away into the haze. A splash of green erupted in the centre of his TI screen and rapidly spread out in all directions. Almost simultaneously, a heavy rumble shook the air and a tremor ran along the earth embankment. A rapid succession of further explosions and bright flashes followed. The crews froze. A moment later, they understood. The artillery barrage on the enemy positions up ahead had opened up. The FOO from the Royal Horse Artillery, operating from his Warrior to the rear of Zero Bravo's Challenger, had wanted to delay the barrage until the tanks were a little closer but his gunner colleagues, he was told, were working to a tight schedule of tasks and were unable to postpone it. It was now or never – and 'now' edged a tight call.

The roar of the barrage was enough to wake the dead, never mind startle the living. With it, the advancing tanks had lost the element of surprise, but the calculated gamble was that the intensity and shock of the assault would soften up the enemy, causing chaos and confusion up and down the line of defence. Captain McLeman ordered his driver to accelerate. Through the murk he could make out a furious orange ball of fire at the foot of a mountain of thick black smoke. The 155mm rounds of the mighty AS-90 guns had ignited the underground junction of Iraq's main oil pipelines that run from the inland pumping stations out to the tanker terminals in the Gulf. The area just to the south of the Taku road interchange had turned into a scene from the Apocalypse: a ballooning mass of flames and sooty smog mingled with the low cloud still blanketing the landscape – dwarfing the column of Challengers, led by Three Zero, now heading straight into the thick of it.

Captain McLeman and his gunner in the seat below were scanning furiously as Three Zero bore down on Taku. Through the churning smoke it was difficult to identify distinct features using the day sights. Equally, it was almost impossible to pick out heat sources in the TI night sights when the area directly ahead of them was ablaze with oil fires. They were about 200 yards short of the junction when McLeman felt his heart skip a beat. He swallowed hard, pushed his face harder into the eye caps and flicked the sights to high magnification. A cloud of smoke and mist obscured his view for a moment but he held his sights on the spot and waited. Then he waited some more. The column was still advancing at no more than trotting pace over the crumbling narrow track but the racing of his heart created the illusion that they were rushing headlong into the maelstrom. Slowly, the smoky haze drifted away and, right there, just north of the junction, was the unmistakable sight of a T-55 main battle tank. Its barrel was slightly elevated and was pointing towards the advancing column of British tanks. McLeman switched to the night sights – yes, the tank did have a heat source, meaning that its engines were either running or had only recently been switched off. His senses raced up the scale to the highest threat level. He was staring down the barrel of an enemy battle tank. They had been warned that a regiment's worth of armour might be waiting for them beyond Taku but somehow it barely seemed possible that he was barrel to barrel with one in the middle of a war zone.

A thousand thoughts tumbled through his mind in the time it took to inhale one deep breath. The Soviet-made T-55 was vastly inferior to the Challenger, but all main battle tanks carry a heavy punch and even if it couldn't penetrate his Dorchester armour at the front of the vehicle, the young captain knew that a round in the right spot could still disable him – and if the enemy managed to get behind him or side on, then he was especially vulnerable. Besides, if the enemy tanks outnumbered them two or three to one as the Intel suggested, then the T-55 suddenly became a far more formidable foe . . . and if this adversary did take him out now and he was unable to advance any further, then Operation Panzer was effectively stillborn. The call signs behind him could not pass. He had to get his FIN round away as quickly as possible . . .

War scatters its assignments and experiences randomly: while one unit is caught up in a ferocious entanglement with the enemy, another is sitting a few miles down the road, dying of nothing more painful than boredom. So it was with 'B' Squadron as they emerged from their sleeping bags for another day of preparatory exercises and humdrum drills in Shaibah airfield. One day's rest had been welcome, a second was tolerable, a third was tedious, but a fourth day of watching the war from ringside was starting to drive the men wild with frustration. Up the road, the other three battle groups were going toe to toe with the opposition and 'C' Squadron had set out on their adventure to link up with the Royal Marines. But in Shaibah 'B' Squadron and the Irish Guards cleaned their weapons and equipment, while the senior officers of the battle group studied maps and aerial photos and ran their commanders through likely scenarios and actions.

Since returning from Nick 104, there had been constant rumours that the SCOTS DG were going to replace one or other of the battle groups, but each one withered and died on the grapevine. The pipes and drums had been unpacked and rousing tunes were played to lift the morale and distract attention from their inaction. But if there's one sound in the world that gets a Scots soldier's blood pumping, it's the rasping bleat of a bagpipe and the steady beat of a drum. The music succeeded in stirring up the men still further.

Lieutenant Colonel Blackman had been doing his best to keep the men busy with various tasks, but the atmosphere was restive, jittery. Coffee and cigarettes were consumed in increasingly large volumes, but they did little to tame the growing disquiet.

That night the tank troops were asleep in the reinforced concrete air hangars, the guards were patrolling on stag and the Squadron leaders were in their 'O' group with the Commanding Officer when the air erupted with a sequence of deafening crashes. Men hit the deck where they stood, or leapt under the vehicles for cover. Some of the crews mounted up, the orders and shouts of the men barely audible above the roar. For a few minutes, there was pandemonium across the camp ... until someone up the command chain chose to inform them that 3rd Regiment Royal Horse Artillery had moved a battery of six AS-90 guns right up behind them and opened fire on targets to the north. The men returned to their sleeping bags cursing the 'bastard gunners' and lay awake watching and listening to the rounds shriek and howl over their heads, deprived once more of a night's sleep.

And just an hour earlier, shortly before first light, Brigade put the battle group on immediate notice to move. Basra, they said, was on the brink of an uprising against Saddam's regime and they needed to get in there to support it. The squadron mounted up, and the Irish Guards piled into the back of the Warriors, the tanks were fully bombed up, the drivers gunned the engines, the whole battle group lined up at the airfield gates to race across the Shatt Al Arab into the heart of the city and . . . Then they were stood down. False alarm. There was no bloody uprising.

The characterization of war as 1 per cent terror and exhilaration and 99 per cent boredom might just have been coined for 'B' Squadron's experience in Operation TELIC. Since crossing the border almost a week earlier the sum total of their war experience was a twelve-hour shoot-out in the dark at Nick 104. So it was that, for yet another day, the men of 'B' Squadron and the Irish Guards tucked into their breakfast rations in silence and prepared themselves for a day of hanging around, waiting for orders, and waiting, and waiting . . .

'Zero, Three Zero, contact, tanks, wait out!' McLeman felt as if he had shouted the report over the squadron net, but to the other commanders and operators he sounded almost unnaturally calm and composed. The words themselves didn't need to be shouted or delivered in a dramatic tone of voice in order to communicate the drama of their meaning. *Contact, tanks!* They had all heard the words many times out on the plains of Canada, Poland and Germany but on those occasions, in spite of the realism of the exercise and the thrill of the moment, in their heart of hearts they knew that they weren't going to be incinerated or vaporized by an enemy round. They were merely going to be lased by a red dot and then all go back to their hide in the woods for a nice hot mug of tea. Now it was for real and those calmly delivered words – *Contact, tanks!* – ran through 'C' Squadron's fourteen turrets like the shockwave from a main armament round.

'FIN, tank!' McLeman said to his crew as soon as he had passed on the contact report.

'On!' barked his gunner, who had already spotted the T-55.

'Loaded!' yelled the loader.

'Fir-ING!'

Three Zero had almost pulled off the dirt track and onto the dual carriageway at Taku when the gunner squeezed the firing button, the muzzle flashed orange and blue, and the bolt of tungsten streaked through the haze. A powerful rush of air and cordite from the bag charge swept through the turret as the main gun recoiled deep into the tank and the Challenger rocked ever so gently on its tracks, belying the violence it had just unleashed. In less time than it takes to blink, a small flash appeared at the base of the T-55's turret and almost at once a white spray of molten metal burst out the other side. The punch of the bolt had smashed a hole through two panels of armour, causing mayhem inside a turret laden with high explosive rounds. Like a bullet, the FIN round, so called because of the stabilizing fins at its base, does not carry any explosive; it's the kinetic energy that causes the damage. Capable of penetrating armour as thick as it is long, on impact it creates a lethal shower of 'spall' – fragments from the armour – that tears through the fighting compartment, killing the crew instantly and shredding and vaporizing everything inside. The crew of Three Zero tried not to picture the scene inside the wounded T-55.

As call sign Three Zero pulled onto the hard surface of the

road, they could see the turret of the T-55 starting to wobble on its base as the ammunition inside began to 'brew up'. And as they had always read and been told, it was just like an old-fashioned kettle reaching boiling point when the lid shakes from the pressure of the steam. Flames and smoke belched from the sides of the tank for a few seconds. The hatches flew open violently and a ball of orange lifted the turret away from the hull and dumped it back down at an awkward angle with the barrel hanging forlornly at the side, pointing at the earth. McLeman found himself hoping that the enemy crew had had the good sense to flee during the artillery barrage. No tank crew relishes the slaughter of another. It's the tank itself they want to annihilate. To die in a tank is to do so hideously. A man doesn't just pass away in a tank; he is blasted into non-existence.

Lance Corporal Bruce Fraser, the loader, opened the breech of the gun and leant into the rack of ammunition behind him and took out another FIN round, in the plastic casing that enabled it to fit the 120mm rifled bore of the gun. He slid the round up the loading chamber, packed the bag charge behind it and closed the protective shield protecting the crew from any recoil and activating the firing system. He completed the entire procedure in under three seconds.

The call signs behind were filing off the dirt track and onto the hard surface of the road junction as McLeman delivered his combat report and scanned for fresh targets through the confusion of smoke. The words 'One T-55 destroyed' had barely left his lips when his driver reported that there were dozens of mines scattered across the road ahead of them. Sitting low down at the front of the tank directly underneath the main armament, the driver had the clearest view of the road but in the maelstrom of smoke and fire he had done well to spot them for what they were and bring the Challenger to a sharp stop. A few seconds later and Three Zero would have driven right over the potentially lethal explosive. The soft, unarmoured underbelly of tanks has always been vulnerable to mine attack – at the very least, just one device could blow off a track and this was the very last place a crew would want to carry out essential, time-consuming repair work. As the vehicle lurched to a standstill, a shower of machine-gun rounds hammered into the Challenger, pinging against the turret and ricocheting into the air in a spray of sparks. The line of date palms a few hundred yards to the north was twinkling with dozens of muzzle flashes and trails of tracer streaked through the remaining wisps of mist clinging to the ground. '. . . Mines everywhere!'

'Blast them off the road with coax!' Zero Bravo's reply was immediate and decisive. 'Then go firm. I'm going to put 2nd troop through you and I'll follow. Cover us!'

The gunner flicked the switch at the centre of the firing controls from 'Main Gun' to 'Coax' and started pumping off rounds to clear a route through the mines scattered across the tarmac. Shaped like fat frisbees, the mines flew up and spun through the air, some exploding, others fizzing and smoking or breaking up without detonating. Like a terrestrial minesweeper, the Challenger slowly, relentlessly churned its way through the potentially lethal litter of explosives. With the initial stretch of carriageway safe, the three Challengers of Captain Rick Le Sueur's 2nd troop, followed by Major Biggart's Zero Bravo, roared off the pipeline and onto the hard surface of the tarmacked carriageway in a clatter and squeal of tracks. McLeman and the rest of his troop provided covering fire as the four tanks surged through the smoke and began the advance east. At the end of the road, eight miles away, the Marines lay in their scrapes and stood by their vehicles and waited. HQ of 3 Commando Brigade came over the radio to inform them that the final phase of Operation Panzer had been launched.

If the enemy had failed to twig from the artillery barrage that some form of coalition attack was underway, there was certainly no mistaking it now as the seven Challengers, one by one, emerged from the thick smoke as if from behind a black curtain billowing in the wind. Most of the incoming fire was emanating from positions to the north of the column, or to their left as they advanced, in amongst the groves of date palms and the undulating expanses of bare earth in between. The mist had lifted high enough to give the Challenger crews a clearer view of the terrain and the Intel had been spot on – a quick scan with the commander's 360-degree panoramic sights revealed a landscape bristling with enemy activity. There were tanks all along the route, most of them hull down with just the tops of their turrets and barrels visible over the crest of the raised ground where they had taken up position. It was just a question of how many there were and whether any of them were the more formidable T-72s. Where there are tanks, infantry will never be far away and, sure enough, lacing routes through the rows of palms to the north were a number of MTLB armoured personnel carriers, disgorging troops to take up position in a chain of pre-prepared bunker positions.

The daring angle and timing of 'C' Squadron's attack through the marshland may have been a tactical surprise, but the enemy were there in considerable numbers, dug in and braced for a British onslaught as and when it came. Even before the tail end of the column had reached the dual carriageway, the fire was pouring out of the trees and bunkers. All the tanks had their barrels pointing to the south and not towards in the Marines in the east, indicating the enemy knew that armoured reinforcements were going to try and reach the cut-off Commandos.

Speed is of the essence in mobile warfare and it is one of the great assets of the Challenger that it can fire very accurately on the move. Its sophisticated suspension system gives it a stabilized gun platform, allowing it to engage targets at pace over rough terrain and making it hard for enemy gunners to strike back. The squadron was making full use of the Challenger's technological superiority as they opened up with an awesome mixture of FIN, HESH and coax. Loaders rammed rounds up the barrel, while commanders and gunners went into hunter-killer procedure, scanning, lasing and firing at a seemingly endless stream of targets. The turrets reverberated with shouts and orders and the traffic over the squadron net became congested as tank after tank reported its engagements and contact reports. The smell of cordite filled the fighting compartments.

There were so many rounds being fired, it was difficult to know which call sign was engaging which target. Captain Le Sueur was now leading the thunderous charge down the road and to avoid confusion and wasting ammunition on the same target, he made the decision, as soon as he saw the battlefield conditions, to divide up the different types of target between his three tanks. He and his Troop Sergeant Charlie Baird in Two Zero and Two One were to keep loading FIN and concentrate on taking out the armour to the north, while Two Two, commanded by his troop Corporal, Dougal, was to load HESH and focus on engaging bunkers and dismounts.

With a good loader, a Challenger can destroy three separate targets in under ten seconds and all seven loaders in the column were close to matching those speeds to ensure the crews were able to get a main round away faster than the enemy. Standing in their stations below to the commander's left, each loader was furiously ramming rounds up the breech, like stokers shovelling coal into an engine. The tanks, muzzles blazing, raced along the southern perimeter of Basra's leafy suburbs.

The battle was everywhere. The line of trees to the north leapt with explosions and eruptions of earth. Tracer streaked back and forth. Mortar rounds fell amongst the advancing column of tanks, fountains of earth burst out of the ground on either side of the carriageway. The deafening roar of guns and hectic crackle of machine-gun fire filled the air, drowning out the yells and shouts of the dismounts on the ground as the opposing forces blasted away at each other over the rolling mud flats. A HESH round wiped the smile off Saddam Hussein's face in a giant stone mural at the side of the road, smashing out his teeth and the end of his nose in a shower of flying bricks. Fires raged out of the turrets of T-55s and hulls of armoured personnel carriers. Smoke drifted across the battlefield.

The crews of the T-55s were proving no match for their counterparts in the Challengers – either that, or they had seen the flaming waves of destruction rolling down their line and, jumping from their hatches, fled into the date palms to hole up with the infantry. Shadowy figures of black-clad Fedayeen soldiers ran in amongst the palms and between the bunkers trying to rally the regular forces. Thousands of 7.62mm rounds kicked up the dirt in and around their positions, shredding the bark from the trunks and perforating the troop trucks and other vehicles parked up behind.

The immense firepower of the British tanks was having a shattering impact on the Iraqi lines. This was mobile warfare at its most effective. The enemy, in its chain of static positions, could barely lay a round on them as they streaked along the dual highway. Whatever weight of fire the Iraqis hurled at them, the Challengers responded with even more devastating volleys of main rounds and withering bursts of coax – and then sped away down the road.

Mines had been strewn across all four lanes for long stretches of the dual carriageway and, alerted by the drivers, the gunners chain-gunned them out of the way as best they could but the tanks still had to weave and swerve their way through the deadly trail. This high-speed raid was as close to an old-fashioned cavalry charge as a modern armoured unit could hope to experience; it wasn't a tank battle in the purest sense but it was as near to it as they were going to get in the complex terrain of Iraq. After five days of negotiating the maze of narrow earth causeways and embankments, constantly fearful of sliding into the boggy morass of the drained marshlands, the sense of speed and mobility they were now experiencing was as exhilarating as it was liberating. Racing along the broad carriageway, powered by its mighty engine, closed down in the soundproofed world of the thickly armoured turret, Challenger after Challenger rolled irresistibly towards objective Coriano, leaving a landscape of smoke-choked desolation in its wake.

To the advance unit of the Marines' Brigade Reconnaissance Force (BRF) positioned at Coriano, exhausted and filthy after a week of fighting and living rough, it was a spine-tingling spectacle as they looked down through their sights and binoculars from their positions a couple of miles to the east of the road junction. The advancing column had all the appearance of a ferocious naval broadside as the Challengers crashed their way through the enemy lines with all guns blazing, the tracer fire streaking back and forth. The burning, twisted wrecks of tanks and MTLBs littered the landscape, palls of smoke were rising up through the air and the rumble of explosions grew louder by the minute as the column hammered towards them. One Marine was standing, bare-chested on the bonnet of his cut-down Land Rover with his binoculars trained on the smouldering horizon in the near distance. 'Here comes the cavalry!' he shouted. He half meant it as a joke, but it was true: the cavalry were riding to the rescue.

In amongst the scene of destruction lay the blazing remains of seven T-55s, six MTLBS, two large bunker positions as well as an indeterminate number of dismount casualties, although such was the speed of the advance as well as the rate and weight of the fire it was impossible to know the true number of targets destroyed. There was only one certainty: the biggest casualty suffered by the enemy was the blow to its morale. Without air or infantry support, half a squadron of British Challengers had just advanced along an eight-mile front, from one end of Iraqi-held territory to the other, making mincemeat of their defensive positions in a matter of minutes.

As Two Zero slowed up and pulled alongside the BRF's vehicles, Captain Le Sueur emerged from his hatch to be greeted by a posse of heavily armed, wild-looking Marines, grinning from ear to ear and applauding the tanks in.

'Awesome! That was some engagement! We couldn't borrow your vehicles for a few days, could we?' one of them shouted.

'Well, we do our best,' replied Le Sueur, immediately aware and slightly embarrassed that he must have sounded so very 'cavalry'.

The call signs spread out and went firm at Coriano, which was no more than a bend in the main road with a few dirt tracks and covered pipelines leading off it into the flat, featureless expanse of earth surrounding it on all sides. The crews gulped draughts of water and air in equally deep measures in an effort to steady their racing minds and pumping hearts. It had all happened so fast. After years of training, the troops' first experience of a true battle had lasted no more than about thirty minutes in the run from Taku, but in that brief period they had each experienced more action than a cavalryman serving during the Cold War years would have experienced in twenty-five years in uniform. Such was the shock and intensity of it that all sense of time had been lost inside the turrets and no crew member would have demurred had he been told he had been fighting for two or three hours. They breathed and sweated as if they had just completed a marathon. 'C' Squadron had just played the central role in the largest and most ferocious tank engagement involving British forces since the Second World War, but it was the present, not the past, that preoccupied them. Operation Panzer wasn't over quite yet. *Where is the rest of the squadron?*

Progress had been nothing like as sweeping along the parallel southern route for Captain Cattermole and the other call signs. It was with a mixture of awe and frustration that they listened over the radio to the contact reports and updates of the battle in which their friends and comrades were embroiled a few miles away. They wanted to be flying through the thick of the action with them, not, as it had turned out, rumbling and revving through a labyrinth of unstable dirt banks in first and second gear trying to avoid 'boggying' their vehicles, wondering if they were ever going to find a way out of the tangled web of tracks and pipelines. Shortly after moving across the line of departure, call sign One Two had got bogged down and thrown a track. The others were forced to leave him there while Squadron Sergeant Major 'Speccie' McIntyre detached himself from Major Biggart's half of the squadron to get him moving again with the help of the engineers of the LAD and their CRARRV.

Captain Cattermole had done well to navigate through the mist and maze with nothing but his eyesight and Intelligence to guide him. The plan had been for his group to provide fire support and reach Coriano before the others in order to prevent the enemy leaking out towards the Marines. It was a sensible plan, but it was wrecked by the unforgiving conditions on the ground. When they finally appeared through the haze, guided into the position by Major Biggart over the radio net, Cattermole and his men were racked with the same, almost physical, sense of anti-climax that a boxer in a keenly antici-pated prize fight might feel if pulled out of the ring just before the first bell. Every man, said Samuel Johnson, thinks a little less of himself for not having been a soldier. Equally, every soldier feels a little less of himself for having missed out on the main action of an operation or campaign – and there was a good deal of muttering and cursing inside the turrets as the tanks went firm alongside the rest of the squadron around the interchange at Coriano.

While 2nd and 3rd troops tried to get their breath back, Captain Cattermole's half of the squadron was then dispatched further along the route to exploit the area between Coriano and the Marines. They quickly arrived at a junction with a road running north to a complex of industrial buildings and ware-houses leading up to the docks along the southern bank of the Shatt Al Arab. Looking up it over the flat open terrain, they saw dozens of black-clad Fedayeen paramilitaries, in a convoy of Hilux technicals and military trucks, shooting out of the residential suburbs to the left. Most probably, they had been flushed out from their original positions by the squad-ron's move east and were either regrouping to launch a counter-attack or stockpiling ammunition before fleeing across the Shatt Al Arab to live and fight another day. They were humping weapons and boxes of ammo into the vehicles as quickly as they could when one of them caught sight of the Challengers and raised the alarm. Immediately, they all leapt behind their vehicles for cover and began pouring streams of small-arms fire down the road at the tanks creeping towards them.

Cattermole and 4th troop accelerated up the road to challenge them, strafing the vehicles with coax and sending the paramilitaries scattering in all directions as they advanced. The other Fedayeen vehicles disappeared further north in amongst the network of streets, cranes and factories. Their actions bore all the hallmarks of a trap: they were trying to lure the Challengers into the built-up area to ambush them. Up close and personal, they had a far better chance of disabling one of them and forcing a *Blackhawk Down* scenario. The packet of tanks ground to a stop and Cattermole reported his findings over the net. Major Biggart was of the same mind: without infantry and without a map, there was no sense in chasing after dozens of heavily armed enemy in a network of streets and dead-ends and industrial units that they knew like their own backyard but to the Challenger crews might as well have been the outskirts of Timbuktu. The risks were too great, the prize too small. Squirting some parting bursts of coax into the technicals, the tanks reluctantly reversed back down the road until it was safe to expose the rear of the vehicles, then spun round and sped off to rejoin the rest of the squadron.

As soon as they'd returned, all fourteen Challengers and the four back-up vehicles formed up into single file and, led by Cattermole, continued the advance along the major road across the peninsula that follows the twists and turns of the

Shatt Al Arab down to the town of Al Faw on the Persian Gulf. Obscured by a stubborn patch of mist hanging over a tributary, the column had momentarily disappeared from the Marines' view when Cattermole switched to 3 Commando Brigade's frequency to announce that the SCOTS DG were about to cross into their territory. With so much armour probing and harassing their area of operation in recent days, and with visibility still poor over some of the terrain, misunderstandings could easily lead to a blue-on-blue disaster. Following the tragedy of the RTR incident, no one closed down in a turret in Iraq needed reminding that it only takes a few seconds for some form of strike to take out a tank.

'Hello, Zero this is Zero Charlie,' said the squadron's Second-in-Command.

'No, you're not,' came the instant reply.

'Yes, I am.'

'No, you're not. We've already got one of those call signs and I can see it from where I'm sitting now. Now who are you?'

Resisting the temptation to announce that they were the Republican Guard's Medina Division, Captain Cattermole sighed and tried to explain that he wasn't an Iraqi jammer trying to cause confusion over 40 Commando's radio network. As they were talking over an open, unsecured frequency, there was a chance that the enemy might be listening. In the battle of El Alamein and other engagements of the North Africa campaign, tank squadrons often communicated over the radio in exaggerated regional and class dialects and bizarre idioms so as to confuse enemy eavesdroppers. Engagements, whole battles even, were conducted in a language derived from peculiarly British worlds of cricket, horse racing and popular music. Feeling slightly ridiculous, 'C' Squadron's 2iC tried his own version of mysterious, veiled tank speech.

'Zero, we are, ahem, the heavy horse ... of Scotland ... ahem, approaching the finishing line of the Panzer Stakes ...'

'You what?'

The exchange continued in this vein for a while before one of the Marine commanders cut in and, trying to hide his amusement, said: 'OK, to avoid any confusion you and your other call signs add the call sign indicator Panzer.'

'Zero, this is *Panzer* Zero Charlie. We are approaching the FLOT, your Forward Line Own Troops. Don't shoot!'

It was an impressive, heart-lifting spectacle for both units as the column of tanks rolled towards the main contingent of the Brigade's Reconnaissance Force, the most forward element of the Marines on the peninsula. It was difficult to say which of the two formations was more delighted to see the other: the SCOTS DG because they had just pulled off an extremely complex and daring operation, or the men of 3 Commando Brigade because the threat of being overrun by Iraqi armour was over and they now had some massive fire-power at their disposal, for a few days at least.

The commanders and loaders emerged from their hatches as they approached the Marines, who were spread out along the side of the road in a convoy of cut-down Land Rovers, Pinzgauer troop carriers and quad bikes. Some were laid up in ditches and banks with their assault rifles and machine guns pointing towards Basra. Their vehicles groaned with an armoury of weapons including mortars, shoulder-held MILAN anti-tank weapons, mounted gimpys with trails of 7.62mm rounds flowing out of the side as well as boxes of grenades, smoke rounds, flares and ammunition. To both units, it was as if they had walked onto the set of a movie as the Challengers slowed to a walking pace and the men greeted each other. To the tank crews, the Marines were as formidable-looking a bunch of soldiers as they could expect to lay eyes on: bare-topped or in T-shirts and wearing shades, to a man they were built like brick outhouses, their faces were covered in thick stubble and their bodies and clothes were streaked with pale mud from living rough. Some were hanging out of the sides of their vehicles, others were stripping down GPMGs and rifles and putting in some maintenance on their huge stockpile of equipment. A handful were sitting up in their muddy sleeping bags at the side of the road as the tanks clattered and squealed by. As a cavalry regiment, the SCOTS DG place a great deal of importance on the discipline of maintaining an immaculate appearance, even out in the field. The Marines, a different breed of warrior altogether, looked positively feral by comparison – and all the more intimidating for it. Just a passing glimpse of them would be enough to make most enemies think very long and very hard about whether it was in their wisest interests to risk a confrontation.

One or two of the Marines were holding up video cameras as the dusty armoured column rolled through their position but the rest were clapping, cheering and banging their chests. Many of them had never seen a working Challenger up close, and the sight of 1,000 tons of British armour, carrying the equivalent firepower of half a dozen regular infantry regiments, was as inspiring to them as it was for the tank crews to be linking up with a formation of British forces regarded, without conceit or hyperbole, as the one of the finest commando units in the world. No British unit, other than the Paras, understands the rigours of a long, difficult march followed by a ferocious battle better than the Royal Marines. Having watched them gallop over the horizon and put their tormentors to the sword, there was gratitude and respect in equal measure in the effusive welcome they gave the squadron.

The SCOTS DG were being given the military equivalent of a standing ovation from one of the most celebrated fighting forces on the planet and there was not a man inside those fourteen turrets that didn't feel a swelling of pride as they drove through their lines.

Night descended quickly over the Al Faw, creating a sense of ill-ease across the 'C' Squadron hide. The Challengers were spread out over half a square mile but, with a strict blackout policy, it was impossible for the crews to see the neighbouring troop just a few hundred yards away in the dark. The only light came from the stars, a sliver of moon and the occasional flash of a lighter from behind a cupped hand. With radio silence also being observed, the men climbed into their sleeping bags on the back decks of the Challengers suddenly dogged by a sense of isolation and vulnerability. After the exertions of the previous twenty-four hours, sleep yanked hard at their bodies, but it was difficult to relax in the almost pitch darkness in the middle of enemy territory. There was a village sprawled in amongst the date palms along the banks of the river less than a mile to the north of their positions. The locals there had seemed friendly enough when the troops had taken it turns to conduct foot patrols there earlier in the day, but a few friendly children and the odd wave from a grinning grown-up was no guarantee that there weren't any hostiles in town. Ordinarily, a tank squadron would have highly trained and well-equipped infantry platoons in intimate support of their positions, but having left the Irish Guards back at Shaibah, the cavalrymen were now entirely respon-sible for their own defence. And it wasn't with the highest degree of confidence that the troops settled down for the night, seeing a couple of their comrades disappear into the darkness to keep watch over them, with limited numbers of night vision goggles and armed with nothing more than an SA-80 assault rifle and a couple of magazines of ammunition.

Inevitably, there was plenty of gallows humour banter about nocturnal throat-slitting as the crews rolled over and tried to expel from their minds images of the enemy leopard-crawling towards the tanks with knives in their teeth and bandoliers of hand grenades over their backs. 'Well, that's the last we see of Wee Davey then . . . Don't worry, trooper, I'll tell the wife you died bravely . . . Seriously, mate, just say you *do* die tonight, can I have your MP3 player? . . . Quiet! did you hear that noise over there? . . .'

As was standard practice, the vehicles of Squadron Head-quarters – the tanks of the Commanding Officer, his 2iC, the Sergeant Major, the Battle Captain and the Forward Observa-tion Officer – had taken up position in the middle of the hide where, with the four troops on the periphery of the position, they were relatively safe from a surprise attack. So it was in a much easier state of mind that Major Biggart took out his personal kitbag from the storage bin at the rear of his Chal-lenger, hauled himself up the side of the tank and prepared to turn in for the night.

After the sun had burnt off the early-morning haze, the temperature had rocketed to around thirty degrees to give them their hottest day since crossing the border, but without any cloud cover the air was cold again. The Squadron leader kept his jersey on as he climbed into his sleeping bag, lit a final cigarette and reflected on the most dramatic day in his Army career. It seemed incredible to him that it was no more than twenty-four hours earlier that he had been handed his orders to lead the march across the peninsula. It seemed even more remarkable that his squadron had achieved their objective without the loss of a single man or vehicle. Before deploying to the Gulf, the Squadron leader had written in his diary, vowing to do his utmost to make sure every one of his men returned alive. When the column set out from Shaibah at the start of the night march, that hope suddenly seemed highly optimistic and improbable. In the distance, the lights of the port city of Khorramshahr and the other settlements on the Iranian side of the river suffused the black horizon with a hazy glow. Two miles away, Iranian border guards stood in their watchtowers observing the British tanks through their night sights. Tossing his cigarette over the side, Major Biggart watched it float to the ground in an arc of orange sparks. He lay on his back and marvelled at the star-studded canopy above him. Within seconds he was asleep.

6. Rockets and Raids

'. . . after what B Company Black Watch witnessed this afternoon, I don't think we need any further motivation to give the Fedayeen a bloody nose when we go in, in a few hours' time.'

It was eleven o'clock at night local time and Major Brown was coming to the end of his 'O' group inside the old Iraqi marine base, close to Bridge Four where 'A' Squadron had set up camp after moving up from Az Zubayr. His 2iC Charlie MacDermot-Roe, the four troop leaders, Battle Captain James Bishop, Sergeant Major Anderson and Staff Sergeant McKenzie, the SQMS, stared back at him grimly. They had saddled up to mount a similar raid two days earlier, only to be stood down at the last minute, leaving the men deflated and irritable. Now, following the shocking events of the afternoon, the raid was back on and the adrenaline was pumping once again.

'A' Squadron were to become the first regular forces of the coalition to cross one of the four main bridges into Basra since the invasion began eight days earlier.

The plan was for a classic in-and-out raid. They were to head over Bridge Four, the principal route into the city from the south, and race up the dual carriageway known as Route Red, stopping just short of Old Basra, a maze of twisting, narrow alleys and streets. They were to destroy three targets: the city's main TV and radio mast, which was still broadcasting propaganda, the headquarters and main operating base of the Fedayeen, and, in a symbolic gesture, a massive statue of Saddam Hussein situated in the middle of a giant interchange at the 'Gateway to Basra'. They were to be accompanied by a platoon of the Black Watch, roughly thirty men in four Warriors, whose task was to get out and hold the ground if any of the tanks were to come to grief. There was no reason why all three targets couldn't be destroyed from the air without inflicting casualties on the civilian population, but the planners were eager to send out a bold message to the Fedayeen. Dispatching a squadron of tanks deep into their territory told them in no uncertain terms that their days were numbered. More crucially, it told the Iraqi people and the watching world that the Fedayeen's control of the area was loosening.

A few hours earlier, 'Bravo' Company Black Watch had returned from VCP duty on the south side of the bridge, visibly shaken by what they had just witnessed. Streams of civilians had been pouring over the bridge all day long to seek refuge in the relatively safe areas now under the control of the British. When they had failed to stem the exodus, the Fedayeen started machine-gunning the crowd, mowing down people indiscriminately, including women and children. As the casualties lay screaming in the road, British troops set about destroying the paramilitary positions and eventually British ambulances were able to get in and tend to the wounded. Throughout the conflict, there had been dozens of instances of the Fedayeen carrying and dragging toddlers as human shields but shooting innocent civilians represented a shocking escalation in its sinister tactics and *modus operandi*. Media reports of the incident spread quickly, putting Downing Street and Whitehall under great pressure to react.

There had been a lot of negative news coming out of Iraq since the invasion began a week earlier: casualty figures were climbing by the day, Baghdad and Basra were still in enemy hands, there were major problems getting supplies of water and food and other basic humanitarian aid into the areas it was most needed. The British could not now be seen to be sitting on their hands while the Fedayeen scythed down women and children in a hail of machine-gun fire. An audacious, highly visible tank raid into the heart of the Fedayeen's area of operations to take out a handful of Basra landmarks, filmed by a BBC camera strapped to Zero Bravo's gun barrel, was seen by the authorities as the best possible riposte and statement of intent. It was far too dangerous for journalists to accompany them, but Brown had agreed to let their embedded TV reporter travel in the squadron ambulance to the rear.

The audacity of the raid was certainly not lost on the men being asked to carry it out – nor was the honour of it, or the burden of responsibility they were being asked to carry on behalf of the British war effort. While stressing the gravity and difficulty of the mission to his subordinate officers and NCOs, Major Brown did not spell out his worst fears based on the Intelligence reports he had been given. He probably didn't need to. The risks were obvious to everyone present. The worst-case scenario was one of his tanks being disabled three miles up Route Red in the heart of Iraq's second city, surrounded by buildings. If a crowd was to form, the raiding party would be unable to use their weapons and the enemy only needed to douse the tank in petrol to force out the crew. They also knew the Iraqis were hiding their tanks in the city too. The most experienced active tank commander in the British Army was as good as certain that his squadron was going to take casualties . . . but there was nothing to be gained from passing on that fear to his men.

'. . . I cannot think of a better group of men to execute this raid. Your courage and professionalism have been obvious to all over the last few days. So, unless any of you have any further questions, I suggest we all get our heads down and get as much sleep as possible. We leave for the line of departure in five hours.'

The men dispersed into the darkness back to their vehicles in silence, each of them deep in thought about the enormous challenges they faced at first light. Saying goodnight to the men out on stag and to the REME section attending to a broken track on a Challenger in the centre of the hide, they took their sleeping bags from the storage bins at the rear of the tanks and joined their slumbering crews on the back decks. With thick cloud blanketing the sky, it was pitch-black in the camp and impossible to see the next vehicle along in the formation. The Battle Group HQ had been set up slightly to the south of the tanks, further away from the road, with the Black Watch platoons spread out beyond them.

All four battle groups of the Desert Rats had grown accustomed to the roar of the British AS-90 artillery guns that pushed up behind the frontline to launch their nightly attacks. At first they had caused chaos and terror in some camps as the men believed they were coming under attack from the enemy, but now they barely stirred when the barrage opened up and split the air with deafening shrieks and the thunderous crash of rounds landing on a nearby target.

So when late that night the men of 'A' Squadron heard the familiar sound of a nearby explosion, they rolled over and, in so many words, told the filthy gunners to take their infernal racket somewhere else. It was only when the second one landed with an ear-bursting crash right in the middle of the hide that pandemonium broke out. The first two rounds were followed in quick succession by half a dozen further explosions that erupted in giant balls of bright light across the camp.

Deep in sleep just seconds earlier, some of the men rolled off the back decks, bounced off the sides of their tanks and crashed on to the concrete concourse. Leaving their boots, trousers and sleeping bags on the decks, the rest scrambled for cover. Some dived into the hatches of the tanks, but most, including Major Brown, leapt under their vehicles.

The first round had landed short, the second one long and, after a pause for correction, the Iraqi gunners were now firing for effect. As masters of the art themselves, the tank crews knew straight away that they had been bracketed. The accuracy of the fire suggested there was a man or unit holed up outside the perimeter directing the fire for the gunners a few miles away back in Basra. Major Brown's gut instinct was that it wasn't artillery fire: the British gunners would have long since spotted the guns on their radar and it was unlikely the regular Iraqi Army was still sufficiently organized to mount such a co-ordinated, accurate attack. The alternative, though, was no less alarming. The quick rate of fire, the size of the explosions and the sound of the incoming rounds indicated that the firing was coming from a Russian-built BM-21, a weapon that the Coalition tank squadrons feared more than any other. Mounted with a multiple rocket launcher capable of firing up to forty rounds in twenty seconds with great accuracy from up to twenty miles away, the BM-21 can be packed up and moved around at speed.

The Challengers were powerless to respond as the shower of high-explosive frag-shells rained down. Major Brown lay under his tank alongside Sergeant Stuart Watson, his loader/operator, and looked out through wide eyes at the apocalyptic scene around them. An UBRE fuel tanker burned wildly. In the glow from its flames he could see a Bedford truck, shredded by shrapnel, listing to one side. Boxes and tins of oils and lubricants flickered and flared. He could hear men yelling and from the light of the raging fires he could make out silhouettes diving for cover. The air was thick with smoke and the stench of cordite filled his nostrils. There were other, highly pungent smells too that he didn't recognize. 'Please don't be gas!' he muttered. He needed no reminding that shells, fired from a distance, were the best way of delivering gas to the battlefield. They had to get in the tank – fast. If they were under a chemical or biological attack, the NBC filters in the Challengers gave them a better chance of survival than lying out in the open.

'Immediately after the next explosion, let's go for it.' The Squadron leader was shouting even though Sergeant Watson was lying no more than a few yards away. Never had he felt his heart hammering as it was right then, never had he imagined he could feel such lung-squeezing terror. An enormous explosion rocked the earth to the rear, sending a shower of orange sparks, shrapnel and earth in all directions.

'Go!' yelled the Major and both men, wearing nothing but their underpants, scrambled out from under the tank, one on each side, and leapt up the side of the vehicle with a speed and agility neither could ever muster in normal circumstances. They dived in through the hatches and pulled them tight, shutting out the sound of the bedlam beyond. Vince the gunner was already in his seat but there was no sign of Stu, the young driver. All three men sat panting and shaking. They were suffering a mild form of shellshock. Major Brown fumbled for his notebook. His mind was clear enough for him to know that he must put out a Charlie Charlie call to check on his men. 'Charlie Charlie' he muttered to himself a few times as he flicked open the pad and pulled out the pencil from the narrow wire binder along the top. His hand was

1. Complex terrain: an oil fire billows over Basra as a 'B' Squadron Challenger patrols through the traffic on Route Red.

2. Powerful punch: Captain Le Sueur's Challenger, call sign Two Zero, firing the main armament.

3. Lased: a T-55 is lined up in the sights.

4. Fog of war: 'C' Squadron regrouping after their devastating thrust through enemy territory to link up with 3 Commando Brigade.

5. No more propaganda: the TV and radio mast felled by 'A' Squadron during the daring raid deep into Basra.

6. Gathering storm: 'A' Squadron tanks returning from a raid.

7. A Warrior APC of No. 1 Company Irish Guards on patrol during sunset outside of Basra.

8. The Second in Command, Major Charlie Lambert (*left*), and the Commanding Officer, Lieutenant Colonel Hugh Blackman, plan the next move.

9. Recce Scimitar handing out sweets to local children.

10. Call sign 31 flies the flags after victory at Shaibah airfield outside Basra.

 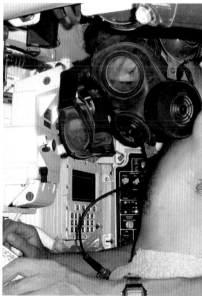

11. (*above left*) Up in smoke: the view from the loader's hatch, as an oil fire chokes the skyline.

12. (*above right*) 'Face welly': fear of a chemical or biological attack was a constant worry for all the troops in theatre. It was, after all, the very reason why they were going to war.

13. Bombing Up: a Challenger's awesome firepower is laid out on the sand ready to be stowed.

14. Major Johnny Biggart, 'C' Squadron Leader, enjoying a break from combat operations.

15. Major Chris Brannigan, 'B' Squadron Leader, stretches his legs during a lull in the fighting.

16. Major Tim Brown, 'A' Squadron Leader (*right*), with his 2ic Charlie MacDermot-Roe.

17. End of the road: The T-55s were no match for the Challengers.

trembling so much he couldn't write properly. It was a struggle to put on his helmet and pull the straps of his radio set over his head. He stopped to compose himself, sucking in as much air as possible and trying to get a regular, lower rhythm to his breathing.

Finally he was able to speak. 'You OK, Vince?

'Yes, boss. As far as I can tell.'

'You, Stuart?

'Getting there.'

As he spoke, there was a loud rap over the loader's hatch. Stuart turned the handle, pushed it open and Stu the driver leapt in, wild-eyed, and, like the others, wearing only his boxer shorts.

'Is this a bad dream or what, boss?'

'It's a bloody nightmare. Get into the driving compartment and run up the engine. We may have to move out.'

With the turret turned ninety degrees and the main gun pointing off to the side, Stu was just about able to crawl backwards through the tiny gap that opened up when the tank was in that position. Immediately he fired up the massive engine and left it ticking over in idle mode.

The silence in the virtually soundproof world of the turret made for a surreal atmosphere; it was difficult to tell if the bombardment was still going on outside. It was only the occasional thud and shudder of the earth that told them that there was still incoming. It was standard practice for the squadron to observe radio silence when in a hide so as not to give away their position. If the troops needed to communicate they did so by means of a primitive but effective telephone system called 'line', rolls of wire linked to receivers and hooked up between the Squadron HQ and the troop leaders' vehicles. But now it was vital that he communicated with every call sign in the squadron and so had no choice but to break radio silence. His hand was still quivering when he took the radio box hanging round his neck and turned the switch to 'A' to activate the squadron net. He cleared his throat, took a deep gulp of air in an effort to steady himself and then slowly and clearly said into the mouthpiece: 'Charlie Charlie One, this is Zero Alpha, report by call sign order, give status.' Usually he would have asked each vehicle to send a 'sitrep' but right then he just wanted to hear that his men were alive.

There was nothing but silence over the air. He gave it five more seconds then cut in: 'Zero Charlie, come in. Are you there?' Zero Charlie was the call sign of the 2iC, Captain MacDermot-Roe's Challenger. Silence.

He moved on to Battle Captain James Bishop.

'Zero Echo, this is Zero Alpha, give status.'

Silence.

He moved on to the four troops, starting with 1st troop leader Lieutenant Graham Craig, the least experienced of his four troop leaders.

'One Zero, this is Zero Alpha, give status.'

Silence.

The major left the space next to One Zero in the notebook blank and scribbled down One One below it. 'One One, this is Zero Alpha, send status.' Silence.

He repeated the call, but still there was nothing. The Squadron leader looked through his sights and saw flames licking the darkness in the distance. His stomach was knotted and he swallowed hard on the bile that was making its way up his throat. When he looked back down at his notes he noticed that his bare legs were covered in blood. He had cut them to shreds diving for cover on the rough, jagged concrete.

Brown tried to expel the worst fears from his mind as he

worked his way through the call sign list in numerical order, pausing for a few moments between each and then repeating the call before moving on to the next. Of the fourteen tanks, only three responded, each of them with the news that their crews were accounted for and unharmed. Of the dozen auxiliary vehicles, again only three came back over the air. It was clear to the few who could hear him that the Squadron leader was battling hard to contain his mounting desperation. He knew that the silence didn't necessarily mean that most of his squadron had been killed – for a start the driver and gunner of a crew are not on the radio net – but given the intensity of the bombardment he also knew it would have been a miracle if they came through the attack without taking casualties.

One of the few to respond was WO2 Ross Anderson, who had been lying on the seat in the back of his Spartan armoured personnel carrier when the barrage began. His soft-skinned vehicle would have been completely destroyed by a direct hit from one of the rounds, but Anderson had instinctively grabbed his helmet and body armour all the same. As usual, he had left the rear door of the vehicle open but when the second explosion burst no more than thirty yards away, he had enough situational awareness to pull the door shut to keep out the flying shrapnel. As he did so, he noticed that Craftsman Burrell of the REME, who had been standing there on sentry duty just moments earlier, was no longer there, not even lying on the ground. He had vanished. When it seemed that the barrage had finally stopped, he put his driver Kenny on the radio and, with thumping heart, stepped out of the back of vehicle to look for casualties and inspect the damage. It was the task of the Squadron Sergeant Major and the Battle Captain, James Bishop, to check the state of the squadron after an attack.

His first thoughts were for Burrell and he shone his torch in the immediate vicinity of where he had been standing, but there was no sign of him. The smoke and reek of explosive drifted across the hide. He could see the beams of two other torches criss-crossing in the darkness like lasers. The air was alive with shouts and orders and men were scrambling up the sides of their Challengers. The fuel tanker was still belching flames.

He shone his torch under the first tank he came to and saw Captain MacDermot-Roe and his startled crew staring back at him.

'You lot all right?'

'I think so.'

'Well, get in your wagon now and report into Zero Alpha and tell him you're safe. The poor man thinks you're goners.'

The Sergeant Major pulled open the rear door of the ambulance, but there was no one inside. Captain Bishop jogged out of the darkness and the two men shone their torches in each other's faces. The Battle Captain was out of breath and had to pause for air as he reported his findings.

'We've got two men down over by the Bedford! . . . Troopers Radredre and Newlands from the SQMS party . . . shrapnel wound and broken bones . . . neither life-threatening, I don't think . . . I'll get them casevac'd asap.'

'Any others?'

'Don't know yet. It's chaos out here. Can't see a thing. Men all over the place. Everyone's stunned . . .'

'Any sign of Craftsman Burrell?'

'No, I'm afraid not, but then there's dozens of others I haven't seen either,' the Battle Captain replied as he jogged away, jumped into his Sultan and got on the radio.

Seeing a shaft of light across the other side of the Squadron HQ position, Anderson strode across and pulled open the rear door and there was Craftsman Burrell, ashen-faced and wide-eyed. He was standing up with his top off while a medic attended to a bright red welt the size of a saucer on the right of his rib cage. He winced as the medic probed the wound.

'The blast blew me clean off my feet, sir! Landed ten yards away on my arse! Just as well I was wearing my body armour. Take a look!' He was talking rapidly, in staccato bursts.

Anderson bent down and picked up the heavy sleeveless jacket. It had a piece of shrapnel the side of a kitchen knife sticking out the side of it.

'Think he's going to be OK,' said the medic. 'There doesn't appear to be any significant internal bleeding. The Craftsman's a very lucky man. Thank god for body armour . . .'

Back in Zero Bravo, Major Brown sat crouched over his notepad with his elbows resting on his bleeding thighs. A stream of thoughts were tumbling and spinning through his mind. He looked down at the list of call signs and long empty spaces between the ticks. In his TI screen, he could see the heat signatures of figures moving round in the dark.

He pointed his pencil to the top of the list and started over again.

'Charlie Charlie One, this is Zero Alpha, report by call sign order, give status.'

Immediately, his left headphone, linked to the squadron net, crackled into life.

'Zero Alpha, this is Zero Charlie, crew all present and uninjured, vehicle undamaged.'

The major exhaled loudly and a smile appeared at the corner of his mouth.

'Zero Alpha, this is Zero Echo. I'm fine, my wagon is fine, dealing with three shrapnel casualties, will report details after Charlie Charlie call.'

'Zero Alpha, this is One Zero, crew all present, vehicle undamaged.'

One by one, the call signs called in and each time he heard the crackle of transmission in his left ear, the major nodded his head in relief. It took twenty minutes and repeated calls to missing crews before finally he knew that his squadron had not suffered catastrophic casualties. The relief didn't flood back, but trickled in bit by bit with each life confirmed. When he made the final tick in his notepad, Major Brown leant back in his seat and clenched his fists in triumph and relief. He lifted the hatch above his head and felt the cool night rush in. Above he could hear the approaching throb of the rotors as the casevac helicopter, sweeping low over the terrain, prepared to land in the hide to take away the injured.

He looked out into the darkness and saw a handful of fires dotted across the hide. The inferno in the fuel tanker was starting to die down but the air was still thick with smoke and the smell of burning diesel, rubber and cordite as well as the less familiar stench of various lubricants and oils from the Bedford support truck. The major shook his head. It was astonishing that no one had been killed. If the attack had come a few hours earlier when most of the squadron was still up tending to their vehicles, equipment and personal affairs, he would have been presiding over a scene of utter carnage. But he may not have survived it himself – one of the rounds had landed no more than twenty yards from where he lay. Leaving aside the human cost, the political ramifications for the war effort would have shaken Whitehall to its foundations.

He looked at his watch. It was almost three thirty in the morning, local time, and his heart skipped a beat. In the drama of the last hour, he had clean forgotten: they had a raid to carry out. Into the centre of Basra! Brown cursed and then bit on his lip as he pondered what to do. *How shaken up are the men? Are they in the right frame of mind to carry out such a dangerous operation? Should I ask the CO to stand them down?*

He felt fine himself. If anything the mild shellshock he experienced – and he could think of no better words to describe it – had, if anything, cleared and sharpened his mind. The adrenaline was still surging through his manically pumping heart. Yes, he was up for it and, he deduced, if that was the case, there was every reason the rest of 'A' Squadron would be feeling just as tigerish. The squadron had taken a massive hit and now they had the perfect opportunity to strike back in the boldest, most spectacular manner possible.

Informed by the 'dicker' co-ordinating the fire on the hide that they had struck their target, the Fedayeen were no doubt celebrating the success of their attack. What better way to crush their sense of satisfaction than to retaliate immediately by demolishing their operating base, knocking out their means of peddling propaganda to the public and annihilating a gigantic statue of their leader? What's more, the enemy would think it was a reprisal raid and, if it all went to plan, they would be stunned by the speed and fury of the reaction.

Brown adjusted the mouthpiece of his headset, switched the radio set back to the Squadron net and said: 'Charlie Charlie, this is Zero Alpha, raiding party prepare to move out at 0200 hours Zulu time.' What he couldn't hear from inside the depths of his turret was the sound of his troops cheering inside their Challengers.

It was still dark when the 'A' Squadron raiding party rolled out of the former Iraqi marine base. The tracks squealed and scraped along the tarmac but there was silence in the turrets. Major Brown had ordered radio silence to be strictly observed until he gave the order to move across the line of departure. There were eleven Challengers in total: 2nd, 3rd and 4th troops, plus the two tanks of Squadron HQ, Major Brown's Zero Bravo and Captain MacDermot-Roe's Zero Charlie. 1st troop were to be held back in reserve at 'DUNDEE', the name given to the Coalition operating base located in a derelict bus depot a few hundred yards to the south of Bridge Four. Behind the tanks were four Warriors, carrying a platoon from 'B' Company Black Watch, one CRARRV manned by the REME section and two ambulances. The Squadron leader wanted both medical vehicles close at hand when the raid began so that they could extract casualties as quickly as possible from the battlefield. Sergeant Major Anderson, tasked with co-ordinating casualty evacuation, joined the infantrymen in the back of one of the Warriors.

Three minutes before H-hour, exactly as Major Brown had planned, the raiding party crawled up behind the LD as quietly as 1,000 tons of armoured vehicles can crawl anywhere. Any earlier and they risked being spotted by the enemy; much longer and daylight would have exposed them to view and the element of surprise would be gone. The dark hulls of the tanks were barely visible as they lined up in formation on both sides of the main road into Basra, a broad stretch of scruffy tarmac without road markings, kerbing or crash barriers. The faint outline of Bridge Four and its towering, obsolete streetlights loomed a few hundred yards ahead of them. The largest and most spectacular of the five bridges spanning the massive shipping canal below, it rose on an increasingly steep gradient to form an arch-like structure that gave sweeping views of the area for miles around.

On the other side, the road became a dual carriageway with a central reservation and it ran through a mile and a half of parched, rubbish-strewn wasteland before hitting the true outskirts of the city. The first buildings on the left were located inside the sprawling campus of the city's Technical College, from where Iraqi snipers and mortar teams had been targeting the troops at DUNDEE over the previous few days. Immediately after that, there was a large office building that Intel operatives reported as being the nerve centre of Fedayeen operations. Behind the three-storey building lay the Al-Hayy-aniyah district, better known as the 'Shia Slums', a network of tumbledown shanty homes, open sewers, markets and shops. It was one of the poorest but liveliest areas of the city, where tens of thousands had fled after Saddam's crackdown on the Shia community in the nineties.

A few hundred yards further up, Route Red reached a major interchange on the edge of the city centre. On a triangular island between the roads sat two large statues: one of Saddam Hussein in Churchill pose, squat and resolute, and one of a fish, twisted into a circular shape, with its face almost touching its tail as if diving out of the water. Over to the right was the bright blue dome of what most presumed to be a mosque but was in fact a planetarium. Tanks were known to be holed up in the streets around the interchange.

On the right-hand side heading over the bridge, directly after a long stretch of squalid rubbish-strewn wasteland, there was a loose conurbation of humble dwellings mingled in amongst dusty industrial compounds and abandoned building projects. This area had been designated the 'Bravos' by the planners who had drawn up the Coalition forces' colour-coded maps. An elusive Iraqi mortar team, operating from the higher rooftops of the Bravos, had been causing mayhem in and around DUNDEE. Firing and moving, the unit was very difficult to pin down and it was becoming a serious threat.

The hope was that the raid would draw them into an engagement and reveal their position, while two soldiers, bearded and dressed in Arab headgear and clothing, split away from the raiding party, infiltrated the Bravos and took them out. Major Brown had met the soldiers tasked with the job the previous day and was struck by the fact that their combat trousers were clearly visible below their dishdash robes.

Beyond the Bravos, almost directly opposite the Fedayeen building, behind a low wall, lay the 300-foot metal television mast, painted in candy-stripe red and white. At the next junction lay the southern perimeter of the College of Literature: a huge complex of one- and two-storey buildings spread out over several hectares and dominated by the blue dome of the planetarium. Reports suggested that 500 fanatical Arab fighters used the college as their base. The total run from bridge to Saddam statue was three miles and, according to Intelligence reports, there were also hundreds of enemy dug into bunkers on either side of the road and in the buildings behind.

The eleven Challengers sat at the base of the slope leading onto the bridge with engines turning over in idle mode, barely audible. On the left-hand side of the road were the three tanks of 2nd troop, commanded by Captain Steve Walters, who had been assigned to destroy the statue. Behind them was 4th troop, led by Lieutenant Ed O'Brien, who was to attack the Fedayeen building. On the right-hand side were the three call signs of Staff Sergeant Hanson's 3rd troop with Zero Bravo and Zero Charlie directly behind them. Their task, to topple the giant TV mast, was strategically the most important of the operation.

Troop Sergeant Will Montgomery, in call sign Three One to the front of the left-hand column, was experiencing the same rush of fear and excitement that had hit him a few days earlier when he had spearheaded the search party into Az Zubayr to find Lance Corporal Baz Stephen. It was an almost physically overwhelming sensation and, remembering how nervous his teenage crew had been when they had set out on that raid, he went on the intercom to see how they were coping on this occasion. 'You all OK, boys? We'll be back in fifteen minutes!' he said with as much cheer as he could muster. As he spoke, he leant down into the turret to give the lads a re-assuring thumbs-up. He was met with a surprising sight: one of his crew was sound asleep, another was reading a lifestyle magazine.

'Oi, you two! What the fuck are you doing? We're not in bloody Noddyland, for God's sake. We're about to go into battle!' he snapped. Both lads sat bolt upright, one quickly tossing his magazine to the floor, the other shaking his head like someone had just poured a bucket of water over him. *It's just as well the young troopers don't have the faintest clue what is about to hit them*, the sergeant thought. There were sound reasons why senior officers and NCOs didn't always pass on to the men the full Intel picture and the risk levels of an upcoming operation. As the squadron's most experienced Troop Sergeant, he knew only too well what kind of reception awaited the first regular forces to attempt an advance into Iraq's second city.

Fifty yards behind him, Major Brown checked his equip-ment for a final time. Rarely in his life had he felt as pumped up and tenacious as he did at that moment. The spotlight of the Coalition effort was trained upon him and his raiding party. This was 'A' Squadron's stellar moment in Operation TELIC. A successful raid would be a propaganda coup, a failure would be a disaster – and a failure with casualties would be a catas-trophe. The moment to move had almost come. He picked up his mug and drained the last slurp of coffee from the bottom – and immediately he felt a powerful twinge in the lower half of his abdomen. 'Oh Christ alive,' he muttered. His bowels were reminding him that it was time for his daily dawn evacuation. Since arriving in Iraq, the major had discovered that his digestive system gave him about one minute to react to the first warning spasm. He looked at his watch. He had two minutes before H-hour. Grabbing some tissues from the compartment next to his seat, the Squadron leader, the man assigned to lead one of the most important, perilous raids of the ground offensive to date, wriggled through the hatch, leapt off the side and ran round to the front of the tank. Crouching as low below the frontal armour as he was able, the 6 foot 2 inch Yorkshireman answered the call of nature in an instant and, pulling up his combats as he went, leapt back into the turret. He was back in under a minute.

'So is that why they call the Al Faw a shithole, boss?' came a voice over the intercom as he fixed his headset back on.

The eastern horizon over to their left was turning a lighter shade of grey and Major Brown was holding his watch and counting the seconds down: 'Fifty-two, fifty-one . . .'

A well-spoken voice erupted in his right earphone. It was Battle Group HQ in the DUNDEE bus depot a few hundred yards behind them. 'Hotel One Zero Alpha, this is Zero, send sitrep.' They had added the prefix Hotel One to distinguish them from the RTR tank squadron in the battle group. The Major ignored them, muttering dark oaths under his breath that they hadn't used the correct procedure to break radio silence.

'Twenty-nine, twenty-eight, twenty-seven . . .'

The second hand seemed to take an eternity as it moved round the dial of his watch towards the 12. He took a series of deep breaths, flicked the switch to the squadron net and . . .

'Charlie Charlie One, this is Zero Alpha. Three, two, one . . . move now!'

H-hour had struck. As one, the drivers stepped on the pedals, the engines of the eleven Challengers and other vehicles let out a collective roar. The two columns of armour began to climb the shallow southern slope of the bridge. Features of the landscape were now just visible in the early morning gloom: a chain of giant electricity pylons stretched away into the distance and the silvery surface of the Shatt Al Arab glinted below them. On the horizon, billowing clouds of black smoke from the oilpipe fires and the dull glow of flames stood out against the gunmetal sky. Straight ahead of them, the crews could see nothing but the rising hump of the bridge. Beyond it, there lay a city of 2 million souls – Basra, where no foreign troops had set foot since the British pulled out after the Second World War.

They were moving at about 15mph when the front tanks hit the crest of the bridge. Basra sat huge and sprawling along the horizon, a jagged outline of distant buildings and towers of belching black smoke.

'Charlie Charlie One, this is Zero Alpha, step on it.' The Challengers responded immediately to the promptings of their drivers, thundering down the northern slope of the bridge. The convoy accelerated towards the 40mph mark, the gunners and commanders scanned the terrain on either side of the road, the scrubland and distant buildings rushed through their sights. In half an hour, the route would be teeming with pick-up trucks, taxis, donkey carts and mopeds, but right at that moment, just before daybreak, the carriageway was clear from one end to the other. The only people on the road were the troops of a British tank squadron swooping down on their targets in much the same way that their predecessors in a bygone era hurtled down a hillside, hooves thundering beneath them, to fall upon the enemy positions with a devastating, deafening crash. The weapons may have changed, the means of transport may have changed, the nature of enemy positions may have changed, but the principles of cavalry warfare remained the same. Centuries on, it was still all about speed, shock and power.

The wasteland was barely behind them when the first wave of enemy fire erupted from both flanks. From a few hundred yards behind, Major Brown watched it crash over the Challengers of 2nd and 3rd troops. Streaks of orange tracer from RPG projectiles and the green trails of automatic fire burst out of buildings and bunkers from both directions, lighting up the grey morning skyline to spectacular, lethal effect. The Squadron leader knew it was going to come at some point, but he was shocked by the weight of the fire, as well as the timing and co-ordination of it. It was as if the enemy knew they were coming, waited until they were in the killing zone and then, when the word was given, opened up with everything they had. Rounds sprayed off the turrets and hulls of the tanks and mortar rounds burst the earth; most of the RPGs flew wide or high of their speeding targets but the odd one that did find its prey caused those following behind to suck in their breath at the sight.

Corporal Dean Gibbs, leading the right-hand column, came over the squadron net. His voice sounded curiously composed considering the maelstrom of fire raining down on his vehicle. 'Zero Alpha, this is Three Two, RPGs left and right . . .' He was simply following the procedure drummed in through years of training, but the information he was passing on had already been registered by the call signs following up. The orange tracer of an RPG was slower moving than that of the small arms and easy to pick out in the gloom. As planned, the infantry and other support vehicles stopped short of the killing zone.

Hammering towards their targets as fast as their 75 tons would allow them, the Challengers immediately responded to the hail of fire with bursts of coax, adding to the laser display with streaks of red tracer. Corporal Gibbs spotted a two-man RPG team sprint across the scrubland ahead of them, kneel down and take aim at the advancing column. He traversed the turret, lased the target and released control over the guns to let his gunner engage it. But, stunned by his first experience of combat, the youngster froze at the controls. 'Engage RPG team left! . . . Come on take 'em out! What are you waiting for?' the commander bellowed. But still there was no response. The lad just sat motionless in front of him, gripping the handles of the fire control system, his face glued to the sights. Gibbs reclaimed control of the guns and began squirting bursts of rounds towards the target. As the shots kicked up around them, the RPG team dived for cover behind an earth embankment and the tank roared by.

Inside the turrets of the Challengers, the crews could not hear the crash and crackle of the incoming fire. Staring down their sights, it was as if they were racing through the set of a silent version of *Star Wars*.

Zero Bravo's crew could see the stream of bullets and rockets ripping back and forth with ever greater clarity as they careered towards the first lines of tracer that marked the beginning of the killing zone. A laconic voice came over the intercom: 'Very wise to have had that dump when you did, sir.' As he spoke, dozens of small-arms rounds hit the Challenger like a bag of gravel and ricocheted into the air; an RPG fizzed over the front of the turret narrowly missing the main gun.

The Squadron leader had been controlling the pace of the advance thus far but as soon as the firing erupted, it was each troop to their own as they sped towards their targets. As the rest of the raiding party approached their objectives and began to slow down, Captain Steve Walters' 2nd troop disappeared out of view, a further mile into the city. Having passed through the heart of the killing zone, the incoming was no longer a virtually solid wall of fire, but rounds were still streaking back and forth as the crews set about their tasks.

'Two Zero, this is Zero Alpha, remember there are enemy tanks up there. Keep an eye out and if you need support, we'll be there to cover you.'

Strictly it was not their job to get involved in the combat element of the operation, but as the fighting erupted, the REME crew in the CRARRV at the rear of the raiding party leapt into action. The rest of the battle group had long suspected that the men of their REME section were a few rounds short of the full bandolier, so to speak, and now they had their proof. Unknown to anyone else in the party, the maintenance men had smuggled into the recovery vehicle two extra men, a pump-action shotgun recovered from a munitions dump and an additional GPMG that they had stripped from another vehicle. No doubt the enemy were surprised to see three of the crew emerge from their hatches into a meteor storm of incoming fire and begin blazing away at their positions. One of them, exposed to the waist, was swinging from side to side on the GPMG mounted on the turret, another, leaning out of the neighbouring hatch, worked the unfixed version of the weapon and the third, on the pump-action shotgun, was cocking and firing as fast as his arms would allow him. The rounds whizzed over and around them, but they didn't seem to notice, or care.

At 300 feet high, the television and radio mast was visible from miles around and the crews of the five Challengers of SHQ and Sergeant Hanson's 3rd troop could barely make out the top of it as they approached through the early morning murk. Forming up along the right-hand carriageway in a roughly straight line, the drivers braked sharply, yanked the right stick of the steering lever and swung the vehicles into position. In order not to present a static target to the enemy, the drivers were under strict orders from their commanders to keep the vehicles moving back and forth while the men in the fighting compartment behind them set about the mast.

As they lined up, Will Montgomery's Three One was engaged from a nearby watchtower, a forty-foot structure with a roofed platform at the top from where soldiers were firing. Traversing the turret around and laying onto the target, commander and gunner shattered the watchtower with a single HESH round. A body arced through the air, the debris burst in all directions and the tower collapsed to the ground in a cloud of dust.

Spread out on the other side of the central reservation, the three tanks of Ed O'Brien's 4th troop had wheeled round to attack the Fedayeen HQ. In doing so, they were also protecting the vulnerable rears of Zero Bravo's group as they laid siege to the TV mast.

The mast, set in a block of concrete the size of a large detached house, was 400 yards away in the middle of a compound of one-storey buildings surrounded by a low breeze-block wall. Hundreds of yards of wires were threaded amongst the latticed metalwork and four giant cables running off each corner like guy ropes secured the towering structure even tighter to the ground. Immediately, all five Challengers began pummelling the base with HESH rounds, aiming for the area around the four stanchions. As a hit-and-run raid deep behind enemy lines, speed was of the essence, and the loaders rammed the rounds into the breech as fast as the gunners could fire them. As their flaming muzzles spat out the rounds, the Challengers, roughly fifty yards apart, jockeyed around their positions, backwards and forwards, left and right. One after another the HESH shells crashed into the rock-solid foundations, kicking up clouds of smoke and dust. But, after two minutes of sustained firing, the tower appeared to be entirely unmoved by the hammering it had taken.

Tracer continued to fly around the turrets from the buildings behind but the rate of fire slowly began to drop as 4th troop pounded the Fedayeen base with HESH and coax. Each main armament punched a hole in the edifice of the three-storey building wide enough to drive a tank through. 4th troop weren't so much suppressing the enemy fire as annihilating it. As the piles of rubble grew and the clouds of smoke climbed higher into the sky, the firing from within gradually fell way as the enemy were either neutralized or fled to new positions.

Captain Steve Walters and the men of 2nd troop may have had the easiest target to strike but, deep in the heart of the city, it was the most difficult and dangerous to reach. Blasting their way through the hail of incoming fire, they wasted no time in attacking it on arrival. The twenty-foot black cast-iron statue, depicting the Iraqi leader in a greatcoat with his arm raised, dominated a scruffy park area surrounded by major routes into the south of the city. For over two decades, Saddam had gazed down on the people from his lofty plinth, but it took just one HESH round from Corporal David Ross in call sign Two Two to bring him, face first, crashing down to earth in a dozen pieces. The round struck the metal figure in a huge bright flash, sending a shower of sparks in all directions, and when the smoke cleared there was nothing left but the stone plinth and Saddam's boots sticking out of it.

As 2nd troop prepared to extract, Major Brown's group continued to pound the base of the TV mast but, to the Squadron leader's mounting frustration, the massive amount of firepower they were bringing to bear on the structure was causing little more than cosmetic damage. They might as well have been firing corks at it. The tank jerked back and forth as Brown yelled a stream of orders at his driver, gunner and loader: 'Left stick, Stu! Left stick! Forward a bit! STOP! . . . load HESH! . . . Vince, aim for the right-hand side this time . . .' At the same time, he was trying to command the squadron – talking to the other troop leaders, receiving and sending sitreps to update the BGHQ back in DUNDEE. The assault on his senses was every bit as punishing as the barrage of rounds his men was unleashing alongside him – and it was starting to take its toll on the Commanding Officer's patience.

Sergeant Watson had been calmly and methodically feeding the main gun with round after round in the area below him, aware of the growing pressure on his commander. In a pause during the Major's tirade of orders, the Sergeant, reaching forward to slide another round into the breech, looked up and, in the mellowest of voices, said: 'All right, boss, just calm down now.'

His long-serving Sergeant was right. He knew he had to clear his mind for a moment, block out the chaos and make a calm, considered judgement. He sat back for a moment to take stock. *Do I admit defeat and call in an air strike?* It was a hard call. The longer they stayed, the greater the risks to his men; but to leave with the mast still standing, with the world's media watching, would have been a propaganda disaster for the Coalition, not to mention a massive morale boost to the enemy and an embarrassment to his squadron and regiment. The image of five British main battle tanks blasting away but unable to bring down a glorified electricity pylon was too humiliating to consider. No matter how unfair, that's how it would have been perceived.

He was staring down through his knees at the body armour on Vince's back when the realization struck him. The solution to the conundrum was sitting two feet away from him. There were probably no more than half a dozen gunners in the British Army with the skill, experience and cool-headedness to bring down the mast with a high-velocity anti-tank FIN round – but Corporal Vince McLeod was one of them. It was a gamble but it was their only chance. The Major and Vince had both joined the Army at the end of the eighties when the Cold War still cast its long shadow across the world; mutual respect and affection had grown up over fifteen years of working together. They had cemented their friendship when Vince was assigned to look after the major's horses during a stint in the Regimental Stables. A cool, unflappable old hand, Vince was just the man any tank commander would want to have in a tight spot.

'Stuart, load FIN! Vince, we're going to take out the metalwork – or rather *you're* going to take out the metalwork.'

As a general rule, HESH is an area weapon for destroying softer targets such as bunkers and buildings, and FIN is used to penetrate armour. But in this instance a FIN round might just do the trick if – and it was a very big *if* – Vince could hit one of the very narrow iron corner stanchions with an even narrower tungsten dart. FIN is far more accurate than HESH, but it would still have to be one hell of a shot – the tank equivalent of a sniper taking out a six-inch target from a distant rooftop. To bring down the mast, Vince would have to hit at least two, probably three, of the stanchions, and he would have to hit them all bang on the money to get some purchase. A glancing blow would be no good. And he needed to work fast. The raiding party had to extract before the enemy, swelled by reinforcements, regrouped and started closing in on the Challengers.

'Vince, I'm leaving this to you,' said the Squadron leader.

'No problem, boss.'

Like a craftsman getting down to work at his bench, Vince leant towards the bank of controls in front of him. He flicked the weapon selector switch to main armament, laid the sights onto the left-hand stanchion of the mast and zoomed in. He was looking at the target in high magnification but it still appeared as a thin metal strip even then. It was no more than a grey pencil line on a grey piece of paper. They say you can put a FIN round through a letterbox; here Corporal McLeod was attempting to put one through a keyhole. 'Las-ING,' he said quietly into his mouthpiece as he dabbed the metal strip in his screen with the red dot and gently pressed the lase button. Instantly the laser bounced back from the target, and the computer digested the information. Vince made a minute alteration with the fire adjustment toggle and the barrel of the main gun automatically elevated the slightest fraction of an inch. Sergeant Watson closed the safety shield on the breech and shouted: 'LOADED!' Vince slid his left index finger up the back of the firing control system and pushed away the safety latch. Beads of sweat ran down his forehead from the effort of concentration. Major Brown stopped scanning for a moment to watch. Vince squeezed the trigger. 'Fir-ING!' he said. The breech burst open unleashing a blast of hot air and cordite around the turret as the dart flew out of the muzzle and smashed into the target at exactly the same time – or so it seemed to those watching. The '-ING!' was still on the gunner's lips as the stanchion buckled.

'Target!' exclaimed Major Brown. Vince said nothing. He was in a world of his own, traversing the turret over to the right-hand stanchion and laying onto his new target with the same precise, methodical movements. The other four call signs continued to hammer the base with HESH rounds as Vince, fast but unflustered, went about his work.

'LOADED!' shouted Stuart, breaking the silence as he reached around to remove a third FIN round from the ammunition rack behind him.

Major Brown heard the battle group net crackle into life in his left ear. 'Hotel One Zero Alpha, this is Zero, send sitrep.' The Squadron leader, his face in the sights, his eyes glued to the right-hand stanchion, said nothing.

'Fir-ING!' said Vince. Bang on again! The stanchion crumpled but the mast didn't collapse. Major Brown wanted to slap the Corporal on the back and yell his admiration but he bit his lip and shook his head in disbelief. Only those who have fired a Challenger 2 could understand the skill of what Vince was doing here. Hours and hours of laborious practice on the simulators back in Germany and in training exercises out on the plains were now paying their dividends.

Vince brought the gun to bear on a third stanchion, the closest of the two in the middle. Something wasn't quite right. Vince pulled away from the sights.

BGHQ repeated their request for a situation report. Barely registering them as he focused on Vince at work, Brown replied: 'Zero, this is Hotel One Zero Alpha, wait out, engaging target.' Steve Walters appeared in his other ear on the squadron net: 'Zero Alpha, this is Two Zero, mission accomplished, extracting under fire. With you very shortly!'

Every two or three shots, the gunner has to make sure that the firing system is aligned accurately. Strictly, a gunner should do it after every shot but in the heat of an intense engagement that was unrealistic. The gunner and commander look at a target from a slightly different angle to the gun and if the alignment between sights and muzzle – known as the Muzzle Referencing System (MRS) – has been shunted even a fraction of an inch out of kilter during firing, it could make all the difference between hitting and missing a target, especially one as small and difficult as this one. He might be the best tank gunner in the world, but Vince could fire all day at a target and keep missing if the system was out. But time was running out. 4th troop had also completed its task: the enemy positions inside Fedayeen base had been eliminated. As the enemy regrouped to block the tanks' exit, reinforcements, alerted by the deafening roar of the fighting, were pouring in to try and disable one of the British tanks.

'LOADED!' shouted the loader once again.

Vince was aware of the pressure on him, but he also knew that he had to make the shot count. Reaching for the MRS lever, he coolly shone the light into the mirror on the end of the barrel and fiddled with the control button. He was right. The gun was out of synch. He twisted the button until he was satisfied that what he was looking at was in line with the light reflecting from the mirror. All the time that he was working the gun controls, the driver was moving the Challenger back and forth in a series of jerking manoeuvres, the tracer whipped around the turret and the other four Challengers continued to pump HESH into the target.

If Vince was nervous, he was showing no sign of it. He lased the stanchion, tweaked the red dot the smallest fraction, paused to make absolutely sure and then squeezed the trigger. The breech burst open again and the dart crashed into the middle of the target, blasting the leading bar of the upright into the distance. Instantly the entire structure buckled forwards as if it was being yanked from the top by an invisible rope.

The immediate reaction inside all five turrets was the same as the massive iron structure began first to list at an angle and then fall rapidly. 'Quick, pull back! It's falling on top of us!' All five drivers rammed their wagons into reverse gear and shot off the carriageway over the central reservation. Vince was the only one to realize that they were witnessing an optical illusion.

'Actually, sir, I think it's falling the other way . . .' he said, matter-of-factly. As he trailed off, the massive red and white metal structure, half the size of the Post Office tower, crashed to the ground, bounced slightly and came to rest in a cloud of dust. White noise and fuzzy screens filled the radios and television screens of homes across the south of Iraq. There were to be no more broadcasts of epic Iraqi victories over the combined might of American and British forces. Saddam's only remaining means of peddling lies and propaganda to his subjects had just been felled. A cheer went up in every turret.

'Charlie Charlie, this is Zero Bravo, extract now. Reverse out! Beware of an enemy counter-attack . . .'

He switched to the battle group net: 'Zero, this is Hotel One Zero Alpha, all targets destroyed, withdrawing in contact.' Spread out over a mile on both sides of dual carriageway, the eleven Challengers began to reverse as fast as they could. With only a limited view of the area in front of them, the drivers were wholly dependent on the eyes of the commanders to guide them backwards. Looking through the built-in periscope arranged around the cupola, the commanders yelled orders over the intercom: 'Left stick, right stick, now keep her straight . . .' As they began to withdraw, only they could see the tracer tearing out of the buildings on either side. The enemy had been waiting for them. The killing zone was reopening for business.

'Zero Bravo, this is Zero Charlie!' Captain MacDermot-Roe was yelling over the squadron net. 'Enemy RPG teams on roof of building to your right!'

Major Brown scanned round and immediately saw a man in a dishdash robe and shemagh headscarf haring along the rooftop of the Bravos in the same direction as the tanks. For a tank commander the fear of being attacked from above is every bit as great as being hit from behind. An RPG through the unarmoured back decks into the engines would stop the tank in its tracks and force the crew out of the turret before it blew. In a killing zone, that effectively meant escaping from a catastrophic explosion to die instead in a hail of bullets.

'HESH! Building! On!' Brown shouted as the gun slaved around. After lasing the target, the computer made its rapid calculations and Brown quickly made the necessary adjustments. He was ready to fire. Vince pushed back the safety latch behind the firing system, put his finger on the trigger and waited for the commander to hand over control.

He was just about to release his grip switch and give control of the gun to Vince, while he prepared to scan for more targets, when something made Brown pause. He held on to the fire control button and in that split second his mind flashed back to the talk he had given in Poland only a few months earlier. It was about how to avoid fratricide on the battlefield, a subject he felt strongly about after all the senseless deaths he had witnessed in the first Gulf War. A keen field sportsman and game shot, Major Brown had drawn an analogy from his favourite pastime. In game shooting, he explained to his mildly surprised audience, a bird erupts from the undergrowth and the instinctive reaction is to raise the gun and fire. But that was wrong, he explained. A man should never pull the trigger until he has identified the bird for what it was. It had to be a positive ID. Now, as the sweat ran round his eyes, he squeezed the controls a little bit tighter as he strained to identify his target.

He could hear Vince in his headphones: 'Come on, boss, are you giving me the gun or what?'

Behind him, the Black Watch Warriors, with their 30mm RARDEN cannons, and Zero Charlie with the 7.62mm GPMG, were hosing the building with coax. Dust and debris burst into the air and masonry fell to the ground as the top of the structure shattered around the man as he sprinted for his life across the flat rooftop. One of the machine guns was strafing the area just in front of the man, punching holes all along the wall. For a split second, he appeared, hurling himself across an opening – and it was right at that moment, to his horror, that Major Brown realized what was happening.

He yelled over the squadron net: 'STOP! STOP! STOP! He's one of us! . . . Man on roof is friendly call sign! Repeat: man on roof is friendly call sign! STOP! STOP! STOP!'

In that fraction of a moment as the man lunged through the gap in the wall, Brown had noticed the camo trousers under his robe and realized it was one of the British soldiers he had met in DUNDEE the day before. He was part of the unit tasked to take out the troublesome mobile mortar team in the Bravos and it was only Brown registering the incongruous sight of his trousers the day before that had saved his life. Half a second later and the HESH round would have razed the building below his feet and he would have plummeted to certain death. Little did he know it, but Major Brown had just saved the life of one of Britain's most decorated and valuable soldiers.

Zero Bravo and Zero Charlie were the last call signs through the killing zone and it was only when they were a few hundred yards short of the bridge that they gave the order to their drivers to swing round and put the tanks into forward gear. As they climbed the bridge, the last of the tracer fire was dying away behind them and first shafts of watery sun were appearing on the horizon to their left.

Major Brown blew out his cheeks, leant down and slapped his old friend on the shoulder, adding through the intercom: 'You're a bloody genius, Vince.'

'You didn't do so badly yourself, boss.'

7. Shaken and Stirred

By the time that 'C' Squadron swept into the Royal Marine positions after Operation Panzer, the logistically hungry Challengers had become dangerously low on fuel and their supply lines were stretched to the very limit of their elasticity. Even when operating in more forgiving conditions, tanks are always hungry for spare parts, oils and lubricants, but after the punishing advance across the peninsula they were positively ravenous. The rubber pads protecting the bolts on the tracks had been shredded and the bolts had worn down, leaving the tracks dangerously close to splitting. But the replacement tracks, road wheels and other heavy spare parts were a fifty-mile journey away, much of it through the same difficult terrain and enemy territory they had just passed through. With the awkward estuary crossing en route as well, it was unrealistic to expect the SQMS to haul that amount of kit from one end of the British area of operation to the other – not least as they had only a couple of GPMGs and some assault rifles to defend themselves. What's more, loaded up with so many tons of equipment, the vehicles were in danger of bogging in the soft terrain of the narrow causeways and they had no CRARRV to support them. Replacing tracks would just have to wait until they were back at Brigade HQ in Shaibah airfield.

When the idea of Operation Panzer had first been mooted, it was imagined that 'C' Squadron, after a day or so to rest and regroup, would return to Shaibah, but now there was talk of them staying and launching a joint operation in and around the fishing town of Abu Al Khasib and the suburbs running west towards Basra. The various components of 3 Commando Brigade, worn out after a week of constant fighting and yomping up and down the peninsula, only had to lay eyes on their newly acquired armoured assets to work out that they would come in extremely handy for rolling up the Iraqi strongholds. Such an operation was all very well in theory, and 'C' Squadron would jump at the opportunity of fighting alongside the Commandos, but the prospect of it was nothing more than a fantasy unless the Challengers could be refuelled, replenished and at least partly refitted and patched up.

Fuel, spare parts, ammo, rations – in that order – these are the priorities of the tank commander. When the Troop Sergeants made their rounds after Operation Panzer to draw up an inventory for a replen, they were not surprised to find that the fuel situation was critical and the need for essential spare parts urgent. More ammunition would be welcome, as would food and water, but they had enough to divvy up between them to be getting along with and, if needs must, they could always procure more through 3 Commando Brigade's logistics chain.

While the rest of the squadron set up a hide in a disused cement plant behind the Commando positions, Battle Captain Colin Dobeson and Squadron Sergeant Major McIntyre went to seek out the Royal Marine Quartermaster about fuel. Unless they could get hold of some soon, then eighty men and assets worth £80 million were going to be left stranded in a very remote, inhospitable corner of the Gulf.

'Yeah, sure, how much do you need?' the Marine Sergeant replied cheerfully. 'We've got masses of the stuff.' He held up a hose connected to a small beige tanker a few yards away as if to confirm his claim.

'Er, I think we'll be needing a dash more than that?'

'OK, how much?'

'Well, we've got fourteen tanks and two CRARRVs, each of them takes about 1,600 litres, plus five support vehicles . . . so let's see, quick calculation, how about 25,000 litres?'

The sergeant dropped his hose.

'I think I'd better go and talk to the boss.' As he walked away, he shouted over his shoulder: 'Don't worry, I'm sure we can work something out.'

Dobeson and McIntyre were not so confident. Where the hell, they wondered, were they going to find 25,000 litres of JP-8 diesel lying around on the uninhabited marshland of the Al Faw peninsula? The Marines needed only modest amounts of fuel for their fleet of light vehicles and keeping them supplied was not a major logistical issue. But 25,000 litres – enough to fill up 500 ordinary cars – that was a different matter altogether.

Two hours later, the Battle Captain and Squadron Sergeant Major returned. A giant fuel tanker was parked up. 'There you go,' the Quartermaster smiled. 'No bother.'

'Where the bloody hell on earth did you get that from?'

'Don't ask,' he replied, winking. 'Anything else you want?'

'Yeah, what about a hundred cases of beer and wine, Sunday lunch for eighty and a troupe of belly dancers?'

'I'll see what I can do.'

The following day, the squadron set out from the Commando positions for a replen from their own SQMS, snaking across the flat, misty marshland into the heart of the emptiness where they were safe from enemy ambush. The replen is a vulnerable moment for a tank squadron, with all of the men and machines congregated in one area. It also took the better part of an hour to carry one out, so it was standard practice to find a rendezvous location as far from potential harm's way as possible. With views for miles around on a clear day, the middle of the Al Faw peninsula, even in the thick of a war, was as good a place as any on the planet.

The task of arranging the replen fell to SQMS (Tech) Mick Lillie, who was in charge of the vehicles' equipment and spare parts, and SQMS Tam McVey, who was responsible for supplying the consumables such as fuel, ammo, water and rations. Known respectively as 'Spanners' and 'Boots', in accordance with the nature of their work, the two men had returned to the estuary crossing point to pick up provisions that were ferried across by their colleagues on the same M3 rigs that had carried the tanks over two nights' earlier. The operation had to take place under the cover of darkness to exploit the enemy's limited night-time capability and this made the task that much more arduous.

With their headlights turned off so as not to draw attention to themselves, the SQMS packet was able to travel at no more than about 10–15mph along the single-lane earth berms. The convoy was made up of two Land Rovers, two eight-ton Bedford trucks carrying ammo and pulling water trailers, a third carrying rations, mail, water and other supplies for the crews, a fourth carrying oils, lubricants and solid fuels, and two UBRE fuel trucks. Lined up in column, with fifty yards between each call sign, the vehicles crawled their way through the labyrinth of tracks. Without maps to guide them, they felt their way through the dark using a combination of inspired guesswork, the position of the moon, a compass and some plain good fortune. It took six hours for the column to make a journey that they could have jogged in half the time in daylight had they known the route.

For the final stretch of the journey, Major Biggart, who had the map, guided them into the location over the radio. The tanks were lined up in immaculate order, troop by troop, along the side of the road with all fourteen guns pointing north towards the enemy positions across the grey expanse like the 32-pounders of one of Nelson's ships-of-the-line. As the replen convoy emerged through the thick early-morning mist, the tank crews sent up a loud cheer and the SQMS men were no less relieved to lay eyes on their comrades. It was difficult to say which group of men looked the more drawn, exhausted and haggard as the faces began to appear from hatches and doors. Even after just three weeks in theatre and one in Iraq, the men had each lost roughly half a stone in weight. Their rations were heavily calorific, deliberately so, but they had been burning up such vast quantities of energy and sleeping so little, that they went about their business in a constant state of hunger. When cases of Coke and boxes of Mars bars were thrown up to the vehicles, they were received with further cries of glee and gratitude.

One by one, the troops pulled alongside the SQMS convoy to be handed up their portions of ammo, water, rations, cigarettes and spare parts, oils and 'lubes'. The driver and commander remained in their seats during a replen in case they had to move off at short notice, and it was left to the gunner to pass down the supplies to the loader through the hatch. The gunner handed back the empty jerry cans and bags of rubbish and once everything had been stowed the tank moved forward to have its fuel and water tanks topped up. The Challenger has four separate fuel tanks, each with a giant sponge inside to stop the diesel sloshing around – a design which reduces the risk of the tank blowing up if it is hit by an enemy round. If levels were low it could take up to ten minutes to fill up all four fuel tanks, but as the Marines had magicked a tanker out of thin air, the vehicles needed only a small top-up and the call signs passed quickly along the line.

Once each troop had completed the replen, it rejoined the others back in the line, and the loaders set about handing out the goodies to their crews. After weeks of eating nothing but bacon and bean rations, the men were delighted to discover that lamb stew and treacle sponge had found their way up the logistical food chain. Like all compo rations, they came desiccated and needed a draught of hot water from the loader's BV to bring them to life. Inside each of the turrets, the men dug into their silver bags as quickly as the steaming contents would allow them. The cans of Coke were gulped down as if they had fallen from heaven itself. Cigarettes were lit like Havana cigars after an emperor's banquet.

But the most welcome delivery of all was the mail bag, carrying the 'blueys' from loved ones back home. Parcels of food awaited them back in Shaibah, but it was the letters from wives and girlfriends, children and mothers, that got the hearts of the men truly racing with excitement. Not every crew member received one – the mail was proving to be frustratingly erratic – but those that did tore them open like a child at Christmas and read them over and over again until the replen was complete and the order was given to move out.

On their return to the squadron hide, Major Biggart was immediately called away for a meeting with Lieutenant Colonel Gordon Messenger, CO of 40 Commando. Operation 'James' had been given political clearance. 3 Commando Brigade, supported by 'C' Squadron Royal Scots Dragoon Guards and a squadron of Scimitars from the Queen's Dragoon Guards, was to launch an attack on Abu Al Khasib and the suburbs of Basra.

Biggart's troops were to be in position at the line of departure in twelve hours' time.

Captain McLeman looked through the large open doorway of the room. Fifty yards beyond his immobilized tank, he could see two Marines sitting facing each other on a plank suspended over a pit. After a few moments he realized they were playing chess while shitting through holes in the wood. He shook his head, unsure whether he was meant to be surprised by the sight.

McLeman was one of roughly a hundred British soldiers and Marines waiting in the abandoned school building and they all stood to when the tall, wiry figure of Brigadier Jim Dutton, commander of 3 Commando Brigade, strode to the centre of the group. With an authority and clarity that held his congregation in captive silence, he laid out the details of the attack they were about to launch. In a long, detailed speech, he paused only once – when the strains of a strong Scouse accent outside interrupted his flow: 'Well, you'll just have to dig a bit fucking deeper then, you useless fucking dickhead.' Captain McLeman bowed his head and covered his eyes with his hand. On arriving for the 'O' group, his Challenger had managed to get bogged down in the Marines' makeshift car park outside. In the efforts to free itself call sign Three Zero succeeded in turning the area into a squally sea of mud before finally giving up and sinking slowly into the treacly earth. As the meeting got underway, the REME fitter section had turned up in their CRARRV to extricate it and it was the voice of their commander that forced the Brigadier to break off from his inspirational speech momentarily.

'. . . Please excuse me, but in expressing our gratitude to the Royal Scots Dragoon Guards earlier for their valiant efforts in coming to support us here on the Al Faw, I had completely forgotten to thank them also for the terrific efforts they have gone to in helping to improve the living conditions of our humble home . . .'

It didn't take long for the graver expressions of the assembly to return as the Brigadier spelt out the mission ahead of them. The largest planned battle of the Iraq campaign so far was, he said, 'an historic moment' in the experience of the British military as Marines fought alongside heavy armour for the first time since the Second World War.

After a feint to the west of the enemy positions by the Marines' Brigade Recce Force, the attack was to be launched on four main axes running from south to north up along metalled roads in the 'complex terrain' of the suburbs: date palms and small urban areas criss-crossed by a network of canals and ditches. Two of the lines of attack were to be supported by a troop of Challengers. Along the most westerly of the axes Captain Le Sueur's 2nd troop were to act as intimate support for the Marines' Manoeuvre Support Group (MSG), a small, highly mobile, heavily armed unit that moved around in Pinzgauer trucks and stripped-down Land Rovers. Their two objectives had been given the names 'Pussy' and 'Galore', key crossroads controlling main routes into Basra from the south. (The operation was named after James Bond and all objectives involved had been termed accordingly.)

Captain McLeman's 3rd troop were to support Alpha Company 40 Commando in their assault to secure Objective 'Moore', a police barracks by a main junction on the outskirts of Abu Al Khasib four miles to the west of Pussy. Each troop was to be assigned a CRARRV, manned by the REME, for the recovery of vehicles and bulldozing obstacles and mines out of the way with the blade attachment at the front. The line of departure for both troops and the Marine units they were supporting was a few hundred yards to the south of the main highway between Taku and Coriano that 'C' Squadron had left strewn with scorched enemy armour two days earlier. Lieutenant Marjoribanks's 1st troop, under the command of 2iC Captain Cattermole, were to establish a block at Taku to prevent enemy reinforcements coming out of Basra. Captain Jameson's 4th troop were to be held in reserve, ready to provide intimate support as and when it was needed across the battlefield.

The Intel picture suggested the enemy would operate in platoon-group sizes, mounting ambushes against the Marine dismounts and the armour. Their plan was to lure the tanks into close terrain, then cut them off by blocking routes and blowing bridges. It was thought that there was roughly one squadron's worth of enemy armour operating in the area, one company of mechanized infantry and several hundred irregular forces. The small relatively affluent communities of Al Jahudi and Hamdan, close to where 2nd troop were to be operating, were known to be Ba'ath Party strongholds. The objective was to defeat the enemy within its boundaries, squeezing them up against the Shatt Al Arab as they advanced north.

For 'C' Squadron, Operation James was an even more perilous undertaking than Panzer. The hardest part of that operation had been the march; the fighting – a speedy gallop through open terrain, firing on the hoof – was exactly what they trained for. Fighting in close terrain, in amongst buildings along narrow streets, was a tank crew's nightmare. And for one of the 'C' Squadron crews, that nightmare was a few hours away from becoming a horrifying reality.

*

Corporal Dougal crouched next to the mangled, smoking stump of his GPMG machine gun. Pinching the sweaty dust from his eyes, he steadied himself to make the six-foot jump from the side of his Challenger. The tank commander swore under his breath as his heavy black boots hit the grit track with a thud. To his left, dozens of fully laden Marines were laid up in ditches and scrapes in the baked scrubland, every last man of them caked in filth from head to foot. Sodden with sweat after humping their own body weight in kit all day in the glare of an increasingly hot sun, they were busy making final checks to their weapons and pulling hard on plastic bottles of water. A few hundred yards to the north, the ammunition dump destroyed by the Challengers earlier in the day continued to smoulder.

'So what's the damage to your wagon, Corporal?' shouted Captain Rick Le Sueur as he adjusted his body armour and strode as quickly as his stiff legs would allow up the dirt track. They had been closed down now for the better part of eighteen hours since moving up to the forward assembly area and his body had gone to sleep from the waist down. He tried to sound upbeat, but the young Captain's patience was wearing thin. 2nd troop's advance north through the Al Jahudi area of the suburbs in support of the MSG had been beset by problems from the moment the Forward Observation Officer had called in the artillery to lay down a pre-attack barrage at first light. Simply nothing had gone right for them in the nine hours since the first shells crashed around the enemy positions in the thick line of date palms, making the ground heave and burst under the maelstrom of hellish ordnance. H-hour had to be delayed by an hour while four Marines two miles to the east were casevac'd for emergency treatment after their unit had advanced too far forward and was caught in the barrage.

When 2nd troop and the MSG finally crossed the line of departure, the element of surprise had been well and truly lost and they quickly found themselves up against the most concentrated and well-organized resistance along the entire front.

Outnumbered five to one and out in the open against an enemy dug in among the date palms, the thirty men of the MSG were forced to abandon one of their Pinzgauers and became involved in a ferocious engagement with the enemy lasting several hours before making a fighting withdrawal. 'Delta' Company, advancing on the axis over to their right, were ordered to re-route on an eight-mile cross-country march under almost constant contact to reinforce the MSG. Fully laden with kit and toiling under the midday sun, it took the better part of three hours to fight their way through a series of ambushes and enemy positions. The two Marine units were now spread out over the baked, undulating earth, weapons and ammunition hanging off their massive upper bodies, gearing up for an advance to contact and an all-out assault on the heavily defended positions shimmering in the afternoon heat two miles to the north.

The three Challengers of 2nd troop had just gone forward to clear the route, but without infantry support they were forced to beat a hasty retreat when Dougal's tank, leading the column up the narrow causeway, drove into a wall of fire. Clearly, the enemy had used the lull in proceedings to bring in reinforcements.

'It was RPGs, boss!' said Dougal, still trying to get his breath back. 'The good news is that the rockets just bounced off our frontal and side armour. The bad news is that they smashed the gimpy in half, broke the fume extractor on the main gun, shattered half my day sights, riddled the fuel drums at the back, made half my crew shite their combats with disbelief, and just when I'm thinking: *How much bloody worse can this get?* the coax machine gun has gone and jammed when we tried to return fire . . . Oh! and worst of all, my fold-down camping chair strapped to the bins at the back has been shredded to fuck, sir, if you'll pardon my Geordie. Apart from that I am happy to say that Two Two is in fine working order, sir.'

The troop leader strode back down the track. 'Right, Sergeant Baird,' he said, looking up to the slight, bespectacled figure sitting in the commander's hatch of call sign Two One. 'Corporal Dougal's wagon has taken some hits. When the Marines are ready to move, you'll lead us back in.'

'Aye, nae bother, boss,' Baird replied, after a pause. The crash of three mortar rounds in quick succession instinctively made everyone crouch down and place their hands on their helmets. Arms reached out of the Challengers and quickly slammed down the hatches with a series of metallic clatters. Captain Le Sueur jogged further along the track and heaved himself over the armoured dust skirts onto the turret and slid into the hatch.

Three miles to the east, Captain Fraser McLeman was experiencing contrasting fortunes to those of his old friend Le Sueur. Under his leadership, 3rd troop and 'A' Company 40 Commando were making such short work of the opposition that they were in danger of getting too far ahead and finding themselves cut off behind enemy lines. With 120 Marines fanned out on either side of them, advancing through the date palm plantations on foot, the three Challengers were clearing the route ahead with such clinical efficiency that they had reached the outskirts of Abu Al Khasib several hours ahead of schedule. They had encountered reasonably stiff resistance all morning, but it was sporadic and disorganized compared to the more co-ordinated threat confronting 2nd troop.

The enemy, many of them army regulars bullwhipped into action by the Fedayeen, were employing hit-and-run guerrilla tactics after abandoning most of their established bunker positions. Softened up at first light by waves of artillery fire, the subsequent sight and sound of attack helicopters over their heads and Challenger tanks advancing towards them through the weak early morning light was too much for the less fanatical among them. Those that chose to stand and fight – or were coerced to do so by the men in black – were simply overpowered by the superior firepower and combat skills of the Marines and the SCOTS DG. As the three tanks demolished bunker positions with HESH, the Marines ducked in and out of alleys and suspect houses to mop up the remaining pockets of resistance. Amongst the dozens of prisoners of war they rounded up were a Lieutenant Colonel and a Major, who were both immediately removed from the battlefield for questioning by Intelligence Officers.

Like all the British tank troops, McLeman's was accompanied by two US Marines from Anglico (Air Naval Gunfire Liaison Company), sandbagged into the top of the CRARRV. Working with a Cobra attack helicopter hovering above them, it was the task of call sign November Bravo Six to co-ordinate artillery and close air support. In the middle of the advance, the Americans reported sightings of a dozen 'bogeys' – enemy armoured vehicles – a mixture of MTLBs and T-55s, some hull down, some out in the open. They were spread out over a mile along a roughly linear front facing the advancing British troops. The subsequent artillery barrage called in by November Bravo Six was as spectacular as it was shocking

– even for the troops and crews laid up a few hundred yards short of it. An entire ridge of earth, complete with date palms and any armoured vehicles in amongst them, appeared to be lifted into the air in a cloud of dust, smoke and flames as the deafening shower of rounds fell upon it.

The moment the last shell landed, Captain McLeman dispatched Troop Sergeant 'Spider' Dudman in call sign Three One to one side and Corporal 'China' Ward in Three Two to the other, and the three tanks moved forward to engage the vehicles that had survived the onslaught. In the event there turned out to be fourteen bogeys, but within ten minutes of the first being spotted every one of them had become a twisted, scorched wreck, smouldering amongst the trees. There was no sign of their occupants. All the vehicles had been showing heat signatures from their engines on the TI but not one of them had fired back at the Challengers, suggesting that the crews had abandoned them shortly before being engaged.

When the advancing Marines were engaged from a line of buildings in amongst the trees, they hit the deck while the Challengers surged forward. Call signs Three One and Three Two used their coaxes to devastating effect as the enemy dismounts scampered for their lives through the rows of trees. A manned roadblock from where the Iraqis had been firing RPGs and small arms was quickly overrun as the tanks, spitting thousands of rounds, rolled forward with irresistible momentum. Captain McLeman was prosecuting the attack as aggressively as possible. He didn't want to be going firm for the night in complex terrain with the enemy still at large. He wanted them rolled up by dusk. The bullish mood of the troop was embodied by Lance Corporal Bruce Fraser, Captain McLeman's loader, who emerged from his hatch to engage the enemy with the gimpy mounted on the turret.

3rd troop's rapid progress was all the more impressive given the disconcertingly complex conditions in which they were operating. It wasn't so much the undergrowth and trees that worried the tank crews as the villages and scattered buildings where civilians were cowering from the battle raging outside. Every now and then, the troops glanced down a side street or scanned the horizon and caught a glimpse of local people running for cover, or peering curiously round the corner of a building at the British troops advancing towards their homes. The high-magnification sights were proving to be invaluable in this close terrain where the enemy had embedded itself amongst the civilian population. Seeing the targets from such long distances, the Challengers were engaging them long before the enemy knew what – or who – had hit them. By mid-morning, the weather was beautifully clear, but with so much vegetation to hide amongst, the TI was still proving more effective than the day sights in helping to spot targets.

By lunchtime, 3rd troop found itself in the chaotic, noisy heart of civilian life when it reached the main road junction on the western edge of Abu Al Khasib. Hundreds of cars and crowds of civilians clogged the main road that ran through the centre of the town like a high street and then continued westwards through the suburbs up towards Basra. Drivers beeped their horns and smiling locals waved and cheered as the Challengers rolled forward and pulled up at the T-junction. Children ran forward to get a close-up of the mighty main battle tanks. It was as if no one in Abu Al Khasib, a community of 50,000 people, had the first idea a war was going on in their midst. They appeared pleasantly surprised to discover that a party of British soldiers, for whatever reason, had decided to join them going about their daily lives. Captain

McLeman was feeling less inclined towards happiness right at that moment. As he emerged from the commander's hatch, a battered red Cadillac-style car pulled out of the traffic and raced erratically towards his tank. The troop leader put up his hand to order the driver to stop, but the car just kept coming.

Sergeant Baird pushed his eyes into the rubber caps of the magnification sights and felt the sweat trickle down the side of his face as he traversed the turret away from the date palms on the left back to the straight, dusty road ahead of him. His sodden shirt clung to his back as he wriggled in his seat to shake out the cramp. He flicked the sights from thermal to ordinary day vision – and instantly recoiled in his seat, as if he'd just been poked in the eye.

It was a shock to have human faces suddenly appear before him like that – the smiling faces of children, what's more, about a dozen of them, swarming around and crawling over the ambushed Pinzgauer troop carrier. They were boys mainly but there were a couple of mop-haired girls too, all wearing colourful shorts and T-shirts, covered in a film of pale dust. The oldest of them can't have been more than thirteen and the youngest no more than eight. The smaller of the girls was skipping around the vehicle. In normal vision the group looked like a colony of ants getting to work on a piece of discarded fruit, but through the Challenger's sights it was as if they were sitting right on the nose of the tank, so close that Baird felt he could reach out and pat them on the head. In reality, they were well over a mile away and completely oblivious to the three tanks of 2nd troop crawling towards them. Half a mile behind the small column of armour, 'Delta' Company and the MSG were emerging from their scrapes and ditches on the 'advance to contact', wild in appearance from their week living rough, armed to the teeth and angry after the morning's casualties and setbacks.

Baird sighed and leant forward again into his primary sights, his knees brushing against the back of the helmet of his gunner, Ferguson, in the seat below. At once his eyes were drawn to the only two adults in the gathering, two young men, roughly his age, dressed head to toe in black with shemaghs wrapped around their heads, AK-47s slung diagonally over their shoulders and ammunition belts across their chests and around their waists. The sweat dripped off his chin as he steadied the image of the two Fedayeen operatives. With both left-side tyres shot out and rammed to the roof with equipment, the Pinzgauer was listing slightly towards the middle of the road.

The two men were gesticulating wildly and exhorting the kids to hurry up and finish stripping the truck. The MSG had managed to salvage some of their equipment when they had been forced to abandon it earlier and make a fighting withdrawal, but there was still plenty left to plunder. Some of the youngsters were busy untying the Bergens from the sides of the vehicle, each of the heavy rucksacks crashing to the ground in a puff of dust. The smallest boys stood and watched as two of the older ones leant out of the canvas-covered back of the truck and bundled out a small armoury of weapons. Amongst the haul, Baird could make out a GPMG, a mortar and base plate, dozens of brown metal boxes of ammo, an assortment of other cases and objects he couldn't identify and . . .

'Shit . . .' Baird gasped as he watched a cylindrical launch tube connected to what looked like a video camera being passed down. He had only the merest glimpse of it before the two Fedayeen seized the apparatus and disappeared around to the front of the vehicle. *Is that really what I think it is? A MILAN anti-tank weapon?*

'What's up, boss?' said Frazer, the loader, leaning on the rail in the hold below to his left. Baird paused as his brain made a series of quick calculations. Even if it had been an anti-tank weapon, he figured, the Fedayeen guys probably haven't got the faintest idea how to operate it and they certainly didn't have the time to learn – in a few moments the tanks would be setting about them and, anyway, they were safely embedded in a Challenger 2 tank groaning with Dorchester armour . . . What was the point in unsettling his volatile, vocal crew still further?

'Er, nothing. It's just some kids,' said the commander, watching the trail of children struggle back down the street under the weight of their deadly bounty.

The grit of the road crackled and crunched under the heavy metal treads as the Challengers continued their steady advance, with Baird's tank on point, Corporal Dougal a hundred yards behind him and troop leader Captain Le Sueur at the rear. They were moving at a fast jogging pace now, but it still felt painfully slow for the men inside as the line of date palms up to the left loomed ever closer. Nervous banter erupted between the loader and gunner. Beset with problems, human and mechanical, since arriving in theatre, call sign Two One was not the happiest tank in the Royal Scots Dragoon Guards and tensions had been running high in the fighting compartment.

'Shut the hell up, you two, will you?' Baird snapped as he watched the last of the children disappear down the side street off to the left of the main road of the village. The thunder and crack of distant engagements rumbled through the air and massive palls of thick black smoke from burning oil wells and pipelines hung over the horizon. Baird was surprised to see that the residents were getting on with their everyday life. It was as though they had become accustomed to the sound of a foreign army blasting its way through the surrounding neighbourhood.

This was the hottest time of the day and most of the locals had already sought the relative cool of the indoors, but there were still a few dozen civilians in the main street going about their business. A hunched-back, elderly man led a train of donkeys on a string slowly across the street, from left to right, each of the mournful animals swishing its tail and flicking its ears to shake off the flies. A few yards away, a mother with a young child in tow stood before a wooden barrow of vegetables and rolled what looked like a tomato around in her fingers as the owner leant against a telegraph pole and blew cigarette smoke into the air above him.

To the left-hand side of the road, just outside the hamlet where the thicket of date palms began, Baird's eyes were drawn to the bizarre spectacle of a large fishing trawler, brown with rust, with its bow pointing down the road away from the buildings. A barefoot boy ran out from behind it kicking a half-deflated football and raising his arm to celebrate his imaginary goal. As he went to give it another boot with his bare foot, the kid stopped dead in his tracks and pointed straight up the road, almost touching the barrel of the British gun – or so it seemed to Baird with his eyes glued to the sights. The boy spun on his heel and shouted to the rest of the street behind him. Immediately there was a rush of activity as the locals scampered in different directions, throwing anxious glances down the road before disappearing from sight. Within thirty seconds, the street was deserted. The tanks were a hundred yards from the date palms.

Baird took a deep breath in an effort to force his heart rate down. As the commander it was important for him to concentrate and make judgements with a clear head. Over the intercom, he told his driver, Trooper Ilivia 'Mac' Macawai, to slow down as they approached the Pinzgauer. The vehicle was riddled with bullet holes down its left-hand side and its windows in the driving cab had been shot out. The truck was over to the right, at a very slight angle, and there was barely any room, two feet at best, for the Challenger to squeeze between it and the deep ditch running alongside. It would have been easier to bump the ambushed vehicle out of the way, but the Marines were keen to try and recover it and salvage what kit they could.

Mac squirmed in his seat to try and make himself more comfortable. He was by no means the largest of the Fijians serving in the regiment, but there was still precious little wriggle room down in the driver's compartment at the front of the tank, an area the size of a bath tub, separated from the rest of the crew in the turret. The soft earth of the levee crumbled and rolled into the ditch on the left as Mac, the Royal Scots Dragoon Guards' newest recruit and one of its most promising, began to ease 75 tons of armour past the vehicle. Unable to see the 'blind spot' area immediately around the tank when closed down, Baird fidgeted nervously with his helmet strap as the young Fijian edged the Challenger forward using his two steering sticks to try and keep the tracks dead straight. Inch by inch, Mac nudged the mighty tank past the truck. There was nothing the other three could do but pray that their new crewmate would keep his head – and keep his hands steady on the levers and his foot easy on the accelerator. For once, silence filled the turret. After half a minute or so – an eternity to the crew – they felt the tracks grip as Mac applied some gas and, with a loud rev of the engine, the tank jumped past the front of the Pinzgauer and back into the middle of the road. All four exhaled as one.

'Brilliant, Mac. Well done,' said Baird over the intercom. Mac's English may have left something to be desired, but in the short time he had been with the regiment he had impressed everyone with his appetite for hard work, his cheerful attitude and his willingness to learn.

Baird looked through his rear episcope and saw the tank's tread marks no more than six inches from the deep trench to the side of the road. He glanced at the Pinzgauer and saw an unexploded RPG stuck in the grille below the driver's seat.

'Thank God for th—' came a lugubrious voice over the intercom.

Following a few hundred yards to the rear, Captain Le Sueur and Corporal Dougal had the clearest view as the first RPG scorched out of the date palms and streaked towards Baird's tank. It had barely crashed into the frontal armour of the turret in a shower of fluorescent sparks when one . . . two . . . three . . . four more rockets ripped out of the vegetation, leaving arcs of tracer over the hundred-yard expanse of scrubland as they raced towards their target. At exactly the same time the air erupted with the crackle of machine-gun and automatic fire. Hundreds of rounds tore out of the palms, peppering the hull like hailstones on a corrugated-iron roof and kicking up a wall of dirt along the ridge of the road to the front and left of the tank.

'Contact, wait out!' yelled Baird into his mouthpiece, but there was no need to tell the rest of the troop.

As soon as he saw the first RPG whip over the barrel of the main gun, Mac instinctively rammed his foot on the brake bringing the tank to a juddering halt that made the three behind lurch forward and put out their hands to steady themselves. A stream of automatic fire smashed his vision block and suddenly his small window on the world had disappeared. All he could see was the crazily shattered glass of his unitary periscope. Almost instantaneously, another RPG crashed into the commander's cupola in a burst of orange and white sparks, shattering the central and left side periscopes. Instinctively, Baird ducked as the round erupted inches from where he was sitting, the shock of the explosion, so close to his face, stunning him into momentary silence and inaction. Ferguson returned fire with some coax but after a couple of bursts the chain gun jammed and he beat his fist against the controls in wild frustration.

They were trapped in a killing zone. Blinded and unable to fight back with nowhere to run, panic seized the tank. The turret filled with a riot of voices, screaming orders and swearing. Outside the tank the air was filled with the rattle of machine guns and automatic rifles, the fizzing of rockets and the yelling of men. The RPG teams were working in pairs, one carrying the launcher, the other the grenades. Crawling through the undergrowth and trenches with the weapons slung over their backs and sticking out from behind their heads, their silhouettes looked for all the world like Red Indians encircling wagons of the Wild West. The enemy dismounts were everywhere – no longer just in amongst the date palms fifty yards away but crawling through the network of ditches and hollows in between – and they were closing in fast, concentrating all their fire on Two One. Not a single shot had been directed at the two tanks behind. It was obvious to Captain Le Sueur what they were trying to do. The Iraqis had lured them in, now they were going to take his sergeant's tank – dead or alive.

It took Baird a minute to regain the power of speech. He

tried to sound calm but it was impossible to hide the desperation in his voice when he came over the squadron net: 'We're getting hit big time here, all my sights are out, I can't see a thing, we have to withdraw! We need help here, Two Zero. Where are you? Where the hell are you?'

The troop leader could hear the shouts and screams filling the turret in the background, almost drowning out Baird, and tried to picture the chaos of the scene within.

'We're right behind you, Sergeant Baird. Now listen carefully . . .' Le Sueur spoke in clear, firm, measured tones as he watched the rounds pouring into Baird's wagon, streaks of tracer shooting towards it like a giant laser show. 'We're right here and we're not going anywhere without you. You must regain control of your crew. We are giving you covering fire. Repeat: try and calm the turret.'

Rounds hammered into the thick armoured shell of the Challenger, scorching and stripping the freshly laid desert paintwork from the metal below. The AK-47 rounds and RPGs were never going to penetrate the armour to the front and side of Britain's main battle tank, but hearing the hail of bullets and rockets clattering on the outside, the raw fears of the crew told them otherwise and they instinctively buried their heads in their hands.

As Le Sueur and Dougal raced up the road, the gunners hosed the enemy positions with coax. The entire line of trees on a 200-yard front quivered as if in a gale. The steep earth bank in the midst of the palms, where much of the firing was coming from, leapt and spat as the rounds poured in from the Challengers. Debris flew through the air as the bark was ripped from the tree trunks and palm fronds disintegrated like paper in a shredding machine. An enemy dismount, racing for cover, spun round like a ballerina and collapsed to the earth in a lifeless heap.

Le Sueur reached for the radio set hanging around his neck and flicked on to the squadron net. 'Zero Alpha, this is Two Zero, we are engaging multiple enemy dismounts at grid 805729. Wait out!' Sitting in his Challenger five miles along the motorway to the south-east, Major Biggart pressed the headset to his ear and waited for the sitrep. The fighting was everywhere now.

Baird turned the switch on his radio box to the intercom setting in the middle so that only his crew could hear him and tried to restore some order, but he could barely make himself heard above the row in the turret. He told Mac to reverse slowly back past the Pinzgauer.

'Sorry? What, Sarge?'

The young tank commander could only just make out the Fijian above the shouting and it was doubly difficult over an intercom system that had been malfunctioning all week, and had chosen now to start playing up again.

'We're going to REVERSE! REVERSE! PULL BACK!'

Baird could only hope that he understood.

'Yes, Sarge. No problem!'

Baird still had a partial view through the vision blocks behind his seat and he turned in his seat to squint through them to guide Mac past the abandoned Commando vehicle. He could just about make out the reversing antenna above the fuel drums and storage bins at the back and it was wobbling from side to side as Mac put the tank into gear and gripped the steering sticks. Down in the cramped bowels of the tank, the driver could see nothing and hear only a little.

Behind them, the other two tanks of the troop, their main guns traversed off to the left, were putting in a blaze of repressive fire with their chain guns to cover the withdrawal of their comrades. Dark figures appeared on the periphery of Baird's vision for a split second as the enemy bounded and crawled from ditch to ditch, bearing down, closer and closer, on the beleaguered British tank. His sweat-drenched T-shirt clung to his skin as he peered through his rear scopes to help Mac guide the Challenger back past the Pinzgauer.

'OK, keep her straight, keep her straight, Mac. Bit faster. That's it. OK, now slow down, slow down . . . Left stick! Left stick! Left stick!'

'No, right stick! Right stick! RIGHT stick!' screamed his gunner and loader as one.

In the confusion, with all three of his crewmates shouting at him, the young Fijian yanked the right stick – the wrong one. It wasn't his fault he didn't know who was shouting what. Fifty yards away, the other two commanders looked on in horror as they saw the rear of Two One slump sideways off the road into the trench to the left of the road with such force that for a moment it looked as if it was going to topple onto its turret. 'Oh Christ, she's going over!' Corporal Dougal shouted. Two One wobbled for a moment on the edge of its tracks before the right side crashed back towards the road and came to rest at a 45-degree angle, exposing its soft-skinned unprotected underbelly. Mac jammed the tank into forward gear and put his foot flat down on the accelerator. The engines roared, but there was no response. Both tracks were thrown and the giant sprockets at the back spun crazily but uselessly. The main armament hung limply over the side, pointing down at the earth. An RPG streaked out of the window of a small derelict building a stone's throw to the left, skidded off the sloping armour at the front of the turret and burst in a shower of sparks and flames on the nose of the gunner's sights. The Challenger was blind, disabled and unable to defend itself.

The enemy had her exactly where they wanted and they swarmed out of the trees and the trenches for the kill.

'Two One, this is Two Zero . . . Two One, this is Two Zero, can you hear me? . . . Two One, come in . . . Two One . . .'

8. The Longest Night

Corporal Fraser swung the gimpy round at the approaching car, forcing it to brake sharply twenty yards short of the Challenger. Two men in shemagh headscarves were sitting in the front seat. The driver got out and began to walk towards them. The crowd backed off a few yards.

'Where are you going in such a hurry?' shouted Captain McLeman from his hatch.

'Market! We go market in Basra!'

'Why the rush?'

'Fish smell.'

'What? Fish smell?'

'Yes, must hurrying. Fresh best. We are car of fresh fish.'

'Yeah, and I've got a tank full of bananas,' the young troop leader muttered under his breath as he lifted himself out of the hatch, took out his little Browning pistol and began to lower himself down the side of the Challenger. 'Keep your eyes open, Corporal Fraser.'

As he walked towards the car, Major Justin Holt, 'A' Company commander, appeared up the road. The Marines had marched twenty miles, fully laden, since the operation began and the sweat was running off his hollow-cheeked face. The odd crack of gunfire split the air behind him. They had advanced so fast that they had left a few enemy stragglers in their wake, who would have to be mopped up before the day was out.

The driver of the saloon car smiled and beckoned to Captain

McLeman to follow him to the rear of the vehicle. He put a key in the boot and, with a loud creak, lifted the lid. McLeman stared in amazement. There, lying loose in the rusting compartment, amongst an assortment of petrol cans, fishing tackle and ropes, were hundreds of bright, silvery fish.

'See, mister. Fish go market. All cars go market. Fish fresh . . .'

As he spoke, McLeman looked down the main road running into Abu Al Khasib and saw that it was emptying rapidly. That could mean only one thing: enemy were on their way. He climbed back into the Challenger and, with a troop of Royal Marines following them in, he led the other two tanks slowly down the street, lined with shops and advertising boards in Arabic on both sides and a row of date palms running down the central reservation. The rickety metal anti-theft shutters had been pulled down on most of the shops and where there had been hundreds of shoppers and traders just moments ago, there was now only a handful of people left in the street – and they quickly disappeared from view as the Challengers ground and squealed towards them with their turrets and main guns swinging from side to side.

A statue of Saddam Hussein stood in the middle of a roundabout pointing accusingly at Iran. At the far end of the street a beautifully ornate wooden house with balconies stood out from the rows of two-storey concrete buildings on either side of it. A two-man RPG team shot from a side street. Almost instantly bursts of coax from the Challengers kicked up the dust around them. The men fled back between the buildings, chased by a column of Marines. The sound of gunfire crackled through the air, and moments later the Marines re-emerged onto the main street and nodded up at the tanks to confirm the threat had been extinguished.

By the time they returned to the T-junction, the sound of

fighting in the immediate vicinity had died away. To the south of the junction lay their objective: two buildings of the local police precinct which, being on the corner of the main roads into town, was as good a place as anywhere for them to overnight. The barracks had been abandoned just minutes before they arrived; the coffee pot in the kitchen was still warm and there were half a dozen half-full mugs and an ashtray full of freshly stubbed cigarette butts on the table. Stretching their numb limbs as they emerged from the Challengers after eighteen hours closed down, the crews slowly and quietly set about addressing their personal needs. Most were too tired to talk. Some sat against the trunk of a tree or the shade of the building and smoked a cigarette, others cooked up a meal or boiled up hot water for a wash and a shave.

Captain McLeman was standing naked in a washing-up bowl of hot water with his face pointing up towards the branches of the tree as he reflected on the events of another tumultuous day. It was the first moment of peace and relaxation he had enjoyed in days, perhaps even weeks, and the sensation of the water on his clammy, weary feet was having a pleasantly soporific effect. He had closed his eyes for no more than a few seconds when he was startled by the sound of a man clearing his throat. Before him stood the imposing figure of a Royal Marine groaning with weaponry and equipment. Sweat ran down from under his helmet through a cut on his cheek and soaked his thick stubble. He was panting heavily.

'Hi, I'm 2nd Lieutenant Butch Buczkiewicz.' McLeman stayed in his washing-up bowl as the two men shook hands. 'We've secured the immediate area and put men out on stag. We should be safe here tonight. Anyway, on behalf of all of us, thanks for all your good work today. The tanks were brilliant.'

'No problem, any time,' the young captain shouted, cupping

his hands over his groin. 'We'll be right here if you need any assistance. You know where to find us.'

'Yep, location logged. In the washing-up bowl under the tree in the police station of Abu Al Khasib.'

As the Marine strode away to rejoin his platoon across the compound, Corporal Fraser, who had remained in the tank on radio stag while his commander dismounted, shot out of the loader's hatch like a meerkat out of its burrow. His face was a picture of alarm as he pressed the headset to his ears.

'I wouldn't get too comfortable in your wee bathtub, sir!' he shouted. 'Two One's down and out and there's a right old scrap going on down the road!'

Sergeant Baird sat slumped in his sloping seat, his left shoulder pressed against the side of the cupola. He was too stunned to respond to his comrades' promptings over the radio. He had lost all concept of time: it may have been just a few seconds, it may have been several minutes since he felt his tank sink down the side of the causeway and crash onto its side. Now he was dimly aware of his gunner and loader screaming at him. 'Get us out of here! We're going to die!' one of them was shouting, virtually hysterical.

Outside, the bursts of suppressive fire that Le Sueur and Dougal were putting in had succeeded in beating back the initial onslaught. The fighting was continuing with the same fury but the enemy had withdrawn into the line of date palms that ran along the fringes of the small community. The immediate danger of them swarming on top of the tank had passed, but the situation remained perilous. Relatively safe behind a high earth embankment, the enemy continued to launch a succession of RPGs at the stricken Challenger in the ditch, some streaking wide of the mark across the scrubland, others hitting their target with a blinding crash. To the crew, the impact generated a small thudding noise and an almost imperceptible jolt, but in the claustrophobic atmosphere of the listing turret, with minimal situational awareness and no ability to fight back, each round sounded like a death knell.

Human instinct told them to get out of the vehicle, but common sense said 'stay put'. They were sitting in the best-protected tank in the world, entombed by two-foot-thick slabs of the most effective armour ever invented. Outside, it was flesh and blood against rocket-propelled grenades and a storm of small-arms fire. But it was the fear of the unknown that was causing the panic. *What if they bring up armour or an artillery piece or a BM-21 rocket launcher or a shoulder-launched anti-tank weapon?* It would only take one round into their soft, exposed underbelly and they would all be burnt alive. There was no telling what weapons the enemy were procuring. No Challenger had been destroyed by enemy fire since the invasion began ten days earlier but several US Abrams main battle tanks, awesome machines in their own right, had been taken out.

'You're the commander! What are you going to fucking do? . . . Come on, Sergeant, what's your fucking bright plan, that's what you're paid for . . . You're gonna get us all killed . . . Come on, think of something, do something! Fucking do something! . . .'

'SHUT THE HELL UP, WILL YOU?' Baird shouted over the voices of his gunner and loader. The turret fell silent except for the shower of small arms that fell upon the turret like rain on a corrugated-iron roof.

But they all knew the truth: there was nothing they could do but sit it out, wait to be rescued and hope to high heaven that their Challenger held out against the onslaught.

Captain Le Sueur had ordered Corporal Dougal to get in

front of Baird's vehicle leaving room for his own tank to take up position directly behind him. The two of them were now less than a hundred yards from the enemy positions, within shouting distance. They barely needed the magnification on the sights to get a good view of the men they were fighting.

So far at least, 2nd troop held the advantage in firepower, but the Iraqi paramilitaries were there in such strength and stretched out over such a wide area that the two tanks were having to fire near constantly to keep them at bay. It was difficult to gauge exact numbers, but the colourful canopy of tracer over the scrubland suggested a minimum of fifty dismounts, with heaven knows how many pouring into the position on hearing the news that a British Challenger was there for the taking. In addition to the dozens spread out along a 200-yard stretch of the wooded bank, enemy were also appearing in windows and on the balconies of a residential building that looked out through gap in the treeline. A bus stop structure close to the rusting boat and a small concrete hut, possibly a disused electricity sub-station, out in the scrubland were also providing protection for the mobile RPG teams.

It was taking a combination of coax, HESH and smoke to keep the paramilitaries from overrunning their position while reinforcements and a REME recovery team were scrambled to assist them. Firing their two mounted multi-barrelled smoke grenade dischargers as well as smoke rounds from the main gun, the crews created a screen, but the respite from the all-out assault was only partial and temporary. Call sign Two One had become a magnet for fire and, short of JDAMing or carpet-bombing the treeline and the residential area behind, there was not a lot they could do about it other than sit and fight it out and pray the CRARRV would be able to winch the Challenger from the ditch and drag it to safety.

The enemy were certainly enjoying their moment of supremacy over the British forces. Two men emerged from behind the boat and began walking down the middle of the road into the village away from the tanks. They had AK-47s in their hands and bandoliers of ammo slung over their backs. Corporal Dougal squeezed a burst of coax as a warning shot, making the track behind them dance with dust. Neither of them flinched. The one on the left, without looking round, stuck up the middle finger of his right hand and raised his arm above his head, nonchalantly telling him to 'fuck off', daring him to shoot them in the back as a coward would. Almost immediately, they both disappeared from view behind the row of buildings in the treelines.

'That arrogant bastard might just live to regret that, but I doubt it,' snapped Dougal as he traversed the turret back to the enemy positions on the left. Immediately he caught sight of a figure in black burst from the bank and race through the drifting smoke to take cover behind a mound of earth out in the scrub. When he reappeared, the young Geordie was waiting for him with the sights on high magnification. The man's face was so close that it took up the entire screen and Dougal could see that he must have washed and groomed himself very recently. Most of the paramilitaries were dressed in civilian clothes, an assortment of tracksuits and sports shirts, trainers and sandals, and they were scruffy and unkempt in appearance but this character was turned out immaculately in the black uniform of the Fedayeen. His hair was clean and combed and his dark moustache neatly trimmed. As Dougal homed in on him, the young man dropped to one knee, pulled the RPG launcher over his shoulder and pointed it at his turret. The firing system was still set to coax and Dougal lifted the safety latch and squeezed the trigger. Nothing. He squeezed even harder. Still no response.

'The coax has jammed again! Oi, Cherry! Sort that fucking chain gun out!' he shouted at his loader. Dougal turned the weapon switch to main armament and dabbed the earth below the Fedayeen soldier. The computer made a slight realignment of the barrel, Dougal released control of the gun, gunner Todd squeezed the trigger, the ground flew upwards in a shower of earth and high explosive, throwing the man and his weapon through the air in different directions. Almost simultaneously, more enemy swept over the main embankment.

Dougal was screaming: 'Hurry up with that bloody coax and screw the dry cycle! There's dozens of them coming!' Using his combination tool, Lance Corporal 'Cherry' Woodcock quickly cleared the round that had jammed in the breech of the chain gun, reattached the magazine of 7.62mm rounds and slammed the gun cover shut. Usually after a stoppage, the loader ran a dry cycle to make sure there were no other rounds stuck in the barrel that might cook off with lethal consequences. But as soon as Cherry shut the cover, Todd seized the grips again and began blazing rounds into the wave of advancing enemy. A two-man RPG team, both in black, crumpled to the ground like rag dolls under a withering stream of rounds. A third emerged from over an earth mound only to be flung backwards into the hollow below by the force of the bullets hammering into his chest. Still they kept coming. Behind him Captain Le Sueur's tank was strafing the treeline and building to the left from where most of the small-arms fire was coming. Hundreds of rounds tore into the dry earth, kicking up walls of dust along the top of the embankment and perforating the adobe walls of the house behind. A HESH round erupted at the base of a tree, removing a great chunk of earth.

Over to Dougal's left a fourth RPG operator was kneeling down getting his loaded launcher into the firing position. As

Dougal brought the turret round, the man appeared through the sights to be staring straight at him.

'When are you lot going to bloody learn?' the Corporal muttered to himself, noticing as he spoke that he was short of breath and that his chest was rising and falling in rapid rhythm. His lungs worked like bellows to give him the oxygen his body was demanding. 'You've just seen three of your mates get bleached, so why don't you just fuck off home?' As he was speaking, Dougal traversed the turret and gun back and forth, like a man shaking his head. 'Don't make me do this.' The paramilitary put the sight to his eye and raised the launcher so that it was level with Two One's turret, Dougal squeezed the trigger himself and twenty rounds of 7.62mm shredded the man where he knelt. He fell backwards, a heap of lifeless black, bloodstained cloth.

In the fury of the engagement there was so much fire criss-crossing the scrubland that no one saw the high-explosive rocket from the anti-tank weapon coming. But Baird and his crew certainly knew all about it when it careered into the right-hand side of the sloping front turret above the smoke grenade charger. Where the rocket-propelled grenades had been making a barely noticeable thud on the tank's armour, the shocking impact of the ATW on the area right in front of where Gunner Ferguson was sitting triggered a fresh bout of pandemonium. When blue sparks from the spall sprayed across the fighting compartment, as one, the crew yelled in alarm, convinced that the Challenger had been penetrated and they were about to be vaporized.

In the chaos, loader Frazer injured his hand against the breech of the gun and was shouting as much in agony as in fear of an imminently hideous death. Mac, who had crawled through from the driving compartment, was showing a composure under fire that belied his inexperience. When the spall flew through the air he merely crouched down and covered his head. Whatever ATW had hit the Challenger in one of its softer spots, it certainly wasn't the dreaded MILAN missile. In all likelihood, it was the less powerful LAW – a weapon capable of taking down lesser main battle tanks, but not the Challenger. After a few moments the crew realized that the Challenger had survived the strike but it was too late: the resolve of the crew had been broken. Fearing another hit, there was a noisy scramble for the hatches. All tankies know there is no such thing as a painless, tidy death inside the turret of a tank and their instincts told them they had a better chance of surviving a gale of gunfire on the outside than a catastrophic ATW kill on the inside.

When Captain Le Sueur saw the hatches of the stricken Challenger fly open, he switched on the radio net and snapped: 'Two One this is Two Zero, get back in the tank NOW! You will not, repeat NOT, leave your tank. The safest place for you to be right now is where you are!' In the background, he could hear a voice screaming: 'Let me out! Get the hell out!' His heart went out to Baird, a good man, a willing soldier and popular character in the regiment, who had perhaps been promoted to sergeant a year too early. It was further bad luck that during the hectic rush to deploy not all the cards had fallen in his favour when the complicated configurations of the crew arrangements were worked out. Now the young, modest family man from Ayrshire found himself having to deal with the tank commander's worst-case scenario, the equivalent of a submarine coming to grief on the seabed with its crew in mutiny.

At the very moment that the crew began trying to scramble clear of their tank, Major Biggart, roaring up the track from the south in Zero Bravo, arrived on the scene and immediately cut into the squadron net. Where Le Sueur had barked his order to stay put, Biggart positively bellowed at Baird to keep his crew in the turret. Following behind Zero Bravo was the CRARRV, call sign Juliet Three Three Bravo, commanded by Corporal John Morgan of the REME's Light Aid Detachment. Biggart's and Morgan's hearts sank simultaneously at the sight of the Challenger wedged at a 45-degree angle in the steep ditch, its gun hanging forlornly over the side. They were even more shocked by the proximity of the enemy positions and the sheer weight of fire that was pouring out of the treeline.

As the Squadron leader, Major Biggart automatically took control of the rescue operation from Le Sueur – and the young captain couldn't help but feel a stab of disappointment as he handed over. As troop leader, he wanted to sort out the mess that one of his call signs had caused. This could have been his defining moment not only as a soldier but as a young man; a junior officer sorting out a truly senior disaster. Le Sueur was the fourth generation of his family to serve in the regiment; his grandfather had been 'A' Squadron leader in the war and his great-uncle had commanded the regiment. None of his relatives had ever encouraged, let alone coerced, him to join the family regiment, but he knew they were proud that he had chosen to follow in their footsteps. Taking a backseat role now, he would never discover if he had inherited his ancestors' leadership skills to manage a crisis of such towering magnitude – and he was surprised by how deflated he felt.

The CRARRV pulled up just short of the crippled Challenger, with Zero Bravo taking up position twenty yards behind. Biggart and his loader immediately opened up their hatches to make a proper examination of the scene. Using the primary sights was fine, but for full situational awareness a tank commander prefers to be sitting up in the hatch. Pushing the hatch open just a fraction, Biggart's first reaction was one of astonishment at the deafening noise of the engagement. Inside his turret, the battle was no more than a muffled boom; outside it was uproar. The crash of the main armament, the eruption of high explosive, the crackle and spit of machine-gun fire, the whoosh of RPGs, and the yells and screams of men filled the air with a hellish commotion. The moment his helmet peeked out of the cupola an RPG screeched across the front of the turret, no more than two yards from his head; another whistled through the gap between the road wheel and the drive sprocket – the only part of the tracks not covered by the armoured dust skirt. Instantly, the two men ducked back down and slammed the hatches tight on their near-silent world within.

'Well, it's always comforting to know that you're in other people's thoughts,' said the major looking at his startled loader.

As the commander of the unit, the Squadron leader's principal role was to oversee the operation in hand; to stand off a little, give himself the best possible view and understanding of the situation, and then call the shots accordingly. What he didn't need in such a complicated and pressurized incident was to get sucked into the fighting. He needed to be the eyes and the ears of the operation, not the fists and boots. But judging from the welcoming reception, it seemed he had little choice but to join the furious melee.

Putting his eyes into the sights, he traversed the turret over the scrubland and brought them back sharply when he caught sight of a man with an RPG in his hand sprinting towards them over the undulating scrub, brushing aside the tufts of long grass and reeds, knees and elbows pumping, wild eyes popping out of his head. 'RPG dismount, coax, on!' he said, releasing control of the firing system to his gunner. The man was running so fast that by the time his gunner pulled the trigger, he was virtually under the arcs of the coax and just seconds from reaching the Challenger. Zero Bravo had flicked the sights to high mag, bringing the dismount so close he was almost inside the tank when the gunner squeezed the trigger. The short killing burst didn't just stop the attacker in his tracks – it cut him in half across the waist. For the briefest of moments gunner and commander sat frozen in the sights, horrified by the sickening image pressed up against their faces.

But there was no time to dwell. A company's worth of irregulars was swarming all over the terrain and without any infantry in support to tackle them, all three tanks were hosing the landscape with coax in a desperate effort to keep them at arm's length. In the space of half an hour, the three tanks fired more live rounds than they had done in two years of training and it quickly became obvious to the Squadron leader that unless they could drag the tank from the ditch quickly, then they were going to need a lot more firepower: infantry, artillery as well as more tanks and more engineers. The only alternative was to rescue the crew and stick a FIN round in the vehicle to deny it. That was the simplest and safest option, but it was also a defeat. That was the last resort.

The most concentrated fire was coming from the upper floor and flat roof of the building in the middle of the treeline. Tracer fire streaked out of the windows and muzzles flashed along its entire length. The Challengers were putting in bursts of suppressive fire to keep their heads down for brief periods, but they couldn't stop it altogether.

'Two Zero, this is Zero Alpha, we need to HESH that enemy position in the building!' Within seconds both 120mm guns of the two tanks, the barrels raised at exactly the same angle, roared and recoiled in unison as if choreographed for artistic effect. Blue, orangey flames shot out of the muzzles as the Challengers lurched backwards on their haunches. The upper part of the building exploded in a burst of brick, dust and high explosive as the two rounds made impact simultaneously. Two further rounds followed five seconds later, followed by two more and another two . . . A minute later, when the cloud of smoke cleared, the top half of the building no longer existed. In less than half a minute, the enemy's principal firing platform had been reduced to a smouldering, rubble-strewn bungalow. A man staggered out of the wreckage, his black hair and black uniform caked in a film of dust, staggering and wheeling, then slumped to the ground.

Like iron filings to a magnet, the rounds continued to pour into Two One. The close fighting was akin to the trench warfare of the First World War, only with far heavier weapons. With the enemy closing in and nightfall no more than ninety minutes away, the imperative of extracting the vehicle was quickly becoming critical. But first the crew had to get out of the vehicle in case it rolled when the CRARRV attempted to pull it up the bank. Although the other three tanks had been firing near continuously since the battle began, they would now have to increase their weight of fire while the four men scrambled out of their hatches, and hope that the chain guns didn't suffer any further stoppages. Inside the claustrophobic metal compartment containing enough explosives to raze an entire village to the ground, hearing the rounds peppering the hull, the crew's survival instincts were screaming at them to get out. No vestige of reason remained in their agitated, fearful minds to remind them that what they were about to attempt was, by far, the most dangerous moment they had experienced since the disaster had unfolded. By leaving the protection of the world's most effective armour, they had nothing but the shirts and light body armour on their backs to shield them.

'Three, two, one . . . go!' When Zero Alpha gave the order, the three Challengers laid down a blanket of chain gun fire all along the treeline. Sacrificing accuracy for weight of fire, the gunners held their fingers on the trigger in long ranging bursts. A canopy of red-coloured tracer arced over the scrubland, hitting the embankment and trees like a sudden gust of wind. Dirt, leaves and bark flew through the air under the maelstrom of fire and for a few moments the enemy was silenced up and down the line. Trying to reveal as little of himself as possible, Sergeant Baird slithered out of the commander's hatch and lay down on the back deck behind the turret. At the same time, the bulky figure of Frazer emerged awkwardly from the loader's hatch. With his damaged hand unable to take any pressure, he used an elbow to lever himself out, then rolled off the back and took cover at the rear. The men of the REME fitter section leapt from their CRARRV, pulling the winch rope behind the ditched Challenger.

Gunner Ferguson scrambled out behind his tank commander and jumped to safety, while Mac used his powerful arms to hoist himself out of the loader's hatch in a single effort. In the few seconds since the hatches were opened, the enemy who still had their heads up and could see what was going on immediately trained all their guns on the turret. As Mac emerged from the commander's hatch and positioned himself to leap to the ground a volley of small-arms fire hammered against the turret, riddling the side storage bin below him with a line of perforations in a metallic clatter, just inches below his right foot. Leaping through the air with streams of machine-gun fire ricocheting off the side of the tank, Mac landed on the slope of the crumbling embankment and fell backwards. Struggling to stop himself falling back into the enemy's line of fire, he dug a boot into the soft earth and flung himself under the shadow of the Challenger. The men sat or crouched against the vehicle trying to get their breath back as shots thumped into the earth just a few feet away.

The CRARRV is specifically designed to recover and repair tanks on the battlefield. In effect, it is a Challenger 2 tank without the fighting capability. Its only armament is a 7.62mm GPMG and a smoke grenade discharger. Manned by a three-man fitter section on attachment from the REME, the Challenger Armoured Repair and Recovery Vehicle plays a crucial role in the operation of a tank squadron. The dozer blade is used to clear obstacles such as land mines, walls and vehicles as well as to create defensive positions in a hide; the crane lifts the engines out of the tanks for essential maintenance while the main and auxiliary winches are used to pull bogged tanks from the mire. And it was these that the REME section immediately set about attaching to the disabled tank. Working under fire, the men crawled back and forth between the vehicles while the Challengers fired smoke to cover them and kept up a heavy stream of chain-gun fire and HESH rounds.

It didn't take long to hook up the two vehicles and the REME crew soon scrambled back into the CRARRV along with Troopers Ferguson and Frazer, while Sergeant Baird and Trooper Macawai took cover behind Major Biggart's vehicle. The CRARRV driver reversed a few yards and the crew activated the hydraulically driven winch. The heavy cable sprang from the earth and went solid as a metal rod as the hydraulics heaved with all their might. The CRARRV revved and grunted and the winch quivered with the effort, but the Challenger did not budge. The tension inside the neighbouring tank turrets was every bit as great as that running along the cable between the two giant armoured vehicles. Watching the CRARRV struggle, it didn't take a mathematics prodigy to work out that part of the difficulty was that the CRARRV's freedom of movement was extremely limited on the narrow raised embankment. To avoid sliding into the ditch behind them, thereby turning a crisis into a catastrophe, they were only able to pull at a very oblique, shallow angle. Compounding the problem, the shed tracks had jammed solid around the suspension, effectively making the tank a 75-ton dead weight, a giant boulder wedged into the earth. The winch creaked and strained and the CRARRV revved and roared with the effort but the Challenger was not interested in yielding so much as an inch. The tension along the cable proved too great – and it snapped. Such was the energy being exerted in the pull that the two ends of the heavy metal winch whipped high up into the air before crashing onto the track in a cloud of dust.

The hopes of Major Biggart and the rest of the troops snapped just as spectacularly as they watched the winch slump to the ground. *What the hell now?* The Squadron leader rested his chin on his hands and exhaled loudly. *Why don't they just put a FIN round through the bloody thing and be done with it?* It was five million pounds' worth of kit he'd be writing off, but that was nothing compared to the propaganda value to the enemy of such a move. The cost to the morale of the squadron and the reputation of the regiment was incalculable.

When 'C' Squadron was reattached to 3 Commando Brigade, Major Biggart argued the case strongly with Brigade for taking two recovery vehicles with them across the peninsula. The terrain, he figured, was going to be every bit as hostile and unforgiving as the fanatical enemy they were fighting. Now his judgement had been vindicated. With its winch now useless, Three Three Bravo was effectively out of action, but the other CRARRV was sitting in reserve just ten minutes away at Taku. It was worth making one last effort, Biggart reasoned. He turned on the radio and called forward call sign Two Four Charlie, commanded by Corporal James Garrett and manned by recovery mechanic Corporal Justin Simons and technician Corporal Rick Parker. Call sign Four One, commanded by Sergeant Lamb, was to escort the new team the two miles up the track and then stay with the rescue package to provide covering fire. Corporal Parker had been working on the malfunctioning TI system in Lamb's tank and he hadn't quite finished the job when the call came in to drop what they were doing.

When the two recovery vehicles pulled up alongside each other on the wider section of track closer to Taku, Corporal Morgan jumped aboard the ingoing vehicle to resume his efforts with the new team. The sun was in rapid decline when Two Four Charlie arrived at the scene and was met with the same storm of incoming rounds that had greeted Zero Bravo and Three Three Bravo an hour earlier. In all likelihood, the forces that had escaped 3rd troop's advance a few miles to the east had heard the news of the stricken Challenger on the bush telegraph and raced to join their comrades in an all-out bid to claim its scalp. When the REME crew opened the hatches and appeared from their soundproof armoured bubble, they were greeted by an equally heavy volley of small-arms fire. As the rounds fizzed past their ears and cracked against the armour, they quickly ducked back inside and battened down the hatches. The message from the REME crew to Zero Bravo over the radio was unequivocal: *We're not stepping out into that. We're mechanics, not infantrymen.*

This was the critical moment of the operation and Major

Biggart knew he had to act fast before the morale of his men imploded. First he contacted the FOO, parked further down the track in his Warrior, to call in a fire mission of smoke. The Challengers had used all their own grenades and rounds; the large shells of the artillery would provide a far more effective screen anyhow. He then called up the REME boys and told them to meet him at the rear of Two One, where Sergeant Baird and Trooper Macawai were sheltering.

It is one of the oldest rules of combat that the Commanding Officer keeps out of the firing line as best he can so that he can carry out the job he was asked to do – namely, command his men. A commander's no good to his men if he's dead; history shows that their chances of survival are diminished by his absence. These, however, were exceptional circumstances calling for an exceptional response. Major Biggart knew he had to lead by example. He pushed open the hatch, lifted his lanky frame out onto the turret and lowered himself down the side of the Challenger, leeward of the incoming fire. The intensity of the enemy attacks had abated only a little since the fury of the original onslaught. The rest of the troop had been doing an impressive job in subduing the enemy positions but the treeline was still twinkling with a string of muzzle flashes and the air was singing with the whizz and snap of automatic weapons and the dull thud of mortar rounds and RPGs into the soft earth.

Pausing before making his move, Major Biggart was aware that if he wanted to communicate a sense of calm authority to the men, it was no good running the twenty yards between the two vehicles. That would serve only to acknowledge the peril they were going to be facing so, with a deep breath and his heart beating on his ribcage to be let out, he jumped from the side of the tank and strode down the track with the air of a man stepping out of a London taxi. The tempo of gunfire from the date palms increased the moment he appeared: At 6 feet 2 inches, Biggart presented an attractive target. Sergeant Baird, Mac and the REME crew were as impressed as they were surprised by the sight of their commander walking towards them. In spite of the gunfire whistling over the scrubland, the Major appeared to be moving just a little faster and more purposefully than had he been heading down Piccadilly, running a few minutes late for lunch with an old friend.

With the enemy dug in no more than a hundred yards from where they were standing and the bullets ricocheting off the armour they were sheltering behind, Biggart stood tall to address the six men with their backs pressed up against the leaning Challenger. From the outset, he made it clear to his audience that they weren't going to be leaving the scene without the injured tank in tow. 'We are all of us going to do whatever it takes. Come hell or high water that tank is not falling into enemy hands!' He reassured them that they would be given whatever support they needed to subdue the enemy while they worked, but if they were feeling heartened by the Major's pep talk the men certainly didn't show it. All six stared back at him wide-eyed and silent. Sergeant Baird's hand wobbled a little as he lifted his cigarette to his mouth, his nerves still shredded by his ordeal inside the turret. 'The sooner it's done, the sooner we can get th—' Instinctively, they all ducked and clutched their ears when the deafening boom of Two Zero's main armament burst the air just a few yards away. '. . . we can get the hell out of here,' Biggart shouted. The shockwave from the round squeezed some air out of his lungs as he spoke.

At the moment he turned to leave, a wave of artillery rounds exploded in the sky above their heads like a massive thunderclap, filling the air and the scrubland with clouds of thick white smoke. Holding his helmet and hunching his shoulders, Biggart strode out through the haze and he was a few feet short of his vehicle when a smoke round crashed on top of one of the external spare fuel drums, setting light to the 175 litres of diesel as it gushed from the rear of his Challenger. A giant wall of flame leapt into the air as he clambered over the dust skirt and slid into the hatch with the sound of AK-47 rounds fizzing through the smoke. His driver immediately jockeyed the vehicle away from the blazing pool as Biggart put his headphones back on and switched to the Marines' frequency. He wanted Lieutenant Colonel Gordon Messenger, Officer Commanding 40 Commando, to push his men forward and dig in on either side of the road to prevent the enemy creeping up on the REME team as they worked in the open. Two minutes later his wish was granted. The Marines had been desperate to get involved in the battle from the moment it erupted but, fearful of a blue-on-blue incident in the very close quarters they were fighting, Biggart had requested they were held back until it was safe.

Now as the giant orange sun slid over the treetops to their left and the last of the light drained from the sky, the tanks needed as many boots on the ground around them as possible. Moments later two platoons of the Manoeuvre Support Group were on their way to assist. Within twenty minutes, the sixty Marines were spread out across the scrubland. Some took up position on the other side of the road to block any enemy advancing across the mile of drained marshland that rolled to the east, but most were laid up in ditches and scrapes facing the enemy treeline. With the TI system out of action, Sergeant Lamb's tank was effectively blind once night fell, so Biggart ordered Captain McLeman's Three Zero to join them.

By the time the reinforcements had arrived and the REME

crew got to work, the fighting had slackened slightly. The two sides continued to exchange bursts of machine-gun and assault rifle fire, but the RPGs and mortars had fallen silent. It went unmentioned, but privately every man was confident that the ferocious exchanges earlier had broken the Iraqi onslaught, the arrival of more units had punctured their morale altogether, and now only a few diehards and stragglers remained.

But that was no more than wishful thinking. Shortly after a coal-pitch blackness had cloaked the terrain, the treeline suddenly erupted in a blaze of muzzle flashes and tracer fire. It was as if someone had just turned on a giant light switch. The enemy was not yet finished. During the lull in the fighting, they had simply been regrouping, rearming and reinforcing, just as the British forces had been. Instantly, the Challengers and Marines launched a devastating reply. The muzzles of every coax, mounted GPMG and assault rifle flashed as one as the rounds hammered into the date palms, painting the black canvas of the night sky with stripes of bright red tracer. The smoke from the artillery rounds was still lingering in the air covering the REME team as they unhooked the broken winch and attached the new one. The Illumination flares, or 'looms', fired by the Marines bathed the trees in an opaque yellow light and lit up the clouds of smoke as they drifted slowly across the brush between the two enemy lines.

While Corporals Morgan, Simons and Parker worked on attaching the winch, Garrett sat in the hatch of the CRARRV giving his men close protection with the mounted GPMG. Exposed to the waist and with the tracer fire giving away his position in the gloom, he was more vulnerable than anyone involved in the operation and his bravery didn't go unnoticed by his colleagues as they scurried back and forth below him between the two vehicles. Further down the line of vehicles

Lance Corporal Bruce Fraser in Three Zero and Trooper Gillon in Four One were also out of their hatches on the gimpys, but being that much further away from the treeline they were more remote from the centre of the action and less likely to take a hit than Garrett.

As the fighting raged, the engineering team switched on the hydraulic winch and stood back. Looking through his sights, Biggart, in the next vehicle along, watched anxiously as the winch tensed and began to tug. To his surprise, the stricken Challenger appeared to respond as the CRARRV yanked with all its 100-ton might. As the recovery vehicle edged backwards and the winch slowly reeled in its catch, Baird's wagon slid along the ditch for a few moments.

It flipped over the edge of the ditch – and suddenly, there it was, horizontal on the causeway again.

A broad grin broke over the young sergeant's face as he watched his troubled vehicle rise from the dead. The cheers of the REME team were drowned out by the roar of the battle, but inside the turrets of the tanks there was unfettered relief. 'Thank God for that!' exclaimed Captain Le Sueur, rubbing his eyes with thumb and forefinger.

The three tanks south of Two One began to reverse slowly to give the CRARRV the room it needed to start dragging the Challenger down the road to the safety of Taku. Hauling the 75-ton lump of metal along the grit was only fractionally easier than pulling it clear of the ditch and it had taken ten minutes to drag it fifty yards when, to the horror of those looking on, the bank on the left suddenly gave way. The Challenger lurched sharply to its side and as the CRARRV responded by pulling harder, the winch cable tensed even tighter and then snapped. The two halves of the thick flexible metal cable shot in different directions and the left side of the

Challenger disappeared from view as it tilted and sank. Two One came to rest on its side in almost exactly the same position it had been stuck earlier, only more deeply wedged.

Major Biggart hammered his fist against the side of the cupola and Sergeant Baird, standing behind the CRARRV, put his face in his hands. He was too tired to weep. A bullet pinged against the armour a few feet away, but he didn't even flinch. He was almost beyond caring now. For about ten seconds, no one said or did anything. There was silence in the turrets and the REME team outside stared in disbelief at the bogged Challenger. The sound of the battle taking place a little over to their left faded to a muffled, distant roar. Major Biggart took a deep breath and called up Corporal Garrett over the radio. The Liverpudlian engineer told him he had only one option remaining: to cut off the tracks and try and reverse the tank out on its road wheels. The tracks, Garrett explained, were jammed so tight that the only way to remove them was to use arc-welding equipment. It would be a slow, painstaking procedure and as the bright sparks of the rotating welder would give away their position, it was highly dangerous too. There was no guarantee they could pull it off either but, he said, the only other option was to abandon it.

The sight of the Challenger coming to grief a second time galvanized the enemy as much as it demoralized Biggart and his men. Almost as soon as it came to rest in the ditch, a wave of dismounts swarmed out of the palms and raced towards the tanks. But they didn't get far. The Marines and Challenger crews, using their night vision capability to great advantage, cut them down before they had advanced more than twenty yards. The TI sights of the tank commanders and their gunners were swimming with hot spots, enabling them to bring accurate fire onto the enemy positions. It seemed that the Iraqis had no idea that the Challenger crews now had better eyes on them than they had in broad daylight.

In an effort to hide the sparks from the arc welder, the REME team hung up a poncho as a screen as they set about trying to cut the tank free of its tracks but its effect was negligible: the glow of the grinder was too bright. Baird and Mac lay alongside the vehicle, lending a hand when asked. Every few minutes they were forced to dive for cover when an RPG streaked towards them, a mortar shell exploded close by or a shower of bullets sprayed against the hull like a bag of grit on a window.

For two hours, the men braved the incoming rounds as they tried to slice through the central connectors, cursing their durability as they worked. Sparks lit up their grim faces under the helmets as the rotating cutter blade ground against the tracks. But no matter how hard the REME team tried, the tracks refused to give. The mud and water at the bottom of the ditch were making it impossible for the men to get a good arc with the welder but the main difficulty was the unbreakable tension of the tracks.

The most depressing aspect of the whole operation – and every crew member and engineer was painfully aware of it as the rounds flew back and forth – was that a small packet of plastic explosive would have blown the tracks and freed the tank in a matter of minutes. Until recently, all British tank support units, including those in the Second World War, carried plastic explosive for the very purpose of blowing thrown tracks, but it was withdrawn from use for Health and Safety reasons owing to the number of accidents it had been causing in training. A small lump of plastic explosive costs next to nothing, but in the absence of any here, a tank worth £5 million was in danger of being lost.

Corporal Garrett had been keeping up a steady stream of suppressive fire on the gimpy and overseeing the operation from the hatch of Two Four Charlie. It was nerve-shredding work but he never once harassed his team to work faster. When, finally, the men climbed out of the ditch, shrugged their shoulders and shook their heads, he knew the game was up. He called up Zero Bravo on the radio to give him the news.

'Is there *nothing* left we can try?' asked Biggart wearily.

'The winches are both gone, the grinders are making no impression, there's no plastic explosive . . .' He paused. 'Well, there is one very small chance.'

'Do it.'

Five minutes later, Three Three Bravo was back at the scene, complete with two metal A-frame drawbars and a pile of chains. Whether it was resourceful or just plain desperate, the unorthodox ploy was the very last chance. If this failed, they would have little choice but to stick a round in the Challenger, withdraw from the scene to regroup and continue Operation James without her at her first light. For 3 Commando Brigade and the Desert Rats, such an eventuality was no more than an operational setback. For the British war effort, it would be an embarrassment but one that would be quickly washed from the memory in the wake of other events. For the Fedayeen and the other Iraqi irregulars, it would be a stunning victory. But for Major Biggart, Captain Le Sueur, Sergeant Baird, Trooper Macawai and the six men of the two REME crews, rightly or wrongly, it would feel like a personal failure and a blight on their regiments. But after twelve hours of trying and twelve hours of fighting, it was shaping up as a likelihood they were just going to have to live with.

Unlike the winches, the A-frames were completely rigid and the CRAARV would only be able to pull on the tank along the angle at which they were fixed. When a tank became bogged, it was the more flexible winches that the crews turned to. Using A-frames to drag out bogged tanks was not part of the training manual. There was simply no give in them, so if the angle was right they had a chance – so long as they could put the bulky, cumbersome equipment on in the first place.

Putting an A-frame on a vehicle was difficult enough in a flat position and in ordinary circumstances. Immensely heavy, they are very difficult objects to move around with only a handful of men and hooking them to vehicles involves a certain degree of precision and patience in the most forgiving of circumstances. Shortly before deployment, an A-frame had been accidentally dropped while it was being moved and though it only fell twelve inches, it clean broke the thigh bone of one trooper. To attach one to a tank listing at over forty-five degrees, while under heavy fire, was immeasurably harder. That they managed to hook it up in just fifteen minutes was down in large part to the brute strength and determination of Mac. From the moment that the young, raw Fijian had rammed the tank into reverse earlier in the day, he had been at the heart of the day's drama and it was inspiring for his comrades to see him straining every fibre and muscle in his exhausted body to help pull his vehicle clear in one last-ditch effort. Without his strength, it was unlikely they would have managed to attach it. A mortar round burst just short of their position and an RPG streaked overhead as the last chains were attached between the two CRARRVS. The men jumped for cover.

'Three, two, one . . . now!' yelled Garrett.

As the drivers of the two CRARRVS stepped on their accelerators, the engines responded with a huge roar. The chains and A-frames stiffened under 150 tons' worth of tension. With the REME crew exhorting it out with shouts of encouragement, slowly, inch by inch, the tank crept up the side of the embankment. As it was raised onto the cusp of the ditch, the Challenger wobbled for several moments, uncertain which way to fall. The rescue team could barely bring themselves to watch as it teetered on the edge before, finally, its right-hand side collapsed on to the causeway with a slight bounce of its suspension amid a cloud of dust. Baird punched the air as it landed. Biggart switched on the radio: 'This is Zero Alpha. All units prepare to withdraw. Two One is clear. Well done the REME. Now let's get the hell out of here.' The entire group immediately began to make a fighting withdrawal. The six tanks and two CRAARVS, all still facing the enemy, slowly reversed away from a treeline still twinkling with muzzle flashes. Alongside them to the left, the Marines emerged from their scrapes and began to pull back.

A bright moon appeared from behind the clouds to reveal the dark silhouettes of the Marines, covering each other as they retreated in small packets over short distances: firing, running a few yards back, then hitting the deck, over and over again. Moving at no more than five miles an hour, the toiling CRARRVs took over ten minutes to drag Two One the mile to the bend in the road out of harm's way as the last streaks of tracer fire faded into the darkness. It was two thirty in the morning by the time Two One was hauled into the squadron hide at Taku from where it originally had set out almost twenty-four hours earlier. To the exhausted crews emerging from their hatches, it felt like a week earlier. But their work wasn't finished yet. As soon as they arrived they had to get to work on freeing Two One's jammed tracks so that it could make the twenty-mile journey back to the Battle Group HQ at Shaibah airfield, where it would undergo comprehensive repairs. It was dawn by the time the job was complete and one of the CRARRVs towed the battered, pock-marked main battle tank onto the tarmac and slowly disappeared from sight along the main highway, escorted by a fellow Challenger. At the same time, the Marines, supported by Captain Jameson's 4th troop, returned to the scene of the drama to complete the unfinished business of the day before. Within half an hour, the junctions of Pussy and Galore had been seized and the area secured.

Baird's Challenger had taken fourteen direct RPG strikes and an unknown amount of glancing hits; it had been hit head on with an anti-tank weapon in one of its softer spots, penetrating three inches into the armour, and it had been peppered with thousands of small-arms rounds from machine guns and automatic weapons. The extensive damage included the destruction of the commander's and gunner's sights, the met sensor, the commander's rear episcopes, the driver's periscope and sights, one smoke grenade discharger, the front headlights and horn, and the side tool bin. It had a hole the size of a large fist where the ATW had hit and its tracks and suspension were completely mangled.

But less than seventy-two hours later, call sign Two One was back in the frontline with all its component parts in full operational order.

9. Complex Terrain

By the first week of April, after ten days of relentless fighting, Basra was there for the taking. From Bridge One in the north to Bridge Five in the south, the Desert Rats of 7th Armoured Brigade were pressed up along a fifteen-mile stretch of the Shatt Al Basra shipping canal, overlooking an urban landscape choked by oil fires and towers of thick, black smoke. 3 Commando Brigade, supported by 'C' Squadron SCOTS DG, had mopped up the resistance in the suburbs along the Shatt Al Arab and pushed up to the eastern outskirts of the city. Repeated ground raids and precision air attacks had degraded the infrastructure of the Ba'ath party and the regular army to the extent that little physical evidence of them remained in the south. The headquarters and operating bases once occupied by these all-powerful institutions now lay in giant piles of rubble, eloquent symbols of the regime's implosion. But the fighting was by no means over – as Major Brannigan's 'B' Squadron and the Irish Guards were quick to discover after finally being called forward.

Held in reserve at Shaibah, the SCOTS DG Battle Group had spent six days watching the skyline erupt with explosions and listening to BBC World Service reports of the battles and raids involving every element of the Brigade – except them. Hearing all about the adventures of 'A' and 'C' Squadrons from the SQMS boys returning from replens in the field to restock at Shaibah only heightened the men's sense of redundancy. The traditionally healthy rivalry between squadrons and regiments was in danger of turning sour. There was only so much light jogging and lubricating of machinery that a man in a war zone can do before he begins to question his purpose as a soldier – and it wasn't a day too soon when the call to action from Brigade came through.

The battle group, minus 'C' Squadron, had been assigned to relieve the 1st Battalion Royal Regiment of Fusiliers and the 1st Battalion Black Watch. As Major Brown's 'A' Squadron returned from their dramatic raid up Route Red, Lieutenant Colonel Blackman and Major Brannigan, heading in the opposite direction, swept out of the airfield gates to lead their men up to the frontline. Warrior after Warrior full of Irish Guards, together with the echelon vehicles, followed them out in a convoy that took ten minutes to pass through. Stoked by a week of waiting in the wings, the battle group was radiating a palpable sense of purpose. It wasn't so much that they were desperate for a fight; they just wanted to *do* something, to get involved, to make their own contribution towards the effort of liberating the Iraqi people. They didn't want to return home with an empty box of experiences.

The designated area of operation for the SCOTS DG Battle Group covered Bridges Three to Five, but it was obvious from the moment they arrived there that Bridge Four and the area around Route Red was going to be the focus of their operations. It was here, along the principal route into the heart of Basra, that the Iraqis had dug in for what both sides knew was going to be the decisive encounter. Intelligence reports and aerial reconnaissance had revealed that the area at the northern end of Route Red had been turned into one massive system of layered defences, including a complex network of trenches, concrete 'Toblerone-style' barricades, oil fire ditches, with tanks dug in around every major junction and a series of operating bases on either side of the road. The defences were marshalled by several hundred highly trained Fedayeen militiamen, supplemented by up to 500 fanatical fighters from across the Arab world and backed up by a far larger but less committed force of Iraqi army regulars. Word was that the regulars, most of them already in civilian clothes in line with Fedayeen tactics, were likely to melt away into the city if and when the British began to squeeze the city harder.

Over the previous ten days the Fedayeen had stepped up the intensity and improved the quality of their attacks on the British based on the other side of the bridge. When the SCOTS DG arrived to conduct their relief in place with their combat-weary comrades in the Desert Rats, they were given an immediate taste of life on the frontline. The vehicles had barely pulled up at their operating base in DUNDEE when four mortar rounds fell through the bombed-out roof of the derelict Iraqi army transport depot. The Iraqis had witnessed the changing of the guard from their positions across the water and dropped in a small welcoming gift for the new incumbents. The shells landed just seconds apart in a succession of sharp blasts that echoed around the hangar-like building. The men dived for cover, while dozens of squeaking rats streamed out of the rubble.

'You'll get used to it after a while,' said one of the Black Watch, climbing into the back of his Warrior.

'What, the rats or the mortars?' asked Brannigan.

'Both. It's the flies, the heat and the stench of shit that gets you down,' he said cheerfully. 'There must have been over a thousand turds dropped in here over the last week.'

'Well, thanks.' Brannigan looked around at his squadron's new home. The 2,000lb JDAM had certainly had the desired effect. The remains of the roof and wrecked vehicles had been bulldozed to one side into giant piles of twisted metal, concrete and rubbish. Four leaning walls of twisted metal rods, beams and crumbling concrete, crazily distorted by the shattering impact of the strike, framed the blue sky. The reek of human excrement, made worse by the recent steep hike in the temperature, filled his nostrils. DUNDEE was indeed one mighty big shithole. The squadron's first task on arrival was to clear out and burn every last item of potentially hazardous waste – not for their personal comfort but to prevent an outbreak of disease.

For a week the two forces on either side of the canal had been squaring up to one another, each trying to tease the other out into the open. Day after day the mortars had rained down on the British positions in and around DUNDEE and the VCP on Bridge Four, fired from mobile units operating out of the residential and light-industrial areas a mile or two away over the bridge. The attacks had been slowly increasing in frequency and growing in accuracy as the enemy perfected their hit-and-run tactics and tried to lure the British into the city.

Often the attacks were aimed at the large crowds of civilians that congregated around the British positions during the day and the medics were kept busy tending to the many wounded. The enemy's default setting was to make life as awkward and uncomfortable for the British as possible, and if that meant shelling a few Shia women, children and elderly people in the process, then what the hell? Collateral damage was not an issue for the Fedayeen, but for the British it shaped the very way they fought. They were, as the media buzz phrase of the time had it, trying to win the 'hearts and minds' of the Iraqi people, to show them that they were there to help not harm them. It was an unintended, ironic consequence but, to some extent, the Fedayeen's actions were actually helping the British achieve that end. When the Fedayeen mortared the locals, the British came out to treat the casualties. It didn't take a professor of psychology to work out who the locals were going to look towards for protection.

Although the shelling was causing only moderate damage and a handful of casualties among the soldiers, it did succeed in unsettling the troops by depriving them of the few opportunities they had to sleep. And at night the tank crews faced a tough dilemma: did they sleep on the back decks as usual and risk being hit by a mortar or did they lie under the tank with dozens of massive rats running over their sleeping bags? Most chose to risk the mortars. Either way, they got next to no rest.

Squeezed at every angle by the Desert Rats and the Commandos, from the air and on the ground, the enemy's area of operation had shrunk by the day. Holed up in their labyrinth of defences, they were now ready for a fight to the death to thwart the Coalition's bid to take the city. The Fedayeen, which means 'those who sacrifice themselves' in Arabic, had nothing to lose but their lives. In the Shia-dominated south, the reviled enforcers of the Sunni-dominated regime, once commanded by Saddam's sons Uday and Qusay, had little to look forward to in a post-liberation era. In all likelihood, they were going to be seized by the mob when, if, Basra fell to the British. It was better then to die for their cause than be battered to a pulp by vengeful Shias. As for the foreign fighters, fired by religious zeal, they had the consolation of certain martyrdom to soften the blow of any military defeat they might suffer. In a way, they couldn't lose.

As a fighting force, the enemy may have been a motley collection, but they were diehards. Over the previous week they had shown a high degree of combat skills as well as – and their British opponents were the first to admit it – a great deal of courage. Or was it lunacy? That depended on how you defined the quality of character that motivated a foot soldier to hurl himself into the path of an oncoming main battle tank. Either way, the fourteen Challenger crews of 'B' Squadron, supported by two companies of Irish Guards, were going to have to fight for every yard of territory along the five-mile stretch of Route Red from Bridge Four up to the major road junction just south of Old Basra where 'A' Squadron had blown up the statue of Saddam Hussein.

In Major Brannigan, a bullish Londoner of Irish background whose father had served in the Paras, the SCOTS DG had just the man for the job.

There are a number of Army officers who don't enjoy the combat element of being a soldier as much as laymen may suppose, but for Major Brannigan there were few things he enjoyed more about his job than a good skirmish from time to time. Brannigan had fought in the first Gulf War, where he had served as an infantry platoon commander with the Royal Scots before transferring to the SCOTS DG in 1996 following the post-Cold War restructuring of the Army.

When the deployment of British forces was announced in the Commons on 20 January, Lieutenant Colonel Blackman turned to Brannigan to carry out the highly unenviable, complicated task of merging 'B' and 'D' Squadrons, both of them under-strength, into a tight, well-drilled fighting unit. His bruising style of management was not popular with everyone at first, but he soon gained the respect of his men for his fairness, loyalty and lack of airs. It was perhaps his infantry background that meant he was just as comfortable getting his hands filthy in the tank park with his men as he was enjoying a glass of Pol Roger leaning on the mantelpiece of the offi-cers' mess, holding his own with the Oxbridge graduates and other intellectuals of the regiment. With a BA in Classics and an MA in Defence and International Relations, he had the brains to complement the brawn.

Whereas 'A' and 'C' Squadrons had enjoyed the luxury of a full training year, Brannigan and his 2iC, Captain Matheson, had less than two weeks to get their men and machines ship-shape and Bristol-fashion. It was an extremely daunting task but twelve days after Blackman had given him the nod, the fourteen tanks of 'B' Squadron, all in perfect working order, rolled onto the wagons at the railhead outside the Fallingbos-tel barracks, ready to be transferred to the ships at Emden docks on Germany's North Sea coast. The machines of the squadron were one challenge but overhauling the men was even more taxing. For that, Brannigan made the most of the softer diplomatic skills of Captain Matheson as much as his own force of personality to bring it about without too much damage to egos and reputations. Though very different char-acters, it was obvious after only a few days that they were going to enjoy a solid working partnership.

In Captain Ally Gemmell and Captain Ran De Silva, he already had two extremely professional and competent men in place to lead 1st and 2nd troops, while Lieutenant John Stone, whom he brought in from 'D' Squadron to lead 4th troop, was one of the best young officers in the regiment. He could hand tasks to those three all day long confident in the knowledge that they would carry them out without difficulty. That left 3rd troop – and this is where it got complicated. Overlooking the claims of several eligible officers, Brannigan went for the controversial call by opting for Staff Sergeant Jamie 'Dodger' Gardiner.

Alongside 'A' Squadron's Staff Sergeant Hanson and 'C' Squadron's Sergeant Lamb, Gardiner was the stand-out NCO at the time. But in order to bring the man into his inner circle, Brannigan was going to have to spill some diplomatic blood on the officers' mess carpet by sacking a young, well-connected subaltern who, understandably, was not at all amused about being removed from his post. It was not, to say the least, a decision taken or received lightly – and it was the talk of the barracks for some time – but, if nothing else, it sent out an unequivocal message to the men under his command that the new Squadron leader was prepared to do whatever it took to carry out his job. Even Gardiner, grateful for the vote of confidence, was forced to tell him privately: 'You are one ruthless bastard, sir!' And that from a man who once laid out two US Marines for bad-mouthing the British Army and taking too long in the shower.

'You're right about that, Dodger,' he admitted. 'And I've put my neck on the line and taken a big gamble on you. Don't let me down.'

Two months later, looking out across the Shatt Al Basra at the city smouldering on the horizon, the two men were about to discover whether they could deliver on the reputations that preceded them.

When to take Basra was the big question facing the General Staff and politicians. In spite of a number of false alarms, the Shia-led insurgency – the trigger for British troops to enter the city – stubbornly refused to materialize. With the locals flooding back and forth across the bridges every day, there was no shortage of Intelligence coming out of the city. From what they were hearing on the ground, the British quickly gleaned that, mindful of the Coalition failure to support them in 1991, the Baswaris were too frightened to risk a repeat of the bloody crackdown that had followed their uprising then. The message grew clearer by the day: if the Brits wanted Basra, they were going to have to go in and take it for themselves. Whether the British had the forces to hold the city was another matter altogether, but they certainly had enough boots and firepower on the ground to capture it. The challenge was to do that without killing any of the swarms of non-combatants trying to go about their daily lives.

The approach adopted by Lieutenant Colonel Blackman was to sit on the outskirts, soak up the enemy fire, probe their positions and gradually wear down their defences, their manpower and their will to fight on. So it was that for several days a Mexican stand-off gradually turned into a mutual battle of attrition. The two sides duelled and sparred across the waterway, with the British using coax, main armament and the odd air or artillery strike. The enemy deployed snipers and mortars and the occasional packet of assorted armoured vehicles.

The battle group mounted two or three raids a day – or 'thunder runs' as they became known – up Route Red and into the surrounding districts; the Iraqis responded with RPGs and a barrage of mortars. Most of the raids were carried out at first light before the civilians began to pour out of the slum buildings of the Al-Hayyaniyah district in the centre of the city. The Fedayeen had built a huge makeshift barricade and firing platform at 'Red 4' – a junction halfway along the four-mile route leading up to the so-called Gateway to Basra – and on one or two occasions a raiding party of Challengers or Warriors was able to push right up to the positions without receiving a single incoming bullet. On other raids, through what appeared to be quieter, non-militarized districts, all hell broke loose. The situation was fluid, volatile and unpredictable. With the enemy mingling among the civilian population, the British troops were having to be especially vigilant, and especially careful.

Within a few days, each troop, each call sign, had been involved in significant engagements. Some of the most intense exchanges took place at night when the civilians had retreated to the city centre and the battle group had greater freedom to engage targets. On the first night, Gemmell's 1st troop, sitting on the south side of the bridge, directed some artillery onto a troublesome sniper bunker inside the Technical College – at just under a mile across the bridge on the left-hand side, the campus buildings were the closest ones to the British operating base. Two weeks earlier, the college had been home to thousands of students, attending lectures and tutorials. Now, it had effectively become the enemy's Forward Operating Base (FOB), a hornets' nest of paramilitary activity. The next night, Lieutenant Stone's 4th troop teamed up with a passing US AC-130 Spectre gunship to take out some armoured vehicles and a mortar team they spotted inside the college. Sergeant Andy Pearce, of Gemmell's 1st troop, destroyed a small raiding party of Russian-built light tanks and armoured personnel carriers that had foolishly tried to creep up on the British positions from the Bravo residential area opposite the College on the right-hand side of Route Red looking into Basra. Staff Sergeant Gardiner dispatched a mortar team that had been tormenting a platoon of Irish Guards with an inch-perfect HESH round. When the harassed platoon commander came over the radio to ask if anyone had spotted the mortar unit, Gardiner replied laconically: 'Aye, it's aboot 200 yards up in the air reet noo.'

At the end of each day, every tank crew had a tale to tell. The inactivity and relative comforts of Shaibah airfield quickly became a distant memory. And day by day the temperature climbed a degree or two higher towards the mid-thirties. The oppressive heat and humidity coincided with an eruption of black flies and an outbreak of D&V amongst the troops that left half the squadron badly dehydrated and debilitated. Most, however, refused to admit to it in case they were removed from the frontline and sent back to Shaibah to recuperate. The fighting intensified as the four troops of 'B' Squadron, led by Brannigan and Matheson, operating between eighteen and twenty-two hours a day, in conjunction with the Micks, kept probing the enemy defences. In between the raids the REME fitter section, commanded by Staff Sergeant 'Tiffy' Hinson, were playing a vital role behind the scenes. While the Challenger crews snatched an hour's sleep, Hinson and his men, covered head to toe in oil and grease, cheerfully set to work on patching up the tanks and handing out the brews. Ninety-five per cent of the battle group had never previously experienced combat, but after just three days of fighting the men had settled into the rhythms of war as if they were veterans, months into a campaign. The exhaustion and physical strains, the illness, the heat, the filth and flies, the fear and exhilaration of combat, the weight loss, the wreckage of battle, the choking black smoke of the oil fires, the desperate civilians . . . in no time, all this had become part of the daily routine; the huge experiences and emotions marshalled and kept in check by the discipline drummed into them by years of training.

The intensity and complexity of the fighting on Route Red was dramatically illustrated by an incident involving the two tanks of Squadron HQ on the fourth morning. Major Brannigan and Captain Matheson were conducting security overwatch at the entrance to the Technical College halfway up the dual carriageway, pulling over the various models of pick-up trucks that the paramilitaries were using to get around the battle area, and searching them on the side of road. It was mid-morning and waves of civilians were rolling up and down the road, some of them on foot, others in cars, a few on donkeys and carts. Most of the vehicles the soldiers stopped contained nothing more sinister than boxes of fresh tomatoes from the outlying farms – but, as always, there were a small number of rotten ones amongst the good majority. Parked up amongst the bustling throng in which they knew the enemy were mingling with the civilians, the tank crews and the Irish Guardsmen working alongside them had to be especially vigilant.

Brannigan and Matheson, positioned either side of the central reservation, were keeping watch from their tanks and the dismounted Irish Guardsmen were busy overseeing the inspection of a truck when the numbers of people in the street moving down the road suddenly began to swell dramatically. At the same time more vehicles began to appear from the side roads. From previous experience, they knew this could mean only one thing: the Fedayeen were on the move. The Fedayeen often sent crowds, at the point of a gun, rushing down the road towards the British positions in order to cover their own movements of men and equipment. A mile away three cars, one of them a red pick-up truck, were careering erratically in and out of the traffic, racing towards the vehicle checkpoint on Brannigan's side of the central reservation. Veering out onto the side of the road for a few seconds before ducking back into the traffic, it was as if they were trying to conceal their approach. Brannigan alerted Matheson over the radio, giving a target identification, and both call signs immediately acquired the vehicles in their gun sights. The day before, the battle group had been warned about the threat of suicide car bombers targeting British troops following a series of incidents involving US forces in which decoy cars advanced with the real threat. This bore all the hallmarks of such an attack.

'I don't like this. They're getting too close, too fast. Fire some warning shots,' Brannigan ordered his own gunner and Zero Charlie, Matheson's Challenger over to the right.

Almost immediately, bursts of coax flew over the top of the oncoming vehicles. Two of the cars instantly pulled over to the side of the road, but the red pick-up just kept coming. The chassis of the car was low to the ground, suggesting it was laden with something considerably heavier than a few pounds of tomatoes.

'Charlie Charlie One, this is Zero Charlie, suspect car bomber, red pick-up truck, heading towards us!' said Matheson, warning all call signs in the area.

With rank comes responsibility and this was a major decision, with lives hanging on it, that had to be made in a matter of seconds. Opening fire with heavy machine guns in the vicinity of innocent, frightened civilians was not a decision to be taken lightly, but given the threat of a suicide bomber slaughtering dozens of bystanders and British troops alike, they were fast running out of options.

'Fire into the ground in front of them!'

The vehicle was now no more than 500 yards away as the rounds kicked up the dust and a spray of sparks on the carriageway – but still the pick-up kept coming. It was just seconds away from their positions – so close they could see that there were two occupants, both in white dishdash robes and red headscarves.

'Take out its engine!' shouted Matheson to his gunner. Brannigan's tank, head on to the pick-up, opened fire simultaneously.

Two streams of coax shot from the Challengers, riddling the bonnet and grille and sending a shower of sparks spraying over the windscreen. The pick-up petered to a stop ten yards short of the checkpoint with steam and smoke rising from the engine.

'Casualties! Get the medics!' Brannigan shouted at his loader, Sergeant Al Hainey. The Major could see the passenger slumped against the door. The driver got out of the car with his hands up and walked round to the other side. He pulled open the passenger seat door and the blood-sodden corpse of his travelling companion fell out into the dirt. One of the rounds had passed through the engine and killed him instantly. There were no explosives or weapons in the car but the officers' instincts had been right. When the Irish Guards searched it they found thousands of dollars in cash and a hit list of targets – mainly Az Zubayr 'collaborators' known to be hostile to the Saddam regime. The body of the dead man was taken away by medics, the driver for questioning, and the suspect items were passed on to Intelligence Officers. There was stunned silence in both turrets. Back at base, commanders and crews talked through an episode which had illustrated so alarmingly the complexity of the conditions in which they were operating and the speed with which they had to make life-and-death decisions. It is in these difficult, upsetting instances that a tank crew pulls together even tighter and the men of both call signs broke up from their meetings in a better state of mind and soul for having aired their feelings.

During a ferocious week of raids and counter-attacks, each tank had fired dozens of HESH rounds and thousands of rounds of coax – and the stress of combat was starting to take its toll in all manner of ways. Most servicemen don't see the consequences of their firing. They simply fire and forget.

But for the tankie, the fighting is very immediate and very graphic. The magnification sights quite simply magnify the experience of killing people. For the commander and the gunner, the enemy is right in their faces. The images are often shocking and nauseating: when a gunner fires a burst of coax into a human body from close range, it explodes heads, shreds flesh, takes off limbs and cuts torsos in half. For most gunners and commanders caught up in an engagement, the instinct to survive, to kill rather than be killed, overrides the natural feelings of revulsion. But that's not the case for everyone, and for one or two of the younger gunners, barely out of school and exhausted by weeks of little or no sleep, the brutality of the engagements on Route Red overwhelmed them on occasions. Unable to concentrate properly, they froze up occasionally or began firing erratically.

For one, the moment he baulked came when he saw a stray dog carrying away the arm of a man he had just dismembered with a stream of coax. When the commander realized what was happening, he took control of the gun himself – and once they returned to base, he took the young gunner aside for a quiet word of reassurance and encouragement. Every young man responds differently when the bullets start flying and the rounds start landing, and there was no shame or disgrace in the reaction of the small handful of men who, from time to time, found themselves shocked and disgusted by the bloody reality of battle. The incidents were kept within the crew so as not embarrass the men involved. A tank crew sticks together, whatever. What happens in the turret, stays in the turret.

Fighting a war in the midst of a local population was an enterprise fraught with all manner of risks, dangers and surprises as the experiences of 1st troop reminded them the following day. Patrolling through one of the impoverished residential areas close to the Technical College, the tanks were rumbling slowly down the broad main street, scanning for trouble. The slums were a densely populated area and the streets were busy with shoppers and traffic. The locals waved and smiled and there was not a hint of trouble in the air. When the small armoured column slowed and came to a temporary halt at a junction, the driver of call sign One Two, commanded by Corporal Martin Smith, opened his hatch at the front of the tank. A woman crossed the road in front of him and, in a strong Birmingham accent, turned to him and beamed. 'Morning! You lads enjoying yourselves in Basra then?' The startled driver fell into conversation with the woman, who explained she had married an Iraqi and moved to Basra to raise a family. 'I'll never go back. Basra's much nicer, even when there's a war going on.' She smiled. 'I would ask you all in for a cup of tea, but you look quite busy. Anyway nice meeting you, tara for now!' And with a little wave and a flash of teeth from under her headscarf, she disappeared into the crowd. A few minutes later, the column turned a corner and re-emerged onto Route Red – and straight into a hail of small-arms and RPG fire from a posse of Fedayeen. 'Complex terrain', as the military term has it, didn't come much more complex than Route Red.

This was the pattern of life on the main route into Basra from the Al Faw. When the opposing forces weren't engaging each other, hundreds of civilians emerged onto Route Red from the residential side streets, coming and going as if there was nothing more menacing happening in their midst than a football match. One minute the soldiers were talking to groups of grinning children at the side of the road, the next they were scrambling for cover and exchanging fire with a mobile mortar unit.

The good humour, warmth and hardiness of the majority of locals never ceased to amaze the British troops, but the 'normal life' around them made for a strange and awkward setting for a war.

At first light on 3 April, the fifth day since being called forward, Major Farrell's No. 2 Company Irish Guards attacked the Technical College to try and flush out the dozens of snipers, mortar teams and other dismounted combatants that had been causing endless problems for the better part of two weeks. Braced for a major encounter, to their surprise, the only resistance they met was a lone gunman. The enemy, it turned out, had seen them coming and withdrawn to their deeper, better defensive positions to fight another day. After securing the College for the battle group to move into as their HQ, Farrell's party raided further up the route, where they were met by far stiffer resistance but still succeeded in destroying a number of enemy positions and seized large stockpiles of weapons.

At the same time, pushing as far north as they could, a packet of 'B' Squadron tanks, led by Captain Matheson, mounted an aggressive raid into the rundown residential area known as the Bravos on the other side of Route Red from the Technical College.

They too encountered only light resistance in amongst the broad, dusty streets, the single-storey buildings and light-industrial units, but as they pulled back onto Route Red, Corporal David 'Thommo' Thompson, commander of Three Two, reported the sighting of a fuel tanker, a mile to the north, parking up close to the barrier structures at Red 4. Half a dozen men, with weapons slung over their backs, were dashing around the vehicle while a crowd of civilians looked on. Two of the men were removing the filler hose from its fastenings.

Captain Matheson knew he had to act quickly. Oil fire trenches had caused constant problems for raiding parties in the days previous. Once lit, they burned for days, filling the air with thick acrid smoke. When the wind was in the right direction they were effective in obscuring the activities of the para-militaries behind and they played havoc with the tanks' thermal-imaging capabilities, making it impossible for the commanders to pick out heat sources against a background or foreground of raging fires. A number of fires had been burning all week up and down the route, but if they succeeded in lighting one next to the Red 4 barricades, it would prevent the CRARRVs from getting close to the barricades to shove them aside. The barricades needed to be removed at all costs in order to open up the route for the battle group to make deeper incursions into the enemy's defensive positions.

'Three Two, this is Zero Charlie. Fire warning shots, and then engage the tanker,' said Captain Matheson. The two tanks pushed further up the road, making themselves more visible to the crowd, firing long bursts of coax high over their heads as they advanced. Instantly, all the civilians in the immediate vicinity sprinted for cover, but the shots had the opposite effect on the armed men, who started working even faster to start releasing the oil. The Challengers spat out two further streaks of coax, but still the men refused to move.

Captain Matheson gave the order to engage.

'HESH! Tanker HESH!' the two commanders barked over their intercoms, as they lined up the centre of the tanker in their sights and lased it. The gunners fired and the tanker instantly erupted in a spectacular ball of orange flames and a cloud of black smoke that steepled high into the air. Such was the scale of the eruption that both men instinctively pulled away from the raging flames that filled their vision and appeared to envelop their vehicles. As the fire raged wildly, Matheson saw his opportunity. There was not a civilian in sight and the enemy had either fled or been incinerated in the spewing flames. Over the radio, he called up the CRARRV from the rear and began to advance.

Great slabs of reinforced concrete made up the bulwark of the obstacles, but they were augmented by all manner of large cumbersome objects that the enemy were able to tow to the location: trailers, trucks, vans, old cars, and indeterminate lumps of scrap metal and hardcore. Whenever they were within range, and provided there were no civilians in the area, the Challenger crews had taken every opportunity to fire HESH rounds into the concrete blocks. Dozens of rounds were brought to bear on the monolithic structures, but they succeeded in taking no more than a few lumps out of them. The barricades were too close to residential housing to call in an air strike, so the only option was for a CRARRV to shunt the obstacles out of the way with its dozer plough and fill in the neighbouring oil trenches with earth before the enemy made a further attempt to get at them.

Route Red was empty when the Challengers began to roll forward but when they were half a mile from the barricade, a surge of traffic, human and vehicular, suddenly poured onto the carriageways and began to flood towards the pile of obstructions. At the same time, a large truck that formed part of the barricade between the concrete bulwarks was driven out of the way, 'opening the gates' for the traffic to pour through. Captain Matheson looked through his sights at the gathering crowd. 'Bollocks!' he muttered. Ordering throngs of cars and civilians out into the open at gunpoint was a standard Fedayeen tactic. It was dangerous too as it gave the enemy, mingling with the civilians, the opportunity to get up close to the tanks and cause trouble. It would only take a couple of explosives or mines under the tracks of a Challenger to cause a major incident.

The traffic rushed towards the approaching tanks, and the street was suddenly so busy up and down its entire length that firing warning shots over their heads was no longer an option. Unable to communicate with them in any other way, Matheson opened up his hatch, wincing and blinking as he felt the blast of the late-morning sun on his face. As he appeared from the bowels of the tank, the crowd let out a giant cheer and began waving and clapping wildly. Children grinned and jumped down, as if amazed that human beings were to be found inside the massive armoured vehicles. It was an awkward moment for the young captain. The crowd could not have given him a warmer welcome had they placed a garland of flowers around his neck and handed him the keys to the city, but it was imperative that he got them out of the way if they were to have any chance of shifting the barricades. He gestured at them with his arm to move to the side, but this triggered only more applause and celebration. He slipped out of view and back into his seat and began to laugh uncontrollably. 'This is bloody absurd!' he said to himself, trying to regain his composure and put on a straight face. He stood up again, this time with his face set hard and began shouting angrily and gesticulating with sharp movements that left the crowd in no doubt that they were to move from their path. The mob, suddenly looking crestfallen, began to part and the vehicles swept into the gap. As the CRARRV accelerated up to the barricade, scattering civilians into the central reservation and the side of the road, the tanks went into overwatch. The powerful recovery vehicle made short work of the barriers, shunting the concrete blocks and other assorted obstacles into a pile of wreckage in the scrubland. As soon as that task was complete, the crew set about bulldozing mounds of earth into the oil fire trench alongside the barricades, putting it beyond use once and for all. The unscripted operation was a major breakthrough for the battle group in more than just a physical sense. It had effectively opened up Basra.

Removing the barrier was not just a practical move; it was a symbolic gesture and a psychological blow against the enemy. Watching their heaviest physical defences being brushed aside like debris into a dustpan can only have had a dispiriting effect on the Fedayeen soldiers watching from their observation positions and operating bases further up the route. As the CRAARV cleared the route with a few thrusts of its dozer blade, the message to the diehards of a dying regime was clear and compelling: *You better get ready because we're coming in to get you.*

10. The Battle for Route Red

As soon as the Irish Guards had secured the Technical College, the rest of the battle group, in broad daylight and in full view of the local population and the Fedayeen, roared over the Shatt Al Arab in a giant convoy. For half an hour, vehicle after vehicle swept down the northern slope of Bridge Four and onto Route Red to move into their new operating base. Cheered by passing civilians, the column turned left off the dual carriageway, streamed through the college gates and set up home in the campus buildings. The SCOTS DG HQ was now no more than a mile from the first line of the enemy's impressive mile-deep defensive network. As the British soldiers set up home in the accommodation quarters and tutorial rooms of the campus, Commanding Officer Blackman quickly set about planning the next phase of operations. Less than a five-minute drive away, in a large industrial-style build-ing on the same side of the road, his Fedayeen counterparts, on seeing the opposition tighten the stranglehold on their positions, began drawing up their own plans to try and thwart him. After five days of probing and skirmishing, Blackman determined that it was time to ramp up the intensity of the raids and push a little further north.

The plan was to launch a series of aggressive patrols up to the southern end of the heavily defended positions, assess enemy strengths and positions and gather other relevant Intel-ligence for future operations. The first raids, launched the following morning, began, as always, at daybreak before the civilians had emerged. Major Farrell's No. 2 Company Irish Guards group disappeared into the maze of residential streets close to the Technical College, drawing a weight of fire from RPG teams and snipers that had become standard over the previous days. The 'B' Squadron group – 1st and 2nd troops, led by Captain Matheson – stayed out in the open terrain of Route Red, tentatively pushing north to the junction at Red 4. As the seven Challengers approached the junction, they came under attack from dismounts operating in the scrubland on either side of the road. Captain Gemmell's 1st troop went firm around the junction as Captain De Silva, with 2iC Matheson close behind, pushed through. De Silva took the right-hand side of the dual carriageway, while Troop Sergeant Andy Potter and Corporal Hamilton were on the left. Moving at around 15mph past the massive TV mast felled by 'A' Squadron a week earlier, the raiding party engaged several pockets of resistance operating from within the communications compound on the one side and the Fedayeen operating base on the other. RPGs fizzed through the air, glancing off the sloping armour of the vehicles, as the Challengers responded with bursts of coax. As the tanks approached the next major junction, Red 5, at the southern perimeter of the College of Literature, the fighting intensified. There was not a civilian in sight as the rounds ripped back and forth and the tanks began pushing further north than any had been since Captain Walters' troop had destroyed the statue of Saddam Hussein, half a mile up the road at the Gateway to Basra in the 'A' Squadron raid.

Captain De Silva, in Two Zero, was scanning over to the right, while his gunner pumped streams of coax towards the enemy position that he had lased seconds earlier. At the same time, the two tanks over to the left were engaging a string of bunkers on the other side of the road. De Silva's firing arcs were twelve o'clock to three, while Sergeant Potter covered twelve down to nine. The fighting was as intense as any they had experienced since the battle group had been called forward; the enemy infanteers were proving difficult to pin down as they raced between positions, dodging behind walls, and in and out of trenches and buildings. HESH rounds were brought to bear on some bunkers, sending plumes of soft earth shooting into the air, but the fighting never slackened.

What took place next stunned the raiding party. It all happened in an ace. Captain Matheson, following on the right-hand carriageway, had the best view of it as Captain De Silva's tank crossed Red 5 and rolled forward with its chain gun spitting rounds into the dusty scrubland off to the right. Looking through his sights, the 2iC saw first a small glint over to the left, followed almost immediately by an almighty giant explosion where De Silva's tank had been moving and firing just a moment earlier. A bright flash followed by a cloud of dust, shrapnel and smoke enveloped De Silva's tank. It was no more than a few seconds, but it felt much longer as Matheson stared in disbelief, convinced De Silva and his crew had just been blown to kingdom come. Two Zero had been struck by an enemy tank. But the 2iC's feelings of horror just as quickly turned to heart-stirring elation as the air over the Challenger began to clear and he saw its turret swing round to the left and come to rest with the main gun pointing up the road. Flicking to high magnification on the sights, Captain Matheson could see De Silva's quarry – a T-55 hull down in the scrubland, with only the top half of its turret and main gun visible above the baked earth.

Two Zero, the first British tank to be hit by the main round of an enemy tank since the invasion began, had been struck on its explosive reactive armour (ERA) below the main gun. The ERA tiles, fitted as part of the up-armouring process back in Kuwait, had done exactly what they were designed to do: neutralize the effect of the incoming round. But it was a close shave. A few inches higher, where the turret joins the hull, the damage could have been catastrophic. In exactly the right spot it could even have lifted the turret clean off. As it was, to Two Zero's crew, the impact felt no more uncomfortable than if they had driven over a deep pothole. The problem was that they appeared to have been blinded by the strike. Through their sights and episcope they had seen a giant white flash of flame that made them recoil in their seats – and then nothing. The world outside had gone dark. Unable to see through his sights, De Silva peered through the tiny periscopes fitted around the top of his cupola and immediately realized the problem. The camnet which had been strapped to the front of the tank had been flung into the air during the explosion and come to rest over the turret, blocking the views from inside.

De Silva immediately traversed the turret and the camnet slipped from the tank into the road. As he did so, Sergeant Potter came over the radio: 'Two Zero, this is Two One. T-55, hull down, half a mile ahead, to left of road.' Simultaneously, the two tanks brought their main guns to bear on the T-55. Both had HESH up the barrel. De Silva fired a split second before his Troop Sergeant.

'HESH! Tank! Load FIN!' he shouted over the intercom. Sergeant Potter barked the same order a hundred yards away. Barely had the two high-explosive rounds slammed into the tank when two FIN rounds followed them up the road and sliced through the armour. At exactly the same time, the Challengers of 1st troop, several hundred yards behind, opened up on the brave but hapless T-55, adding their own barrage to an already formidable weight of ordnance that obliterated the target. Fifteen seconds after the audacious commander of the T-55 had taken the brave decision to engage the Challenger, his tank had been annihilated, killing any of the crew foolish enough to have remained inside. As the rounds cooked off, the pressure inside the turret began to build, smoke and flames belched from the sides and suddenly the turret appeared to jump out of the ground in one massive explosion and slumped back down in a heap of twisted, smouldering black metal.

Just over a mile away to the west, the Irish Guards were encountering equally determined resistance. Clearing out a house being used by the paramilitaries, one Lance Corporal was set upon by a knife-wielding Fedayeen as he kicked down the door. The two men were touching when the Guardsman pumped five rounds into his assailant, while holding the door open with his foot to allow the rest of the section to pour into the building. During the withdrawal one of the Warriors received two direct RPG hits from close range, one of which knocked out its sights. As the raiding party pulled back towards the Technical College, they came under heavy fire from enemy positions on both sides of the road. The 'B' Squadron tanks responded with withering broadsides of HESH and coax, leaving a trail of smoke and flames in their wake as they disappeared into the compound of the Technical College.

On their return the raiding parties reported their astonishment at the sheer number and complexity of defensive positions at the top end of Route Red. It wasn't just that the layered trench network was so elaborate and extensive; it was the attention to detail that the parties found most disconcerting. Mortar pits had been dug on and alongside the road, each of them concealed with a metal cover; sniper rifles and RPGs had been laid out on rooftops and other key vantage points. The layout of the defences gave fluidity to the enemy tactics, allowing them to move from position to position, controlled by their commanders using mobile phones. The infantry were trained to operate against this sophisticated, urban guerrilla type of warfare but it was a very far cry from the training exercises that tank crews carry out on the wide open ranges of northern Germany and Salisbury Plain. As one of the commanders commented on his return to base: 'If the Iraqis fight as well as they have prepared, then we're in for a hell of a scrap. We couldn't have built better defences ourselves.'

To the Iraqis, the area around the top of Route Red was known as the Gateway to Basra; to the British soldiers, it was simply Red 6. Whatever people choose to call the location, the raids that day, the deepest and most concerted so far into Basra, confirmed that that this corner of the city, rich in history and symbolism, was where the enemy had chosen to dig in, concentrate all his resources and make the British fight for every yard of ground. The day's incursions towards the heart of the city had given the hornets' nest a good kicking – and the hornets were beside themselves with fury. The plan for the next day was to kick it even harder. In a two-pronged advance, the SCOTS DG battle group would attempt to push up to and secure Red 6, while the Black Watch Battle Group, three miles to the north-west, were to advance into the heart of the city along a parallel road known as Route Yellow. In planners' jargon, the aim of the raids was to assess the command and control capabilities of the enemy and observe how he responded to multiple threats. In squaddie talk, as one trooper put it, they were going to be 'jumping the bags and getting in the face of the Feds'.

The local saying, they kept being told, was: *Who takes the Gateway to Basra, takes Basra.* At dawn, the SCOTS DG battle group were to find out whether there was any truth in the old dictum.

Staff Sergeant Gardiner put his forearm against the rear of the tank, looked around to check no one could see him and then leant forward and spewed a pint of watery vomit into the dust between his boots. Head down and rubbing his cramping stomach, he walked round the side of his Challenger, call sign Three Zero, and bumped straight into Major Brannigan.

'Ah, Dodger, I've been looking for you. You all set? H-hour in five minutes. The Colonel wants us all mounted up and ready to roll.'

'Aye, sir.'

'You all right, Dodger? You look bloody awful!' said the Squadron leader squinting through the darkness. 'I hope you haven't got that bloody D&V! I've got a feeling there's going to be a lot of trigger time today.'

'Nae worries, boss. I'm just a wee bit tired, that's all.' Gardiner felt his stomach spasm and he put his hand to his mouth as he swallowed the sick back down. 'Yep, nae dramas, Major.'

'Good man!' Brannigan said, giving the burly senior NCO a hearty slap on the back.

It was coming up to seventy-two hours since any solids had passed the young troop leader's lips and the bug was showing no sign of receding. He had barely slept during that time either – or for the previous four days for that matter – and his aching body was crying out for some rest. He was one of dozens in the squadron to be struck down with the diarrhoea and vomiting bug since the outbreak had erupted shortly after they moved up from Shaibah. Like the others, Gardiner went through the charade of pretending he was in perfectly good health. Hauling himself over the armoured dust skirt up onto the turret he paused before opening the hatch and clung on to the cupola as his head swooned and spun. He had felt faint and dizzy yesterday as well, but as soon as the first rounds of the day's early-morning raids up to Red 6 had been fired, the adrenaline kicked in and carried him through the day.

As he pulled open the hatch, a cloud of black flies swarmed out of the turret in a chorus of buzzing. He waved his arm across his face, cursing as he batted them away, and slid through the hatch. The now all too familiar smell of unwashed bodies and cordite from the dozens of HESH rounds they had fired recently sat heavy in the small, cramped interior of the fighting compartment. No one said a word inside the turret: they were too tired or ill, and after seven days of raids and aggressive patrolling the crews knew the routine now. The Staff Sergeant took out his two remaining Imodium anti-diarrhoea pills and washed them down with a draught from his plastic water bottle.

'Good morning, crew!' he said over the intercom with mock cheer.

'Morning, boss,' they groaned in chorus.

Gardiner's tank sat at the front on the right of two columns of a huge armoured formation of vehicles lined up in the heart of the Technical College. Fourteen tanks and twenty-eight Warriors, together with ambulances, CRARRVs, Sultans and Spartans, waited in the darkness in radio silence. Gardiner watched the second hand of his watch make the final circuit of the dial towards H-hour. Bang on cue, Lieutenant Colonel Blackman's voice broke the radio silence: 'Three, two, one . . . Move!' As one, the engines of almost fifty vehicles bellowed a thunderous roar, the tracks beneath clenched around the road wheels and bit into the dust as the columns moved forward. At exactly the same time, an identical formation of Black Watch Warriors, with the Challengers of Major Brown's 'A' Squadron leading the way, began to cross the Shatt Al Arab to the north. The biggest raid into Basra so far was underway. It was 0530 local time.

As his Challenger lurched forward into the gloom, Brannigan muttered to himself: 'Three, two, one . . . here we go.' And, as if he was orchestrating the enemy lines himself, the Basra skyline, already belching smoke from days-old fires, suddenly burst into flame. The most recently excavated oil trenches had been lit. Rivers of fire swept across the scrubland on either side of Route Red, and more clouds of thick acrid smoke swirled into the grey sky.

It had been the same most mornings: as the tanks prepared to move out, the horizon was set ablaze almost simultaneously. The timing was always uncannily punctual and either the enemy had an observation post embedded very close to the battle group's operating base, or they were monitoring their radio transmissions. As well as messing with the TI capability, the oil fires were highly effective in obscuring the view of drones, satellites and helicopters. There was a psychological element as well: to the crews advancing up Route Red, it felt as if they were passing through the rings of hell. No matter how many times they had done it, it was difficult for the crews to feel at ease as they moved forward into a landscape of flame and smoke.

The apocalyptic vision greeting the Challengers on the morning of Saturday, 6 April was made all the more striking by the massive artillery barrage on the enemy's positions on either side of the road. Gemmell's 1st troop, supported by a platoon of Irish Guards, led the advance onto Route Red, depositing a FOO close to the Fedayeen operating base a mile up the road to observe and correct the incoming fire. Shortly afterwards, a massive explosion rocked the four-storey building, sending a shockwave that could be felt several hundred yards away, while it was heard and seen for miles around. Airburst shells erupted in the gloom and giant geysers of earth burst out of the ground on both sides of the road in and around the Fedayeen HQ and the broadcasting compound on the opposite side of the road. It was just to the north of those buildings and the surrounding scrub, close to the Red 5 junction, that the enemy had constructed the complex network of trenches and bunker positions that stretched up to and around the junction at Red 6 a mile or so to the north. Off to the right of the road lay the sprawling campus of the College of Literature, an Islamic school which, according to the Intelligence, was the operating base for 500 fanatical foreign fighters.

With 4th troop held in reserve, Captain Matheson in Zero Charlie was sent forward by Brannigan to secure Red 4, while 1st troop waited to push through on the left-hand side. The seven tanks of Gardiner's 3rd troop and De Silva's 2nd, with Brannigan in Zero Bravo, were to advance up the right-hand carriageway towards the forwardmost trenches of the enemy defences. 3rd troop led the way, with Gardiner commanding his men from the middle in Three Zero. A few hundred yards behind them, to the great consternation of his crew, De Silva had chosen to lead his troop from the front in spite of the fact that the ERA panels, blown away by the T-55 the day before, hadn't been replaced. A second main armament strike on the now exposed nose of the Challenger would have a lethal impact. Trails of Warriors, each of them crammed with Guardsmen, followed the small packets of armour as they rolled onto the tarmac.

The three tanks of 3rd troop churned up the baked mud

of the central reservation as they crashed over to the right-hand dual carriageway and straight into a shower of incoming rounds. As Three Zero bounced back onto the carriageway an RPG streaked across the turret and exploded in a bright flash onto the lamp post to their left. Gardiner shivered with fever and the sweat poured from under his helmet as he flicked to high mag on his sights and zoomed in on the bunker position from which it had come. The troop leader had been doing both the scanning and the firing in his tank over the past few days and as he laid onto the target he picked up the two heat sources of the RPG team. Immediately, he lased their bunker position with the red dot and pulled open the safety catch behind the control grips.

'HESH ... BUNKER! ... MINE! ...' he shouted hoarsely as he squeezed the trigger and watched the earth a hundred yards ahead of him heave into the air, sending the two dismounts somersaulting backwards. His mouth and throat were so dry he could barely speak and he sat back and gulped down a litre of water. The adrenaline was coursing through him again and his legs quivered beneath the fire control system. 3rd troop had inflicted dozens of casualties on the enemy during the week, but the crews had never grown accustomed to the lung-busting drama of combat. Gardiner picked up the large plastic bottle at his feet and vomited into it. He screwed the lid on tight, put his face back into the sights and scanned the terrain over a 180-degree arc. The TI screen wriggled with heat sources. The entire scrubland before him was alive with enemy. 'This is going to be one big long bastard of a day this one,' Gardiner muttered to himself as he zeroed in on yet another target. 'BUNKER!' The early exchanges set the pattern for the unfolding battle: 3rd troop were taking the brunt of the enemy's onslaught.

It wasn't long before the fighting erupted on the other side of the dual carriageway as the RPGs streaked and the mortars arced out of the Fedayeen operating base. The Challengers replied with waves of HESH and coax. For the tanks fronting the advance, the weight of fire was far heavier than anything they had experienced in previous raids. It was as if both sides had acknowledged that the sparring and jabbing couldn't go on indefinitely; it was time to start landing knockout blows. The enemy were never going to be able to overwhelm their British opponents and drive them back over the bridge, but victory was still possible if they succeeded in preventing the armoured raiders from securing the route. If they could destroy a Challenger, capture a crew, overrun a Warrior full of Irish Guards or inflict heavy casualties some other way – all in full view of the embedded media – then they would carry the day. For the SCOTS DG Battle Group, victory meant defeating all resistance and capturing Red 6.

In amongst the mass of vehicles, Lieutenant Colonel Blackman assumed a free role. Flicking between troops he was able to analyse the conditions and shape the battle without getting too involved in the fighting – if he could help it. But as soon as the columns pushed through Red 4 the rounds began tearing and screeching back and forth and the CO and his crew found themselves caught up in the shooting gallery. Mortars crashed around the Challengers as they accelerated through the drifting black smoke. RPGs ripped out of the murky light in trails of orange tracer and the scrubland flickered and sparkled with the flashes of dozens of Kalashnikov muzzles. The further the head of the column pushed up, the longer and more fragmented the battlefront became. It wasn't so much two forces colliding head on, rather a series of constantly shifting localized actions and engagements as the tank troops and the Warrior gunners tried to nail down highly mobile, resourceful and courageous opponents.

As the column on the left-hand side of Route Red rolled and mauled its way forward, the Challenger crews were alarmed to find themselves coming under heavy attack from a large fishing trawler sitting in a dry canal set back a few hundred yards from the road. In amongst the usual mix of mortar and RPG teams, the enemy had mounted a 12.7mm Dushka heavy machine gun on the bridge of the boat and set about strafing the columns of armoured vehicles engaging the bunker positions dug into the scrubland in between. Originally designed as an anti-aircraft gun, the Dushka was no great threat to a main battle tank, but some well-directed fire or a lucky shot was capable of damaging its external features – including, crucially, its sights – and it had the potential to cause even greater damage against the less heavily armoured infantry fighting vehicles. The CO, 2iC and 1st troop all engaged the boat, using chain guns and the odd round of HESH, while the Warrior gunners rang and perforated the metallic hull of the boat with bursts of 30mm RARDEN cannon.

The enemy had chosen their firing platform well. Tanks don't enjoy being fired upon from above at the best of times, and whoever was manning the Dushka kept up a steady stream of accurate harassing fire, backed up by mobile mortar and RPG teams, and succeeded in delaying the advance of the Challengers by over an hour. The enemy unit in the boat was an elusive quarry, firing then disappearing from view only to re-emerge in a different position moments later. Finally, a direct hit with a HESH round dispatched the Dushka high into the air and brought an end to the heavy sniping. A further round hit either the boat's fuel tank or the ammunition store. Whatever the cause, the result was as an almighty explosion that sent flames soaring into the sky and two paramilitaries cartwheeling overboard. With the boat engulfed by flames and the ammo exploding in all directions, the Challengers left the colourful pyrotechnic display fizzing and smouldering behind them and pushed up towards the Red 5 junction, 400 yards to the north.

To avoid being pinned down by the enemy gunners, the Challengers on both sides of the dual carriageway jockeyed backwards and forwards, to the left and to the right, as the rounds ricocheted off their armour and burst in the road around them. Steadily, relentlessly, as the sun climbed ever higher into the cloudless sky, they ground their way up towards the Gateway to Basra. The temperature climbed quickly and the Challengers' aircon systems were only so effective inside the closed-down cauldrons of the fighting compartments. By mid-morning the crews were sodden with sweat under their body armour.

Hovering above their heads like kestrels preparing to swoop, Super Cobra attack helicopters (AH) of the US Marine Corps weaved in and out of the plumes of billowing smoke from the flaming oil trenches, picking out enemy vehicles and positions beyond the view of the troops on the ground. Missiles and rockets streaked earthwards from the sides of the aircraft, devastating the targets below. The sight of the US Marines' AHs flying through the British fields of fire to take the fight to the enemy had a galvanizing effect on the troops watching from below.

With the first lines of resistance subdued and the route secured, the battle group, led by Gardiner's 3rd troop, closed in on Red 5. It was here, outside the walls of the College of Literature, that the enemy were concentrated in their greatest numbers. As soon as the first Challenger appeared within range, a volley of fire opened up from multiple bunker positions in the scrubland. Coax from the three Challengers ripped into the earth, puffs of dust chasing the paramilitaries as they sprinted between positions. The ground was softer here and the HESH less effective. Needing a reasonably hard surface to get some purchase for the pat of explosive to spread out, too often the HESH rounds were being swallowed up by the powdery, sandy soil, diminishing their force on impact. The 7.62mm rounds of the chain gun, the coax, were proving to be the most effective weapon. The challenge was to pin down targets that were constantly moving, out of sight, through the maze of trenches. Working out where they might appear became a game of second-guessing for the commanders.

As 3rd troop settled into their cat-and-mouse battle at the front of the advance, the call signs behind took the opportunity to refresh themselves. Inside the turrets, the crews necked bottle after bottle of water and the loaders handed out steaming silver bags of rations. The men were burning up calories at such a rate that the loaders had already got through half of the next day's food allocation. 1st troop had parked up half a mile to the south of the engagement raging ahead of them. Beyond the trenches and over the perimeter wall of the College of Literature, they could see the beautiful bright blue, mosque-like dome of the planetarium glinting and trembling in the midday sun. Around the famous Basra landmark lay several dozen more mundane structures, including five-storey residential blocks, lecture halls, classrooms and administrative outbuildings.

Call sign One Two, commanded by Corporal Martin Smith, was parked up alongside a small concrete hut, to which a donkey had been tied before, presumably, it had been abandoned by its owner when the fighting flared up earlier in the day. Entirely uninterested in the giant main battle tank next to it, the beast flicked the flies from its tail as it tried to squeeze itself into the small slice of shadow that the little building was offering under a fierce sun, now almost directly overhead. Major Brannigan and his crew, sitting fifty yards behind, were chuckling at the slightly incongruous, mildly comic sight of the dispirited donkey sitting in the middle of a battlefield. 'I wonder what poor old Eeyore makes of it all,' said his driver, Lance Corporal Gordy Brown, shovelling a forkful of treacle sponge into his mouth. As he spoke, a figure dressed in black stuck his head through the window of the hut then just as quickly darted from view. Instantly, Brannigan gulped down his mouthful of tea and broke into the squadron net.

'One Two, this is Zero Bravo, suspected Fedayeen dismount in the building to your left.'

Corporal Smith looked through his sights but the building was so close he could only see the top of it. As he did so, unknown to him, but seen by Brannigan, the paramilitary leapt out of the building, lobbed two grenades onto One Two's turret and almost in the same movement, dashed back into the building. One after the other, the grenades rolled off the sloping armour onto the ground and exploded with a bright flash and a small puff of dust. One of the enemy's more optimistic efforts of the conflict had gone entirely unnoticed by the crew within. Neither hearing nor feeling the explosions, they carried on munching on their rations. As they ate, Zero Bravo and the call sign behind opened fire with coax. The small concrete structure quickly began to crumble under the onslaught of hundreds of rounds. Steadily, the hole in the wall grew larger and larger to reveal their Fedayeen attacker. Twin streams of rounds from the two Challengers pinned him to the far wall. Slowly he slid to the ground, leaving a bloody smear on the paintwork behind him. When the Challengers stopped firing and the dust cloud from the rubble had cleared, the donkey was still there attached to the wall, completely unharmed, flicking its tail as if nothing had happened.

By now it had become patently clear to Blackman that he and his men were involved in a battle that could well prove decisive to the fate of Basra. It hadn't quite reached the point where it was safe for the Irish Guards to start dismounting and clearing out the enemy positions, but slowly, bunker by bunker, the battle group was getting the upper hand. Realizing that the siege of the enemy's last major stronghold was swinging in its favour, the Commanding Officer communicated his cautious optimism to Brigade HQ in one of his numerous sitreps via Operations Officer Captain Macmillan back at Battle Group HQ in the Technical College. The information was passed up the command chain and the decision was quickly made to exploit the Royal Scots Dragoon Guards' progress. Devising a hasty plan, Brigade called forward the Fusiliers Battle Group to advance into the centre of Basra on a parallel route between the SCOTS DG and the Black Watch Battle Group, which, with 'A' Squadron SCOTS DG leading the way in, had already deployed into the northern area of the city as part of the original operation.

The Black Watch column had encountered only very light resistance during a rapid advance that took them right up to the dock area on the Shatt Al Arab. Along much of the route they were even cheered in by smiling, waving crowds of Baswaris. The greatest difficulties they suffered were the gruelling heat and humidity, a huge pestilence of black flies and a truly nauseating stench emanating from the rotten vegetation and fetid mudflats flanking the mighty river. When the Fusiliers surged over the Shatt Al Arab a few hours later, they too were met by largely friendly crowds and only the odd lone gunman.

The relative ease of the two advances was confirmation that what serious enemy resistance remained in Iraq's second city was concentrated down on Route Red. More precisely, that resistance, a hundred or so diehards offering themselves to martyrdom, was to be found in and around the College of Literature, hammering Gardiner's 3rd troop with every weapon still available to them. Rarely had war's unequal distribution of tasks been better illustrated than in the scenes on Route Red that afternoon. While 2nd and 4th troops sat further down the road, drinking tea and listening to the unfolding battle over the radio for the most part, Gardiner and his men had been in almost constant contact with the enemy since first light. It was only when they were called forward to relieve Gardiner's men, who had run out of HESH and coax and had to return to the Technical College for a replen, that 2nd troop became fully aware of the intensity of the battle being fought. Not since the Allied advance into Germany sixty years earlier had a British tank exhausted its supply of main armament rounds in a single day's fighting. That, if nothing else, brought home the scale of the fighting and the carnage being slowly visited upon a brave foe determined not to cede a yard of territory. 3rd troop had destroyed over thirty bunker positions.

Once the southern side of the College had been largely subdued by the Challengers, the order was given to the Irish Guards, cooped up in the sweltering interiors of the Warriors all day, to clear out the trenches on foot. The infantrymen had been shielded from the fighting thus far, only occasionally dismounting for a quick glimpse of the battlefield in order to get some situational awareness. The back of a

Warrior fighting vehicle is a miserable place at the best of times. Closed down with no windows, the seven or eight soldiers huddled along benches in full combat gear can see nothing and hear only the dull thuds of the battle beyond. In a battle situation the men rely on the running commentary provided by the section commander sitting up at the front with the driver to keep them abreast of events unfolding outside. As the Challengers fought their way up Route Red for hour after hour, it was especially hard for the Guardsmen as they sat in temperatures hovering around the 100 degrees Fahrenheit mark and listened to the explosions bursting all around them.

Captain Matheson, sitting in overwatch, and ever interested in how other units of the military go about their work, looked on as the Guardsmen, working in pairs, streamed out of the backs of the vehicles and into the baked, barren terrain between the road and the walls of the campus. It was classic trench clearance that he was witnessing: a grenade lobbed into a trench, a small explosion and a puff of a smoke and dust and then the 'double tap' – two bullets to make sure. As he slurped on his tea and watched the infantrymen running and crouching their way through the enemy positions, he caught sight of the battle group photographer, Tony Nicoletti, who had been embedded with them since crossing the border. Brave as a lion, he was never far from the thick of the action.

Matheson shook his head and smiled as he watched the fearless snapper follow a pair of Guardsmen, before slipping out of view into a trench a few yards behind them. 'That man is completely mad,' he said over the tank's intercom. As he spoke, he could hear a voice in the left earphone of his head-set. It was one of the commanders in a Warrior keeping a lookout for trouble. 'There's a Fed following you! He's in the trench behind! We'll engage.' Matheson watched the two Guardsmen's heads turn as they received the news through their headsets and swung round, pointing their assault rifles at the trench. It took a second for Matheson to twig the Warrior was one squeeze of the trigger away from taking out the photographer. Snatching the controls of the radio set hanging around his neck he hollered: 'STOP! STOP! STOP!' The Guardsmen froze and looked up towards the line of armoured vehicles positioned on the dual carriageway a hundred yards away. 'He's the photographer! I've been watching him. STOP!' Nicoletti's blue helmet appeared from the trench and Matheson saw the two soldiers shake their heads; whether in anger or disbelief it was difficult to tell.

As the platoons painstakingly worked their way through the enemy positions, trench by trench, bunker by bunker, one section suddenly found itself face to face with a unit of paramilitaries bursting out of a ditch fifty yards ahead of them. The Guardsmen immediately hit the ground, exactly as they are trained to do, but one of them remained on his feet – a young recruit who had only joined the regiment just over a month earlier. As the enemy shaped to throw a grenade, he was gunned down by the fresh-faced Mick. The grenade he had been about to throw at the advancing section exploded, killing the fighter next to him. The section moved on.

As the Irish Guards mopped up the trenches, Major Brannigan and 1st troop pushed up to Red 6, a few hundred yards to the north. The fighting was suddenly dying down almost as quickly as it had erupted at the start of the day. The marketplace and taxi rank in the centre of the junction were empty and there was not a paramilitary in sight, let alone a civilian, as they accelerated towards what was normally one of Basra's busiest interchanges. The statue of Saddam Hussein, destroyed by 'A'

Squadron, lay face down with the dictator's giant moustache pressed into the dirt. The fish statue next to it, with several chunks taken out of its tail and bullet holes riddling its scales, stood in graphic testimony to the recent fighting. On the approach to the junction there lay a large triangle of scrub to the right with a slip road running down one side of it to the main entrance to the College of Literature. The tanks began to slow up as they reached the designated limit of the area they had been tasked to exploit. The turrets and main guns swung back and forth rapidly, scanning the terrain, but it was quiet. Eerily quiet. Brannigan didn't like it. *Is this not the Gateway to Basra, the final threshold that must be held at all costs?*

He continued scanning. He caught sight of two T-55s hull down in amongst the shrubs and palms of a small park area – and he didn't wait to find out whether or not they were active. Fifteen seconds later both tanks were brewing up as the ammunition began to detonate and the fuel tanks caught light. An MTLB parked up nearby suffered a similar fate as Zero Bravo hammered it with a further round. The USMC Super Cobra overhead finished off the vehicles with rockets. Two artillery pieces opened up on the Challengers from close range but were quickly destroyed by 1st troop. A dozen enemy suddenly appeared from sandbagged trenches in the triangle of scrubland. RPGs and automatic fire streaked in one direction, HESH and coax in the other. One of the RPGs smashed into call sign One One sending the camnet tied to the front flying into the air as high as the lamp post next to it. For ten minutes the two groups exchanged fire. A T-55 appeared from the park area, but before the Challengers could lase it, it had sped away into the depths of Old Basra. Half a dozen dismounts followed it, melting into the alleys, conscious they stood no chance against he combined might of Challenger and Cobra. Wrecked vehicles smouldered around the junction and smoke hung heavy and sinister in the thick, humid air. Red 6 had been subdued. The Gateway to Basra was under British control.

'I think we've done it, boss,' came a voice over the intercom in Zero Bravo. Brannigan said nothing as he swung his sights ninety degrees around to the right.

It was curiosity as much as anything else that persuaded Brannigan to divert down the slip road from Red 6 and investigate the scene beyond the metal-barred gates at the main entrance to the College of Literature. When he pulled up outside and pressed his face into the sights, he was met by the unsettling sight of a dozen or so dead enemy scattered across the forecourt to the compound. By the way they were lying it was as if the paramilitaries had been gassed. There were no visible signs of physical trauma. Usually, dead combatants lay in grotesquely twisted positions. Brannigan tried to remember hearing contact reports over the radio earlier in the day referring to an engagement *inside* the College. There had been so many contact reports throughout the day, it was impossible to recall every single one. There was something strange about the scene. He decided to take a closer look.

Switching to the battle group frequency, he conferred with the CO, who agreed that while there was still daylight, it was right to capitalize on the successes of the day and try to secure the College. The Irish Guards were called forward to act as intimate support. The plan was for Farrell's No. 2 Company to break in and attack any enemy they encountered while MacMullen's No. 1 Company swept through to clear the buildings and secure the area beyond. The Warriors, a hundred yards or so to the rear, lined up facing the compound, with good views over the low perimeter wall. 'Right, Gordy, get her up to ramming speed and smash through the gates,' Brannigan said to his driver.

With its main gun traversed over the back decks to avoid a potentially catastrophic barrel strike, the 75-ton tank drove through the heavy barrier as if it wasn't there. Lance Corporal Nick Brown, the gunner, spun the turret back round, with the barrel of the main gun narrowly missing the roof of the little porter's lodge as it traversed the 180 degrees. The vehicle came to a halt just inside the gates. Three men emerged from a doorway, throwing down their weapons while one of them waved a white shirt above his head. One of the men on the ground twitched. His RPG lay at his side.

Brannigan switched the sights to TI and felt his heart skip a beat. All the corpses were showing heat signatures.

'They're all broon breid,' said Brown. 'I think that one's got rigor mortis, boss.'

'Well, if they are dead, they must have been killed very, very rece—'

As he spoke, the three Warriors of No. 5 platoon pushed forward, led by Sergeant Whiteside. As his vehicle crashed through the low wall, one of the 'dead' soldiers, lying below it, leapt to his feet only to be crushed under the rubble and tracks. As one, the rest of the 'corpses' rose from the ground and began firing RPGs and small arms. One of the grenades smashed into the side of Whiteside's Warrior in a shower of sparks and smoke. In a split second, total bedlam had erupted inside the compound as the rounds flew back and forth. One dismount with an RPG was promptly dispatched by a Guardsman who, worried about shooting up his comrades with the Warrior's chain gun, stuck his head out of the hatch, and shot him with his assault rifle. Another paramilitary brought his

RPG to bear on Zero Bravo, aiming straight at the commander's sights. The coax jammed. Brannigan flicked the weapons switch to main armament. A second later, the HESH round exploded at the enemy's feet, leaving no trace of him.

With so many 'friendlies' in the vicinity the Challengers had to be extremely careful: HESH is an area weapon with a hundred-yard splash, while spraying coax around was only marginally less dangerous. This was the type of close fighting that infantrymen spend their careers training for and the Micks set about the enemy with swift, brutal professionalism. The paramilitaries, about a dozen in total, were trying to rush the vehicles, but they were cut down by the Warrior gunners sitting on the outside. Within minutes, the enemy 'zombies' had been well and truly returned to the afterlife. Dark pools of blood ran into the dust where the bodies lay.

No. 1 Company swept through into the heart of the campus, dismounting from their vehicles, as Lieutenant Daniel O'Connell led No. 1 platoon into the first building at the start of what was going to be a painstaking process of clearing the thirty buildings of the College, room by room. With the light starting to fade, the Guards had to move quickly to work their way through the complex, breaking in, clearing and then remounting time and time again as they systematically cleared the buildings. As night fell, No. 1 Company withdrew into a defensive position in an area of the campus secured earlier. Snipers were put on the rooftops and the first men went out on stag as the rest of the men found a quiet room and collapsed into a deep sleep.

The men of 'B' Squadron were, as Brannigan put it to his Commanding Officer, 'absolutely fucking chinstrapped'. He pleaded for them to be stood down for twelve hours so that they could recover to the Technical College to rest while the

REME set to work on repairing their shot-blasted vehicles. Lieutenant Colonel Blackman agreed and immediately called forward Major Biggart's 'C' Squadron to relieve them. 'C' Squadron had returned from their adventures with 3 Commando Brigade three days earlier and after two decent nights' sleep were in marginally better shape than their shattered colleagues in 'B' Squadron.

As soon as they handed over to Biggart's troops, the column of 'B' Squadron vehicles snaked out of the gates back onto Route Red. In darkness and silence, they returned along the route they had fought their way up for almost twelve hours. On either side of the road dozens of bunker positions lay destroyed and dozens, possibly hundreds, of enemy lay dead. Within minutes of climbing wearily from their vehicles, the men found an empty room and flopped to the floor, stopping only to remove their helmets and body armour. Almost instantly they fell asleep in the delirious knowledge that, for the first time since leaving Shaibah airfield almost eight days earlier, they were going to get more than two hours' rest in a stretch.

And they did: they got three hours. It was three o'clock in the morning when Brannigan was shaken awake by his loader, Sergeant Hainey, and told that the Commanding Officer wanted to see him downstairs.

'First the bad news – and it's very bad indeed,' said Lieutenant Colonel Blackman softly, looking down at the ground as he spoke. 'Shortly after you left, the Irish Guards lost two men and had two wounded. A gunman fired into the back of a Warrior.' He paused for a few seconds to let Brannigan take in the news.

'Secondly, the Paras have been called in to secure Old Basra at first light and "B" Squadron are going to escort them in. You need to get your men in position at Red 6 within the hour.'

When the Challengers rolled back through the College gateway, the first grey light of day was spread along the horizon. The atmosphere was thick with grief. Dozens of men were up and about, but it was almost completely quiet. Only the occasional crack of small-arms fire in the distance broke the silence. Some Guardsmen sat leaning against the walls of the buildings with their heads in their hands trying to take in the loss of their two comrades. Piper Christopher Muzvuru and Lance Corporal Ian Malone were killed when a gunman, who had either been lying low or had stolen into the campus, opened fire with an AK-47 into the back of their Warrior before escaping. Two others were seriously injured: Lance Corporal Martin and Sergeant Holland, who despite his wounds, managed to reach the platoon commander's vehicle and get on the radio to warn the rest of No. 1 Company before remounting and helping to secure the area. Only then did he let the medics tend to him. The deaths wiped out any relief and satisfaction felt at the end of a bitterly fought victory. Every face was a picture of melancholy as they silently went about their business.

By mid-morning the sun was beating down over the Al Faw and 3rd Battalion the Parachute Regiment were beginning their march up Route Red to link up with the Challengers of 'B' Squadron. Dismounting from their vehicles 1,000 yards short of the College of Literature, they made an impressive spectacle as hundreds of men, fully laden with kit, appeared on the horizon and slowly made their way towards the heart of Iraq's second city. It was, if nothing else, a colourful show of strength and a superb photo opportunity for the ranks of assembled media as they prepared to inform the world that the fighting was finally over and that Basra had been liberated.

The Paras were a 'strong brand', and the camera shutters clicked and snapped as they yomped past, sweat pouring off their lantern jaws.

As part of 16 Air Assault Brigade, 3 Para had been tasked to take and hold the Al-Rumaylah oilfields to the north-west of Basra at the start of the ground offensive, but they had encountered only very light resistance there. Of all the components of the 1st (UK) Armoured Division their experience in Operation TELIC had been the least eventful. The Army's most formidable regular fighting unit had barely fired a shot in anger.

A troop of 'B' Squadron Challengers had been assigned to escort each rifle company up to their line of departure, from where they were to disappear into the narrow alleys and streets unsuitable for tanks. Exhausted by a week of hard fighting and distressed by the night's events, the men of the Royal Scots Dragoon Guards and the Irish Guards said little as they watched the Paras advance ever closer. Fearful of a repeat attack, dozens of the battle group had taken up defensive positions. Snipers looked down from windows and rooftops, while others lay in ditches combing the terrain with their assault rifles. Tension charged the atmosphere.

The Paras pulled up alongside the waiting tanks and the two units stared at each other through the heat haze. Major Brannigan and Sergeant Gardiner, pale, drawn and filthy, were standing in silence smoking cigarettes in the shadow of Zero Bravo, too tired to talk. One of the Para Company Commanders, recognizing the Squadron leader, approached them with a broad smile. The two men shook hands.

'Hey, I thought you guys were being held in reserve. Don't worry, we'll finish off the job for you!' he joked.

Brannigan held out a cigarette, trying to muster a weary

smile for his old friend. 'Good to see you. I think you're a little late, though, aren't you?'

'For what? And why the defensive mode? It's been pretty quiet here, hasn't it? . . . Hasn't it?'

Glossary

AFV	armoured fighting vehicle
AH	attack helicopter
AK-47	aka Kalashnikov, Soviet-developed assault rifle
AOR	area of operations
APC	armoured personnel carrier
APFSDS	aka FIN, armour-piercing fin-stabilized discarding sabot
AS-90	British self-propelled artillery piece, capable of firing its 155mm shells up to twenty miles in bursts of three rounds per ten seconds
ATW	anti-tank weapon
A-Zed	slang for Iraqi town of Az Zubayr
BGHQ	Battle Group Headquarters
BM-21	Soviet truck-mounted multiple rocket launcher
BRF	Brigade Reconnaissance Force, a unit of the Royal Marines
camnet	camouflage net
casevac	casualty evacuation
Challenger 2	main battle tank of the British Army; replaced Challenger 1 at the end of the 1900s, but has only 5 per cent commonality of parts with its predecessor
CO	Commanding Officer
coax	aka chain gun. Coax is short for 'coaxially mounted' 7.62mm machine gun
comms	communications

compo	composite rations
CPS	commander's primary sights
CRARRV	Challenger armoured repair and recovery vehicle
CVR(T)	combat vehicle reconnaissance (tracked)
Desert Rats	nickname of 7th Armoured Brigade
dismount	slang for infantryman
D&V	diarrhoea and vomiting
DMZ	demilitarized zone
ERA	explosive reactive armour
FAA	forward assembly area
Feds	Fedayeen, Iraqi paramilitaries fiercely loyal to Saddam Hussein's regime
FIN	*see* APFSDS
FLOT	Forward Line Own Troops
FOO	Forward Observation Officer
GPMG	general-purpose machine gun, aka 'gimpy' (pronounced *jimpy*)
GPS	1. gunner's primary sights. 2. global positioning system
GUE	auxiliary generator
HESH	high-explosive squash head
Humvee	high-mobility, multipurpose wheeled vehicle: large jeep used by the US military
IG	Irish Guards
Intel	military slang for Intelligence (information gathering)
JDAM	Joint Direct Attack Munition. Smart guidance system for precision bombing
LAD	Light Aid Detachment
LAW	light anti-tank weapon
LD	line of departure

LZ	landing zone
M1 Abrams	main battle tank of the US Army
M3 rig	type of pontoon
MBT	main battle tank
MILAN	anti-tank guided missile
MOD	Ministry of Defence
MRS	muzzle referencing system
MTLB	Soviet armoured personnel carrier
NBC	nuclear, biological, chemical
NCO	non-commissioned officer
NTM	notice to move
OC	Officer Commanding
'O' Group	Orders Group
overwatch	one unit supporting/covering another
pax	passengers
Pinzgauer	versatile all-terrain wheeled vehicle
PJHQ	Permanent Joint Headquarters
QDG	1st The Queen's Dragoon Guards, aka the Welsh Cavalry, specialists in formation reconnaissance
QM	Quartermaster
QRL	Queen's Royal Lancers
RAC	Royal Armoured Corps
RAP	Regimental Aid Post
REME	The Royal Electrical and Mechanical Engineers
replen	replenishment of supplies
RFL	restricted firing line
RHA	Royal Horse Artillery
RLC	Royal Logistics Corps
RPG	rocket-propelled grenade
Scimitar	armoured reconnaissance vehicle

SCOTS DG	abbreviation for The Royal Scots Dragoon Guards
SHQ	Squadron Headquarters, including the tanks of the Squadron leader, 2iC and command vehicles
sitrep	situation report given over the radio
Spartan	member of the CVR(T) family, used for a variety of purposes in the field, including as an ambulance
SQMS	Squadron Quartermaster Sergeant
SSM	Squadron Sergeant Major
Sultan	command vehicle, used as a mobile office in the field by the HQ element of a regiment or battle group
SuperCobra	attack helicopter used by US Marines
technical	improvised fighting vehicle, usually a pick-up truck with a cab at the front and an open back
TI	thermal imaging
UBRE	fuel tanker (unit bulk refuelling equipment)
uparmour	fit additional armour, such as ERA tiles (*see above*)
USMC	United States Marine Corps
VCP	vehicle checkpoint
Warrior	armoured infantry fighting vehicle
WMD	weapons of mass destruction
WO2	Warrant Officer Class 2, highly experienced soldier of rank between commissioned officers and NCOs
yomp	march at pace and/or in full kit
2iC	Second-in-Command
2 RTR	2nd Royal Tank Regiment

Index